Mary,
Smile Always,
Ben Nye

Bev Nye's

Year Round Sunshine

Also by Beverly K. Nye

A Family Raised on Sunshine

A Family Raised on Rainbows

Everyone's a Homemaker

The Best of Beverly

Sunshine Notes

Year Round Sunshine

A Guide to Happy, Healthy and Creative Living

By Beverly K. Nye

Artwork by Nathaniel S. Nye

Edited by Kristen N. Seethaler

Sterling Press
Salt Lake City, Utah

Copyright © 2003 by Beverly K. Nye

All rights reserved. No part of this book may be reproduced or utilized in any form or by any means, electronic or mechanical, including photocopying, recording, or by any information storage or retrieval system, without permission in writing from Beverly K. Nye.

For information contact:

www.BeverlyNye.com

Published by Sterling Press

Printed in the United States of America

First Printing: March 2003

Second Printing: February 2004

ISBN #0-9746665-2-1

To order, send check or money order for $24.95 plus $5 shipping & handling to:

Beverly K. Nye
P.O. Box 95124
South Jordan, UT 84095-0124

Dedication

For my Grandchildren — a big hug and many thanks for the constant rays of Sunshine!

Emily — thoughtful, fun-loving and loves the sun.

Nathan — the bird expert and gifted artist with a heart of gold.

Christian — our scholar and sportsman who loves cinnamon rolls.

Cameron — whose hugs warm my heart.

Megan — what a bubbly talent!

Joel — that handsome gentleman.

Kelsey — with a beautiful smile for everyone.

Audrey — whose love of books makes me love her more.

Mary — with a singing voice like the angels.

Leisel — true sweetness and light.

Grady — what a talented young man with a thirst for knowledge.

Logan — Music, art and learning — always excelling.

Cedar — everybody's friend.

Jacob — ingenious "Jake," who has now brought his bride, Manon, to our family.

Jessica — always willing to lend a helping hand or just be a friend.

Amanda — who dances her way into everyone's heart.

Jennifer — my "food" buddy.

Daniel — forever caring and compassionate.

Sarah — special Sarah, our eternal optimist.

Travis — Grandpa's soul mate, with his beautiful bride Taryn.

Keri — full of enthusiasm and ideas!

Tyler — Mr. Personality.

Craig — who loves those "special" recipes.

Acknowledgements

This book has finally reached completion thanks to some very special people in my life:

My daughter, Kristen, who is always available to type, edit or just lend a listening ear and offer encouragement and enthusiasm.

My grandson, Nathan, who caught the vision and message of the book and supported me with the artwork (in the middle of preparing for a Church mission to Venezuela).

A super good friend, Carol Cartaino, who has always believed in me and given me expert advice!

My special family, who always support me in my many adventures but most of all, love me in spite of my many weaknesses.

My mentor for living and life, Lucille Johnson. I have learned so much from her. If the whole world read her books, what a wonderful place it would be.

My brother, Max, who willingly bounces ideas around with me and gives me the motivation to Do It!

Most of all, my husband Roy for his gentle encouragement and support. He has truly been the calming force in the eye of the storm as this work finally came together.

I love you all!

Contents

January
Opening Doors to a Happy Family
1

February
Fun Ideas that Say "I Love You"
31

March
Making Spring-Time Happy Time
63

April
A Month for Cleaning and Organizing
85

May
You Are a Special, Unique and Beautiful Person
111

June
Marriage and Relationships
129

July
Family Pleasing Outings
149

August
On the Road Again, With Kids
171

September
Who Thought Grocery Shopping Could Be Such Fun?
189

October
Learn About Life From Trees
213

November
Counting Our Blessings with Family and Friends
235

December
Peace and Simplicity for the Holidays
253

January

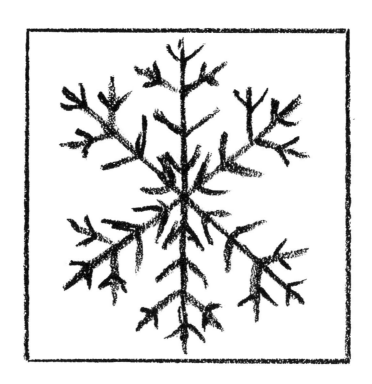

January

Hello, everyone! Come on in, pull up a comfy chair and let's visit. What a great way to start the year, sharing ideas with friends. Don't you just love January? It reminds me of the first day of school, beginning with a fresh clean tablet and pencils and crayons that have never been used. Each year of life is really our school room. Think of all the great things we'll be learning and the exciting adventures ahead. It's up to each of us which classes we'd like to take, but our homes are our schools and our families the most important element in learning and teaching. Aren't we blessed to be part of the structure called family? Whether as a parent, sister, aunt or cousin, it's a bond that makes life worthwhile. Families are "forever" and nothing can be sweeter than that relationship. Let's spend January discussing thoughts on bettering our home and family. I've got some super, homey recipes to share and lots of "food for thought." Make yourself comfortable. It's so nice to share this time with you.

Food for Thought

When our grandson, Christian, was a little boy he had such a fascination for doors. He loved to open and close them and was so intrigued each time he did. As I sat watching him one day, I couldn't help but reflect on how many doors he would open and close in his lifetime. Just as each of us, he has the opportunity to choose and each choice can greatly affect his life. If worry comes our way, we may choose to close the door on the "if onlys" or "what ifs" and remember that the past is just that! Doors also build memories. Who can forget the voice of mother cautioning "Shut the door!" as we ran off to play, or the warm feeling as we heard the door open at the end of the day and a voice calling out "I'm home!" The front door of a friend, Grandma's house or just "home" brings that peaceful feeling of comfort and welcome we all know. Being brought up with strong German beliefs, I was always taught how important the front door was. It was necessary to keep it clean and the step or porch well swept. Still today, women in Germany are seen scrubbing the door and front step each morning! What a nice custom and "welcome" to our home and family!

How thankful I am to have a thoughtful husband who has always opened doors for me, but even more important for the example and message it has sent to our children and grandchildren. As well as the physical doors, do we open the doors to their hearts by listening? I love Thornton Wilder's play "Our Town." Such a message! How it tugs at my heart strings each time I hear little Emily say, as she tries to communicate with each member of her family, "Listen to me! Please listen to me, I'm Emily. Hi, it's me, Emily" and soon she realizes, "Nobody listens to anybody anymore!" It is so vital that we hear these children and validate their thoughts and feelings. They have so much to teach us. If only we could all see the world through the eyes of a child!

One of my favorite sayings is, "Two men looked through the self-same bars. One saw mud, the other saw stars." Many years ago when Roy and I built our first new little home in Sandy, Utah, our son Steve was three years old. His favorite pastime was to play in the dirt and mud in our back yard and find rocks to crack. One day he was busy playing outside and I worked hard cleaning the house. I wanted to be "the best" housekeeper! As I finished scrubbing and waxing the kitchen floor on my hands and knees, I backed into the living room and stood to admire my hard work. Just as I stood up, the back door flew open and in bounded little Steve, mud from head to toe, with a rock in one hand and Daddy's hammer in the other. He raced across the clean kitchen floor, smiling and excited, calling "Mommy, Mommy." Immediately I started scolding him for tracking up my clean floor, getting himself all muddy and besides he shouldn't be using that hammer! As I stopped yelling, with the words still ringing in the air, little Steve, now standing next to me, looked up with sadness and dejection in his eyes and said as he held out the rock, "Look Mommy, I only wanted you to see how the rock shines inside, just like your eyes do when you smile at me!" — talk about seeing the mud instead of the stars!! My mother always said, "A smile is a light in the doorway that says your heart is at home." Are we "at home" for these children?

As we open the doors for our family, one of the most important components of these doors is security. Too often we as parents confuse caring and love with permissiveness. To feel security, children need to learn correct behavior, social graces, respect, consistency, values, and love. Don't get caught up in too many "rules." Instead, teach principles and values. Then the rules take care of themselves. We can't have rules for everything, but knowing and believing correct principles, the choices are already made. Start early, a consistent pattern and life style teaches even babies and toddlers self-discipline. Begin with a bedtime schedule, eating habits, etc. Everyone is happier and life runs smoother. Then an occasional treat becomes appreciated. How well I remember how "special" little Steve and Mark felt when they got to stay up "late" to watch Laredo with Daddy.

Establishing a bedtime is a tradition that can be a big help to everyone. Several of my children's school teachers have told me they can always tell the children that have "set" bedtimes. They are brighter and more alert, as well as being more self-disciplined. Family rules and guidelines sure help develop this. A regular, disciplined bedtime was established in our family council meeting and adhered to faithfully. I think it really takes more discipline on the part of a parent than the child, but it pays off in so many ways. The children respect you more, they feel they are genuinely cared about, and they feel so much better physically for having an established sleeping pattern. As a parent, first show them lots of love, explain the reasoning for an established bedtime, make sure they are comfortable and have all necessary things taken care of (like a drink of water), firmly say goodnight and express your love again. Then comes the most important ingredient — be consistent. It takes effort on your part, but I can't begin to tell you the benefits you will share.

Little ones — and grownups, too — don't always want to go to bed when they should, but that doesn't mean bedtime can't be fun. All children love stories, and it gives parents a chance to exhibit the "ham" in them. As you read or tell stories to your family, don't be afraid to embellish them with sound effects or actions. It can be very relaxing for a parent at the end of the day to "loosen up" and really get into the story. Try it, it really works. A story becomes a lot more real and exciting when the duck is "quacking," the fire truck siren "blares" down the street or the birds are "cheeping, chattering and fluttering their wings." Our favorite story had a character with a strong southern accent, and the kids just loved it when I would do that particular one. After fun story-telling experiences, I guarantee you both a good night's sleep.

Help children to love work. Too often we just expect them to do it! First, show them how to do a job and appreciate the end result. Then work with them and do the job together. Finally, let them do it by themselves and praise them for their efforts. Everybody loves compliments! Don't be critical and correct their work. Nothing crushes an ego faster than to have someone re-do your task! If more lessons are needed, work together a few more times. One of our mottoes was "many hands make light work." If it were Steve's turn to mow the yard, and Mark finished his job already, Mark knew they could play ball together sooner if he helped, so off he ran to get the rake. As we assigned tasks and responsibilities around the house, I tried to choose jobs that coincided with each one's interest, such as gardening, cooking, decorating, etc. It helped to develop their talents, everyone enjoyed their work time more, and it was a big help to me. Which brings up another point. I believe children can see right through "busy work," so give them meaningful chores to do that really benefit the family. Our motto is always help each other. If a child needs help with a school project and you willingly pitch in, they will be much more willing to help when the garden needs weeding. Taking care of a happy home is a family responsibility! Each day we can learn and grow together. It takes patience. I'll always remember visiting my daughter Kristen's home when little Jacob was about four years old. As we were gathering for breakfast in the kitchen, suddenly from upstairs, we heard an agonizing moan. Wondering what was wrong, we hurried up the stairway. There sitting on his bed, with his head in his hands, was this sweet little curly headed boy saying, "Do I have to get dressed every day for the rest of my life?" Yes, Jacob, it takes patience and perseverance!!!

True, life isn't easy, and there are trials along the way. "We can't stop trouble from coming through the door, but we don't have to give it a chair to sit in." The secret is in how we deal with it.

I have always teased Roy about being such a "saver," but through this habit he taught me a valuable lesson. One day as we were doing some remodeling in our house in Kansas City, I went outdoors to take him a cool drink. He was down on his knees picking up some bent nails. As I began chiding him about this silly habit of his, he took me by the shoulders, sat me down on a saw horse and proceeded to tell me a lesson he had used in his church class for teenagers. He held up a bent nail for me to see as he said, "Take a look at this crooked nail. Many would say it was useless, of no worth, but — just hold this nail firmly, find the weak, bent spot and then gently tap and work with it, until it becomes straight. Now you don't want to just pound it on the head or force it, but just gently work with it until it becomes straight again. It will hold stronger than any straight nail ever could!" What a powerful lesson! After relating this story to a group of women in Indiana one evening, I had a sweet little mother come and give me a hug with tears in her eyes. "Thank you," she said, "and now I have to hurry home because I have a teenage 'bent nail' waiting for me!" Never will we regret taking the time and making the most of each moment with our families!

Our family was blessed with a special spirit — Antoinette (my niece). Antoinette was the mother of five children. She may not have been the world's best housekeeper, but she knew how to be a "super" mom. Antoinette was that loving type of mother that could put down the dish cloth and rush outside to lay on the grass with the little ones and watch the funny clouds go by, or sit on the living room floor to play games and sing songs. One day as we stopped by to visit, newspapers etc. were on the floor. Antoinette had stopped her work and was busy building memories with her children. While we visited, the children ran in to share a bouquet of dandelions and wild flowers with her. "Oh, kids," she said, "these are magic flowers!" And she explained to them how they would form "parachutes" and seeds would fly all over the world having an adventure. The children were mesmerized. Antoinette then rushed to the kitchen, grabbed a can, filled it with water and placed her new bouquet on the table with pride. "Golly, kids" she exclaimed as she gave them a hug, "You have made my day!" Antoinette truly knew the meaning of mothering!

When Heidi was a little girl, her most frequently asked question was, "When are we going to get there?" no matter if it were a trip to Utah or to the grocery store. Too often we live our lives like that — thinking we will reach our destination of happiness at some later time. We forget that life is a journey and not a destination. Many, many times as I was growing up, I remember Mom counseling me not to wish my life away. Soon I had a little family of my own and could see the wisdom in her words. Each day should be special, and it can be if we make it that way. It's so sad to see someone work hard toward something only to reach it and realize that life has passed him by. Living happily, usefully, and lovingly is the most important part of "getting there." As homemakers, we have the ability to instill in our husbands and children, as well as ourselves, to do the "little things" that make days memorable.

As I visit with friends and neighbors, they usually say, "Oh, we don't have many traditions." But have you ever stopped to think just how many habits and expected routines you establish in your day-to-day living? Would everyone be shocked if Dad got up in the morning before Mom (or vice versa), or if Mark didn't lick the bowl after Mom made cookies, because this is the way it "always" is? That's tradition. It helps build self-worth and gives a sense of continuity and belonging — a feeling that is greatly needed in our world today. We don't always realize the full impact of these little things until our grown children return home and comment on the good feeling these traditions give them.

Traditions are also that link with the past that helps preserve our heritage. Many of the lasting values of life are learned this way, such as the sharing and showing of affection by the Polish people. At Christmastime, gathered around the table, they give each other a bite of their wafer, embrace and express their love. The Maori people of New Zealand express their traditions in their legends, songs, stories, and dances. Whether your ancestors were German, Irish, American Indian, or Japanese; whether your family lives in the South, the Midwest, or New England; your own unique heritage can be preserved in your family's traditions.

Roy and I had many long talks before we were married about our goals and expectations of marriage and raising a family, so we set up some guidelines right then. Of course, these constantly change and grow as our lives progress. For you young people, I heartily recommend starting this way. It's like building your house on a rock foundation instead of sand. On the other hand, it's never too late to set new goals and ideals. After all, ten years from now you'll be ten years older no matter what, so you might as well start now to make those years happier.

Praying together has always been an important tradition in our marriage. As our children joined our family, we continued to have family prayer, kneeling around our bed at night and around the breakfast table in the morning. Everyone takes turns, and this has brought so much closeness to our family. Sunday dinner is always Dad's turn, though; that's tradition, too.

Traditions can also help you run a more orderly household. The kids always looked forward to bath time, and they had great fun, but at first the clutter of bath toys made a big mess. We soon established another tradition, "three toys only in the tub." Our bathroom always had a fishnet hanging above the tub. We put two hooks on the wall above the tub about four feet apart and bought an inexpensive fishnet at an import store. Then the net was hung from the hooks. The wet toys could be tossed into it as it hung in hammock-style, and any excess water just dripped into the tub. It sure saved a lot of headaches. (Have you ever tried getting all of the water out of a doll's head, and then still found puddles on the closet floor?)

To let each child know how much he is cared about, why not let Daddy spend one bedtime a week for a little private "conference talk." A father can feel left out since we as mothers get to share so many things with our children while husbands are away, and children need a good relationship with their fathers, too. Roy made it a practice of taking each girl out to eat occasionally for a Saturday breakfast (Kristen really loved those special times at the pancake house) or a Friday night hamburger. Often he would take just one boy to play golf or go fishing. I know they had some choice conversations at times like this, and they always will be special memories, too.

As our children grew, we established set times for other activities such as homework. And along with set times, we provided our young scholars with a comfortable and workable area with good lighting for study. This doesn't have to be expensive. We got a big old library table for the boys from a junk store for a couple of dollars. We then worked together to refinish it; and it was a perfect study table. (Now that the boys are gone, we cut the legs down, and have the greatest coffee table. It's such a heavy and sturdy piece — we eat snacks around it, play games on it, rest our feet on it, etc., and we sure have gotten our two dollars' worth! A good coat of wax now and then, and it will last forever.) Anyway, back to the study areas — we picked up a little desk for the girls from a hotel that was changing some furniture. It was free; we just had to pick it up. That little desk was painted several different colors and trims to go with their room décor. It has now been passed on to another young family. The point is to provide everyone with a study area of his or her own, if possible. We also found it was much more conducive to study if we all were reading, writing, or studying. Especially when the kids were little, it was hard to expect them to be upstairs studying if everyone else was downstairs laughing at something on the TV. It didn't take us long to discover that the TV didn't have to be on all of the time. Roy and I could use the time to good advantage, too, by reading or doing some letter writing. So, we all benefited. Like I said before, "it's lots more fun to work or play if someone is doing it with you."

When we sat down with our family recently and asked them which traditions they remember most, our youngest, Heidi, piped up with "We got to start wearing a little makeup when we were thirteen." We have found that by establishing traditions like this, the kids really looked forward to these events and it becomes more meaningful. Some others were group parties at age fourteen, no single dating until age sixteen. These were exciting milestones in their lives, and they knew we cared.

The tradition our boys laughed about was the family haircuts. Every two or three weeks, I set up a barber shop in the garage and cut their hair. (As soon as Roy and I were married, we saved our pennies and bought a set of clippers out of necessity!) The kids and Roy never went to a barber. All the neighbor kids in Kansas City would gather 'round, and we had a great time telling stories just like in the "old days." The boys still laugh about those "burr" cuts, but in time I got to be a pro — no nicks or anything. Roy still prefers my haircuts, so we have our regular barber sessions — I think he just likes the pampering. Don't be afraid to try haircuts on your family. Start first with little trims around the neck or the ears a few times until you get the feel of it. A good sharp scissors (barber scissors are best) and comb is all you need. Work at this until you feel comfortable, then gradually increase working with the complete head. It sure is a saver once you get the hang of it.

We have continued to add traditions with our family as the years pass. We hope they will carry them on in their families for fun and colorful years to come.

Since living in Ohio, the Buckeye State, we have a dish of buckeyes (or lucky beans, my boys call them) sitting out. When we have out-of-state visitors, they are always invited to put one in their pocket to take home. Traditions open many doors for our families.

As our children grow, we can give them everything that money can't buy, by building memories, working together, playing together, listening and sharing. (Remember the word sharing involves both directions!) Learn to organize and plan to enjoy meals together. "It isn't what's on the table that matters, it's who's in the chair!" Mealtime can really bond a family together. Have fun with your family as you gently guide them. A wise person once said, "Kids don't care how much you know, until they know how much you care." Those mealtime conversations will open many doors to caring and understanding!

There are times where discipline may be necessary, but be sure the "punishment fits the crime." Loving firmness is the best approach. Too often parents avoid discipline so they are not disliked. Yet without correction, a child can feel confused, hurt and rejected. We do our children an injustice by being overly permissive. Ben Franklin said, "Let the child's first lesson be obedience." An obedient child is a happy child. If we consistently "expect" obedience, we will get it and we will have a happy and contented home. Each parent needs to set an example and teach right from wrong. If our child is covered with mud, we don't let him wait until he grows up to decide if he needs a bath! We just try to remember the counsel given in the scriptures, "Reprove at times with sharpness, then show an increase of love to him." How swiftly these wonderful children grow up. Everyone of us hear "enjoy them while they're little, they will soon be gone." But we continue to wish our lives away, saying, "I'll be glad when they're out of diapers, going to school, etc." Isn't it a shame the truth never sinks in until we live it?

All four of our children got married in about one year. It was a busy one!!! Our lives felt like a revolving door! Luckily I had a grandmother who taught me to enjoy the moment! We had so much fun with all those wedding activities. How well I remember the excitement we had as a family as we hid silly little notes all over the first apartment of our son, Steve, for them to find when they returned from their honeymoon. They were finding notes for months!

Now grand-parenting has been one of the greatest doors I've passed through. What an opportunity it gives us to share unconditional love and affection. It's our privilege to keep these families together by making the past part of their present and future. Busy families today find it hard to do all the teaching necessary. What a joy (and help) it is to spend time with these little grandchildren. Too often we as grandparents try to hurry and get our chores done so that we can "play" with them, when what they really enjoy is "helping" us do what we are doing. The conversation and the giggles you will share while learning to tie shoes, making a bed, fishing together, or working on a recipe in the kitchen will bring blessings to both of you. Establish traditions with grandchildren, too. Teach them old-time games and songs. I think every child and grandchild in our family can sing "Mairsy Doates!" Be a friend — be a teacher — not a preacher!

One of our most fun projects was the grandchildren's newsletter. With 23 grandchildren, I am always trying to think of ways to keep us close as a family. Five of them live in Iowa, eight in Seattle, four in Missouri and six in Utah. Of course, there are four sets of parents, too, so it seems we always have a project of some sort going on. I titled it "Grandma Bears Good News." (We also collect bears, and they play an important part here, also.) I talk to all the mothers fairly often on the phone, so I got an update on all the sports, school, and other activities involving each child. (This could be done by letter, also.) I did a column on each child including their school picture next to their name in large print. The printer who runs the newsletter off for me recommended silk screening the photos so we could use them each month, and they would duplicate much nicer. I appreciated that tip.

I also added some puzzles, pictures to color (bears, of course) and riddles. They love these! Color books and the library are great sources of materials. Naturally there was the editorial column with a picture of Grandpa and me. This was a perfect place for funny news, teaching "tools," challenges, and interesting tidbits of history of our family — a great opportunity to give a child a sense of really "belonging."

In my first editorial I asked for news and contributions. It really paid off! The newsletters were sent out and greeted with excitement and giggles from everyone. The children all loved to read about themselves and were anxious to see what their cousins were doing. Even the parents couldn't put them down. Since each child got his own edition, there was not arguing over who got to color the pictures and do the puzzles, an important point to remember!

The drawings, poems, stories and jokes poured in. My file was overflowing with clippings, children "tested" recipes, did you know...facts, and puzzles I used in future articles. It's amazing the places in which ideas turn up — magazines, newspapers, even place mats for children in restaurants are a good source.

I then sent a questionnaire for them to fill out and return. They loved it and felt so important. (Of course, I included an envelope and stamp for returning.) Here is a sample of the page I sent.

My name is _____

My address is _____

My phone number is _____

The color of my hair is _____

The color of my eyes is _____

My hands are good for _____

My feet are good for _____

My favorite food is _____

I never eat _____

My favorite color is _____

My best friend is _____

My favorite TV show is _____

My favorite song is _____

I am happy when _____

I am sad when _____

The best thing that happened to me was _____

The worst thing that happened to me was _____

If I had three wishes, they would be _____

I varied the questions a little for the younger ones, and they had Mommy's help. But I got some really choice and touching answers and will always treasure these pages. It's a priceless gift when a granddaughter says her best friend is Grandma, or the little ones say they are sad when they leave Grandpa's house.

The ideas for questionnaires are endless. I also used family history, our country, and nature.

There were theme months, and with holidays in nearly every month, that's a natural. One issue I included $5 with each newsletter for them to buy a book and report back on what they read and how they liked it.

If you have family living away from you, I highly recommend a newsletter. It's amazing the skills it helps to develop in the little ones, and the love it generates in a family. Even older children and adults will benefit. Who does not like to read about himself and his loved ones, and everybody loves to see the mailman come with good news!

Since we do talk to our families fairly often on the phone, the parents have made it a practice to keep our picture close to the phone so the children identify our voices with our pictures. This really helps!

We also use tapes to keep in touch. I often read or tell stories to the little ones. If I read a book, I then send the book along with the tape. It's fun to interject little personal things like "turn the page…quick…the bunny is running away!…Oh! I guess not, silly Grandma!" or "Don't peek on the next page. Oh you did, you did!" I love to tell stories, including all the sound effects. (It's a great exercise to get rid of inhibitions.) Soon they're able to tell the story with you, word for word and sound for sound. Our family favorite is Teddy Bear's Birthday, by Mary Lundell. Gee, by the time we're to the page to sing "Happy Birthday" the excitement is so high they can hardly wait. I think every grandchild has been through that book with us, and it's a real treasure.

Each one in our family enjoys music. So many tapes we exchange are songs we want to share with one another. Anne Murray has a tape for children called "There's a Hippo in the Bathtub." It is excellent and has some real funny and easy sing-along songs on it including "You Are My Sunshine." I have sung that tape so many times with the grandchildren that several of them actually insist that it's me singing on the tape. I'm sure Anne Murray wouldn't appreciate that, but I'm flattered! The older granddaughters are now taking piano lessons, so we love getting tapes of "their" songs. When we visit them, the first place they take me is to the piano so we can play "Chop Sticks" and the older basic duets. It keeps me on my toes, and we have a good laugh at our "goofs." Jessica even had her dad video tape us, so she could practice after I'd gone home. The children's love of music is now opening other doors for them.

Roy and I really hope our grandchildren will find books their "good friends" and will remember our love for books, also. We keep our home stocked with well-used books and a favorite pastime is listening to a child read. In fact, Roy and I enjoy reading to each other as well. When children are beginning to read, it's so important to keep that enthusiasm alive:

1. Give them your full attention, don't let your mind or eyes wander. The nice part of being a grandparent is that you have time to listen.
2. Comment with interest as they read.
3. Don't correct little habits such as using his finger to follow the line while he's enjoying the story.
4. Also, don't have him try to sound out the word as he's reading to you. If he doesn't know the word, he needs help now, and he wants to get on with the story. You can work on sounds later.
5. Supply them with books on subjects they enjoy. If they want to read Dr. Seuss twenty times in a row, let them. We all have favorite things. I'd eat a piece of chocolate cake twenty times to a piece of pie any day.
6. Continue to read to them even when they're old enough to read by themselves. The attention and sharing is worth every minute.
7. Don't make them finish every book before they can start another. How would you like to be subjected to a rule like that?
8. Don't feel just because <u>Elsie Dinsmore</u> was your favorite book as a child that your grandchild will be thrilled with it. You may pique her interest in it by things you tell her, but if not, help her find a title she is intrigued with and enjoy it with her. You'll be a grandparent she'll remember!

When we sold our large home, my greatest concern was that the grandchildren would not have Grandpa's and Grandma's house to come back to. Well, several years have passed and we have had many little visitors to our cozy condo. Surprise! I've discovered any place we are is "Grandma and Grandpa's home." We still have our basket of story books, cookies in the cookie can, Grandpa's silly puzzles in his basket, our big poofy bed, our teddy bears, and our love! When we moved from the house, each child and grandchild got a special memento to keep so our "presence" is with them whether they're at home or visiting us. Every time Keri crawls into that twin bed with the fluffy quilt, she thinks of sleeping at Grandma's, or when Christian reaches for a handful of peanuts from that big blue jar, it's a treat from Grandpa in his mind.

As the grandchildren get a little older, they are able to travel alone or in pairs by plane. Our first fun adventure was when Emily (age 11) flew to visit us from Seattle. With camera in hand, we greeted her at the airport when she arrived dressed up like a sweet young lady with a smile from ear to ear. We recorded her visit on camera taking candid shots of her sleeping like a kitten, having lunch out with Grandpa, learning to sew at Grandma's machine, displaying proudly the six pair of shorts she made (three to take home to her brothers), swimming and playing war in the pool with Grandpa as they dunked each other to their hearts content, visiting with friends, and flying home. I then got a pretty scrapbook and wrote a journal of her trip, complete with pictures of every activity and mailed it to her thanking her for coming and sharing her sweet spirit with us. Her parents told me she looked at it over and over again! Emily is our oldest grandchild and

Gee! the years pass by quickly. She is now grown up. It's so important that we use every teaching opportunity and truly capture the moment.

Excuse me a minute while I write a short letter to this sweet girl.

Dear Emily,

Golly, today's the day! You've become a young lady. We've been teasing you for months about getting old, boy friends and being a "grown-up," but you were always so sweet and good-natured and would just smile. Your loving spirit has helped you put up with the silliness of a couple of "old folks." But down deep you know how very much we love and care about you. From the day we gathered around your crib, four grandparents and a bunch of aunts and uncles, we knew you were a very blessed daughter of our Father in Heaven. We watched you grow and develop, eating dill pickles before you had teeth, but they certainly didn't sour your disposition. Every phase you passed through brought happiness to us. How we loved having you knock on our door with a little bunch of wild flowers or "lick" grass that you had picked, or sit on the cupboard and help bake cookies or arrange pickles on the plate for Sunday dinner (my how you loved pickles!) or combed your pretty hair with my brush. With each year you grew more beautiful inside and out. Now that you are stepping through the door to a new phase of your life, don't run too fast. The more time you spend in each phase, the more you will enjoy it. Don't forget to stop and look back now and then. Remember the joys of being a little child and keep that in your heart always — the challenges, the learning and the excitement of life. There will be times when your parents, and life itself, will not seem fair. When "everyone else" gets to do things you don't, and when things hurt so much that no one understands! Please remember that Heavenly Father gave you parents and a family that love you very much. They have been through the door that you are passing through and know the feelings you experience. They will be there for you all along the journey. You are a bright, beautiful, good and loving girl. There will be many doors before you in life, choose carefully. Have a fun life! We love you so much, you'll never know until one day your child passes through your door with a sweet grandbaby in her arms. Then, think of us.

                                            Love, Grandma & Grandpa

Keri soon followed Emily with an exciting repeat visit to our house. We are so very blessed.

Behind my kitchen door is a supply of aprons. I can't function without one (I have noticed my daughters are now picking up the habit!) If you don't own an apron, I heartily suggest you get one right away. Being a grandmother these past twenty years would not have been the same. When it started to rain, how could we have carried all the toys in from the sandbox without basketing them up in my apron? What would have dried Cameron's tears when he fell down? How would we have carried all those shiny red apples into the house that we lovingly picked from Grandpa's tree? What would have protected by fingers as we pulled the pan of peanut butter cookies from the oven? Where would Craig have to hide when someone came to the door? He was too shy to say hello! How could I help Mary and Leisel gather their Easter eggs in the back yard when their baskets overflowed? What else could the little girls tie around their heads playing house. It served as a veil, long beautiful tresses, or a cape. And what else could I have wrapped around my chilly arms as I watched Jacob and Jessica shoot one more basket, or Nathan and Christian jump one more time in the pile of leaves. I may be teased about my apron, but I couldn't live without one.

Families are quite different now from the family life we remember, but the basic needs for love and approval are still there. As parents and grandparents, we have the opportunity to fulfill these needs and share in the blessings. As a grandma, I'm thankful for my "bigger lap," open arms and happy smile, because each day those sweet spirits open a new door for me! I can't wait until tomorrow!!!

January Food for Fun
Warming Foods for that Budget

When the teenagers come over, this is always a hit for those big appetites.

Mexican Bake

Brown: 1 lb. lean ground beef

Add: 1 large minced onion

Then add: 1 can drained green beans
2 diced tomatoes (fresh or canned)
1 can chopped green chilies
1 clove minced garlic
2 c. cooked rice

Mix well. Heat through or bake at 350* for 30 minutes.

Top with: 1 ½ c. sour cream
2 c. shredded cheese

Serve with corn chips. (I just do all this in my big fry pan. — DELICIOUS & QUICK!)

¤ ¤ ¤ ¤ ¤

Kids and grown-ups alike sure enjoy these sandwiches. So-o-o easy and inexpensive.

Frenchie Dips

Brown well in a large pot: 1 large chuck roast (about 3-4 pounds)

Add: 4 c. water
       1 ½ tsp. garlic powder
       1 tsp. basil
       1 tsp. oregano
       1 bay leaf
       ½ c. light soy sauce
       some coarsely ground pepper

Cover and simmer for 4-5 hours until beef is tender. Strain off the broth and shred the meat. Serve the meat on good crispy rolls and use the broth for dipping. YUM!

I freeze the meat in sandwich amount packages and the broth in small containers, then we're ready for a sandwich whenever the kids drop by.

¤ ¤ ¤ ¤ ¤

O.K. friends, here is the recipe that makes the whole book worthwhile. These rolls are so light, they nearly float off the plate. Your family and guests will rave and want them with every meal. You won't even mind, because they are so easy!

Melt-in-your-Mouth Dinner Rolls

Dissolve 1 pkg. yeast in ½ c. warm water.

Add: 1 T. sugar
      1 tsp. baking powder

Let stand for 20 minutes.

Meanwhile, scald: 1 c. milk

Add to scalded milk: 1/3 c. margarine
                     1/3 c. sugar
                     dash of salt

Stir to combine and melt margarine. Cool, then add: 2 beaten eggs

Combine all with: 4 ½ c. flour

Cover and refrigerate overnight.

Roll out 2 hours before serving. Shape either as butterhorns or as pinwheels in muffin pans. Let rise 2 hours.

Bake at 425* for 10 minutes.

¤ ¤ ¤ ¤ ¤

Everyone can make yummy homemade bread with this simple recipe. Give it a try, you will be surprised. You'll never buy that airy store-type bread again.

Easy No-Knead Bread

In large bowl, pour 5 c. warm water. Add 2 pkgs. (1 T. each) dry yeast.

When yeast is dissolved, add: 8 T. sugar or honey
　　　　　　　　　　　　　　　　8 T. shortening
　　　　　　　　　　　　　　　　8 tsp. salt
　　　　　　　　　　　　　　　　6 c. flour

Beat on high speed for 3 minutes. Then add 6 more cups flour. Stir in with wooden spoon.

Let rise. Stir down and spoon into pans. Let rise again.

Bake at 375* for 45 minutes in large pans, or 30 minutes in small pans.

Take from pans immediately, brush with butter, and let cool on racks.

Makes 4 large (9x5 inch) loaves or 7 small loaves.

¤　¤　¤　¤　¤

You'll never have as much fun as the day you try these EASY sweet rolls. From this simple dough, you can make cinnamon rolls and coffee cakes. You'll be proud and excited with the results, and I promise you RAVE reviews. There is no kneading, just stir it together. It's a soft dough, but with a little flour on the board to "flip" the dough in, you will do fine. Remember the softer a yeast dough, the more tender your product.

Sweet Rolls

Dissolve 1 pkg. yeast in ¼ c. warm water.

Mix together: 1 c. scalded milk
　　　　　　　1 stick melted margarine
　　　　　　　½ c. sugar
　　　　　　　1 ½ tsp. salt

Add: yeast mixture
　　　　3 beaten eggs
　　　　4 ¾ c. flour

Mix together and let rise until double, then follow variations.

Sweet Roll Variations

Cinnamon Rolls: Roll out the dough into a rectangle. Sprinkle cinnamon mixture (1/2 c. sugar and 2 tsp. cinnamon) over dough. Roll up dough lengthwise and slice by sliding a thread under roll, bringing it up and crossing over. Place rolls on greased cookie sheet and flatten with heel of hand. Let rise.

Bake at 375* for 12-15 minutes. Let cool slightly and frost with powdered sugar glaze.

Caramel-Pecan Rolls: Prepare dough as for cinnamon rolls. Slice.

Make caramel mixture by cooking together for one minute: 1/3 c. butter
½ c. brown sugar
4 T. corn syrup

Place whole or chopped pecans in bottom of greased muffin cups. Drop in one spoonful of caramel mixture. Put slices of dough into muffin cups. Let rise.

Bake at 375* for 12-15 minutes. Immediately turn muffin pan onto platter to remove rolls, and let cool.

¤ ¤ ¤ ¤ ¤

In our family's opinion, nothing makes a breakfast more special than French toast. It's so fun to make because there are so many varieties — you can just go with your mood. For a "dynamite" treat for everyone try the "Cinnamon Sticks." Wow! Are they delicious!!!

French Toast & Varieties

Basic Egg Mixture: In a blender, combine: 3 eggs
½ - ¾ c. milk
dash of salt & pepper
pinch of nutmeg

Dip bread slices on both sides, fry in hot oil until golden brown on both sides.

Oven-style French Toast: Butter a large cookie sheet well. Dip thickly sliced bread into basic egg mixture. Arrange slices on cookie sheet and bake in a 400* oven for 10 minutes on each side.

Waffley French Toast: Dip thickly sliced bread in egg mixture. Place in a well-oiled waffle iron. Cook until golden brown.

Deluxe French Toast: Spread one slice bread with softened cream cheese. Sprinkle with pecans. Top with another slice of bread. Dip sandwich into egg mixture. Fry in a small amount of oil until brown and crispy on both sides. Serve with berry syrup. (We especially like raisin bread for this combination.)

Elegant French Toast: Make a batter of:
- 2 beaten eggs
- 2 T. sugar
- 2/3 c. milk
- 1 tsp. melted Crisco
- 1 c. flour
- 1 tsp. baking powder
- dash of salt

Refrigerate batter while preparing other ingredients. Cut one large loaf of French bread into 1 inch slices. Heat oil in deep fryer or electric skillet. Mix together basic egg mixture. Pour egg mixture into one pie plate, batter into another. Dip bread slices into egg mixture on both sides, let stand a minute or two, and then dip into batter on both sides. Deep fry until golden brown on both sides.

Cinnamon Sticks: Cut 1 lb. load of unsliced bread into 4x1x1 inch sticks.

Combine:
- 2 c. milk
- 5 beaten eggs
- 1 T. sugar
- 1 tsp. cinnamon
- ½ tsp. nutmeg

Pour into broiler pan or sheet pan. Put in bread sticks and turn to coat. Cover and refrigerate overnight.

Deep fry in oil for 3-4 minutes. Drain on paper towels.

Our son, Steve's, favorite version of French toast is **Strawberry French Toast:**

Make sandwiches of white bread spread with Strawberry Freezer Jam and softened cream cheese. Dip in egg mixture, fry in hot oil, and serve with fresh berries and whipped cream. WOW!

¤ ¤ ¤ ¤ ¤

At our house we love to create recipes for the grandchildren. This is a real favorite!

Jessica's Glorified Rice Dessert

Dissolve 1 small pkg. of lemon Jello in 1 cup boiling water.

Stir in 1 c. pineapple juice drained from a large can of crushed pineapple (setting aside fruit).

Whip and set aside: 1 c. whipping cream
                      1 tsp. vanilla
                      1 T. sugar

When Jello is jelly-like in consistency, beat with beaters until fluffy.

Stir in: crushed pineapple
       2 c. cold cooked rice
       ½ c. chopped pecans
       ½ c. chopped maraschino cherries
       whipped cream

Refrigerate.

January Grocery Bag

January is traditionally known as "thrift month," isn't it? Whether it's because our budgets are tighter after all the holidays or because we're making New Year's resolutions, it's a good idea to get back to spending and eating wisely. Since groceries are not a fixed expense as is rent or a house payment, this is an area where we can really stretch our pennies, if we plan well and shop wisely.

One of the main things we need to guard against is impulse buying. If a single factor could be pointed out, perhaps this would be the one that makes stores the most profitable. Be aware that the displays at the ends of the aisles and in aisle bins are every often regular price. The stores know that we assume these are sale or special-price items. Often they are regular priced, high mark-up items that they would love to have us buy. Also, don't browse through a grocery store. The longer we are in the store, the more we tend to buy what we don't need. And as we gaze at all the "convenience" this and that, we rationalize and finally convince ourselves of the "value." You know, there was a study done by Vance Packard showing that most people are in a trance while at the grocery store. The people he studied generally blinked less and slower while in the store. This indicated a light trance — we blink more when we are excited. He felt that people couldn't deal with making so many decisions. Let's all remember that good foods are less expensive and more nutritious than junk food — and keep our good new year shopping habits throughout the year.

At the **bakery**, let's not spend "bread and roll money" on air-filled products. Also, remember that dark bread does not necessarily mean it is more nutritious. Much of it is just added coloring. Only if the package says "whole wheat" does the law require the use of whole wheat flour. And even then there are lots of things that can be added.

If you find a good buy on **meat**, remember these figures from the U.S. Department of Agriculture: if frozen at 0* – beef will keep one year, pork will keep six months, and chicken/poultry will keep two months. If kept longer than this, the nutritional value will not go down too much but the meat will become dry. If you get a U.S.D.A. prime or choice rump roast, cut it across the grain for a home version of a tender filet mignon. Mini drumsticks from chicken wings may fast become a family favorite.

In the **frozen food** section, look for the line that runs a few inches from the top of the freezer. The temperature below this line is supposed to be cold enough to keep the food frozen. Be careful of any food stacked above this line.

At the **produce** counter, you'll be seeing a few good buys on **brussel sprouts** as they head into the last month of their season. These are an excellent source of vitamin C and a good source of vitamin A. They will keep up to four to five days in the refrigerator if they are wrapped unwashed. Pick out firm, compact little heads that are green; avoid any yellowing ones. Cut a tiny x in the core to help speed cooking and add a small piece of celery to help eliminate the strong odor. Don't overcook and use only a small amount of water.

Oranges are, of course, still a good buy and should be until April. Tangerines, though, are at the end of their season so take advantage of good prices. Both should last several days in the refrigerator.

January is also a great month to talk about dried **legumes**. Legumes are some of the biggest grocery store bargains available. A one pound bag will usually make eight to ten servings and only costs you about $.40. The dried legume category consists of split peas, lentils, black-eyed peas, chick peas (garbanzo beans), kidney beans, lima beans, pinto beans, great northern beans, navy beans and pea beans. Legumes are probably the #1 meat substitute available to us, as they are rich in protein, riboflavin, iron and thiamin. In much of the world, beans, peas, and lentils are a primary source of protein. Alone they are an incomplete protein because they are missing two of the eight amino acids needed by the body to synthesize protein. Soybeans are the exception; they are a complete protein. When combined with whole grains and dairy products, legumes offer the value of a complete protein. Economically, they stand alone as a protein source. They have almost twice as many grams of proteins per pound for less than half the cost of their meat counterparts. A cup of dried beans also provides a man with half his daily needed iron and a woman with one fourth. They are also one of the richest sources of the B Vitamins. The nice part is that beans are filling, and you can feel full on only 250 calories (1 cup). They also contain no cholesterol and are a terrific source of fiber or bulk.

Most beans, peas and lentils are officially inspected, but the packages rarely show the grade. To do your own grading, consider color, size and defects. Dried beans should have a bright uniform color. Fading indicates age. If the beans are old, they will have less taste. Check also for perforations in the package and foreign material.

Because of the large variety of legumes available, there are many creative possibilities open to you. Lentils are one of the oldest and most nutritious foods. They go well with vegetables, grains and meat, especially ham. They do not need soaking and cook tender in less than an hour. Now is a great time to try lentil and split pea soup, green or yellow. Like lentils split peas cook in a relatively short time and do not need to be soaked. The next time you are cooking rice, throw in some split peas for a rich protein dish. Top with melted butter and some melted cheese. Everyone will love it!

Kidney **beans** are red and kidney shaped. They are especially good in Mexican food like chili. Pinto beans are a relative of kidney beans and can be used in much the same way. They are beige with brown speckles. The next you cook up a Spanish or Mexican dinner, try making your own refried beans. They are so delicious and lots cheaper than the commercially prepared ones. You can do this on the stove or in your crockpot. To make **refried beans** on the stove you first need to soak two cups of pinto beans overnight. The next morning pour off the water and cover with two to three times the volume of water. Cook over low heat with one chopped onion until very soft (three to four hours). Add ¼ tsp. garlic powder and 2T. chili powder and mash. Fry in ¼ c. bacon drippings and add some grated cheese for a great flavor. In your crockpot or slow cooker, put 2 cups beans and cover with two to three times as much water before going to bed. Cook on lowest setting and in the morning add a chopped onion. Stir occasionally throughout the day, then before dinner follow the above directions. For either method feel free to increase or decrease the water while cooking to suit your taste. Sounds easy, doesn't it?

Great northern and pea beans are excellent for use in soups, main dishes, and homemade baked beans. They are small, white and oval in shape. Be creative with your soups and try interchanging different beans for new tastes. Don't forget to add bread, cheese or a glass of milk to make an economical and protein-rich meal.

All cooked beans can be marinated in an oil and vinegar dressing and served cold as a salad.

Once cooked, beans will keep in the refrigerator for about a week or up to six months in the freezer in an airtight container. Since they store so well, cook up a large batch at once, and you will not have to repeat the process as often. This is really helpful if you are a "working" mom and short on time.

Store dried legumes in covered containers after the package has been opened. By keeping a variety of beans on hand in decorative glass jars, you will have a cute kitchen display and be reminded to use them often. Your family's health and budget will both benefit!

Snacks seem to be everyone's biggest downfall. In this area we usually end up eating just empty calories, filling our tummies (and our waistlines) without getting any nutrition and food value for our bodies. Why not take a good look at your family's snacking habits and see what you can do to improve them. Here are a few of our favorites: apples and cheese cubes, frozen orange slices, dried fruit, whole wheat scones (great for after school), nuts, relishes (carrot and celery sticks, turnip slices, etc.) and blender drinks. A combination we really like is:

    ½ c. fruit juice (apple, orange, pineapple or cranberry)
    3 heaping T. yogurt
    1 banana
    2 T. wheat germ
    2 T. bran

By eating the wholesome fruits, vegetables, grains and dairy products, you feel a sense of satisfaction and will be surprised that the craving for all those sweets won't be nearly as strong.

With good shopping, you'll eat better and feel your best!

January Why Didn't I Think of That?

Why not let the little ones read to you as you iron, sew, etc. It gives them good practice. "Telling" family stories is also a good pastime.

¤ ¤ ¤ ¤ ¤

As we put our babies and little ones to bed each night, we always played tapes of classical music (Mozart is great) near their bedrooms. It was relaxing and has instilled in them a love of "good" music.

¤ ¤ ¤ ¤ ¤

Our daughter, Kristen, and her husband, Mark, have 6 children. Mark makes it a practice of spending an hour or so each Sunday with each individual child, a different child each week. They all look forward to it so much, and what a nice way to develop relationships.

¤ ¤ ¤ ¤ ¤

Nothing works better for a teenage girl sharing a bathroom than a "beauty bucket." A brightly colored plastic bucket, trimmed or decorated with paints, is easy to pick up and carry all supplies from bathroom to bedroom and back again. Let their artistic efforts go to work in creating their container!

¤ ¤ ¤ ¤ ¤

As each of our children were born I got a large, sturdy box with a lid at the office supply store (I like the white ones) and labeled it with their name. This became their keepsake box and contains baby shoes, awards won, favorite old toys, special school papers and many, many treasures. As each child has grown and left home, the keepsake box has gone with them. It's so fun to hear them reminisce as they look through their special memories.

¤ ¤ ¤ ¤ ¤

A bored child is a restless, unhappy child. Give him responsibility and he will soon be happier and earn a very valuable lesson. Even little 3-year-olds can pick up in their room, make their bed, empty wastebaskets, put silverware on the table, dust furniture, and scrub the tub. What a help to mommy and child.

¤ ¤ ¤ ¤ ¤

When did you last make "snow angels" in the yard with the kids, or blow bubbles together and have a good laugh?

¤ ¤ ¤ ¤ ¤

Making a family time capsule (to be opened in 5-10 years) is lots of fun. We even enjoyed filling a little box with thoughts, hopes, dreams, etc. in January to be opened and checked on next January. It is amazing how much we change from year to year.

¤ ¤ ¤ ¤ ¤

We like the old Amish saying, "Eat yourself full, but clean your plate empty."

¤ ¤ ¤ ¤ ¤

One of the favorite pastimes for my little children, and now my grandchildren, is my button jar. They sit for hours dividing them in colors or stringing them on a long piece of thread. What fun they have!

¤ ¤ ¤ ¤ ¤

As each grandchild gets their first loose tooth, I can count on a phone call, alerting me to get a tooth fairy pillow made. There have been little pillows like a dump truck, a fish, a duck, a fancy heart, and now the last one was Sarah's, who insisted it had to have a BROWN HORSE on it!

¤ ¤ ¤ ¤ ¤

I buy a large synthetic sponge at the grocery store and cut it into 1 ½" squares. I then soak them in water and freeze them on a cookie sheet. When they are frozen, they're placed in a plastic bag and kept handy in the freezer. My supply of "Boo-boo Sponges" are always in demand when the grandchildren are around. They feel so cool and comforting on that "owie" and never drip all over.

¤ ¤ ¤ ¤ ¤

"Dress up" boxes are a sure hit at Grandma's house. Anything furry, silky or fancy, old costume jewelry, high heels, scarves, purses, even uniforms spur a child's imagination, and they will play for hours.

¤ ¤ ¤ ¤ ¤

Each time Kristen has had a baby (she has six now), I packed up my "Granny's Goody Bag" and headed for Utah to help with the family. It's just a plain, navy duffle-type bag but filled with fun and treasures you wouldn't believe. Last time there was an activity for each afternoon. Everything for making salt-dough figures, simple recipes for a cooking adventure, a treasure hunt list for everyone with a little prize afterward, even materials for everyone to grow a jar of sprouts for salads. Little Jenny could hardly wait until after each meal when we faithfully rinsed our seeds until, at last, we each had a full jar of beautiful sprouts of all kinds. Golly, did we have some delicious salads and sandwiches. The last day of the visit everyone wrote letters on teddy bear stationery for me to take home to Grandpa, and I had a bear in my bag for each of them to remember the visit!

¤ ¤ ¤ ¤ ¤

Our "Lizzy Long Legs," the biggest and softest bear in our collection, is a favorite of everyone. She gets to be adopted when we have little visitors. They take her home for a month and then mail her back. She comes home with some of the cutest notes and letters. Sometimes it a "Help! Let me out of here!" and sometimes it's a letter telling of her adventures on the trip.

¤ ¤ ¤ ¤ ¤

When the grandchildren come to visit, we love to have a "what if..." day. It might be:
    What if we didn't have any electricity?
    What if we didn't have a car?
    What if we have our picnic ready and it rains?
    What if there was a medical (first aid) emergency?
    What if we couldn't see?.....etc.

It's a great learning opportunity. You can use your imagination and have lots of funny experiences together. The electricity adventure is really an eye-opener!

¤ ¤ ¤ ¤ ¤

We like to have "long distance" parties. When someone is having a birthday or anniversary who lives far away, we enjoy their favorite food for our dinner, look at pictures of them, tell favorite stories of their life, and maybe use a memento of theirs as a centerpiece on the table. This is a fun way for children to learn about distant relatives.

¤ ¤ ¤ ¤ ¤

For a fun game to mail to a grandchild, draw a large snowman on construction paper and send it to them along with a bag of miniature marshmallows. A marshmallow is glued on each time the child does a good deed. When the snowman is completely covered, a little gift or prize can be sent.

¤ ¤ ¤ ¤ ¤

When baking those cinnamon rolls, try sprinkling finely grated apples and chopped pecans over the cinnamon-sugar mixture before rolling the dough. Then after the rolls are baked, while still warm, drizzle with caramel topping. WOW! Are they good!

¤ ¤ ¤ ¤ ¤

Often, if I don't feel up to a full family dinner, Grandpa and I will invite one grandchild over to enjoy that special dessert with us.

¤ ¤ ¤ ¤ ¤

Since we have a big dinner on Sunday, Sunday night is "Creative Night" and every one can fix whatever they prefer. The only rule is you fix what you want and clean up your mess. Golly, the kids could come up with some creative ideas, and then again some would settle for cereal! This practice is what developed our sons interest in cooking, so it pays off!

¤ ¤ ¤ ¤ ¤

The grandchildren love to do dinners from other countries. We learn to say "I love you" in that language. We have lots of fun and giggles with "Ich liebe dich." When we do Danish sweet rolls, everyone loves to get their fingers in the dough. Watching them rise and sprinkling on that mouth-watering cinnamon sugar, butter and currants, then seeing them "poofy" up in the oven was always more than little Nathan could bear!

February

31

February

Ah, February, a month of "love" and "hope". Two of the most valuable qualities we need today. Thank goodness for Valentines Day to give us the little nudge and reminder many of us need to appreciate those "special" people in our lives.

Nothing lifts us more than giving love to someone else. Only when we're serving others do we truly "find" ourselves and feel enthusiasm and hope for the future. February really is the month to feel hope. Hope for sunny days, flowers blooming, birds singing, picnics ahead, but most of all, a brighter day each day of our lives. No one is poorer than the person who feels no enthusiasm! If I live to be three hundred there will never be enough hours in the day to take all the walks I want to take, see the things I'd like to see, sing the songs I want to sing, taste the recipes I'd like to taste, and meet all the friends I want to meet! Breathe deeply, and fill your soul with love and hope! This month let's agree to say, "I love you" more every day!

Food for Thought

As I was preparing breakfast this morning, I could hear the hammer and saw in the garage and Roy whistling happily. I knew he was building his first birdhouse of the season, and his heart was full of hope. He feeds his feathered friends all through the winter (and we'll talk about that later), but there's just something about building those little houses and inviting the birds to start their families in our back yard.

These structures are so basic to put together and can be as elaborate or simple as you desire. The two key ingredients for a good birdhouse are the location and if they are able to get in and out of the hole provided. If you have swallows or robins in your area, put the birdhouse near a place where there are often mud puddles. They use mud in their nest building. Scraps of yarn, string, wood shavings or fibers are used by lots of birds. They also appreciate the birdhouses being hung in a protected place, such as at the edge of a wooded area. Items like bleach bottles, gourds and clay pots can be used, as well as lumber, to construct your bird residence. Most birds do their courting and set up their new homes in the middle of February, so now is a great time to get started. Why not run down to the library or book store for ideas and information. You'll soon find a bird is not just a bird. You'll discover there are shore birds, night birds, mountain birds, birds of prey, as well as backyard birds. You will learn their feeding and mating habits and how they migrate, eat or even survive. Their songs and flight patterns are so unique. It's fascinating!!

My two favorite birds are the cardinal and the nuthatch. Watching that little nuthatch run, head first, down a tree trunk is a sight to behold. They are called nuthatches because they wedge nuts and seeds into the crevices in the bark and then "whack" them open with their beaks. It is fun to watch a pair of these tiny birds courting. They are so devoted to each other. I also like watching them "sweep" their nest area. They are such "tidy" birds. The cardinals (many people call them "red birds") are so regal-looking, especially the male with his bright red feathers. However, I think the female is pretty in her own way. Her bill and tail are red, but she is a delicate grayish-rose color. They look so attractive together. They also start getting ready to set up housekeeping in February. They are terrific songbirds, and it's so touching to watch the attentiveness of the male as he cracks a seed and feeds it to his mate. Once you start learning about these amazing birds, a walk or drive in the country will never be the same. I highly recommend a book called America's Favorite Backyard Birds, by Kit and George Harrison, to get you started. And of course, Roy doesn't go anywhere without his copy of Roger Tory Peterson's Field Guide to Birds. Birding is such a terrific hobby to develop with your mate, children and grandchildren.

While Roy is busy in the garage working on those birdhouses, it's a good time for me to get my herb seeds started. My herb garden isn't very big, but I couldn't cook without running out to the patch to gather extra flavor for my recipes. My favorites, and most used, are — dill, basil, oregano, mint, tarragon, parsley, sage, rosemary and thyme. These are all easy to grow, and the more you pick the better they grow. I always start my dill and basil from seed. The others are perennial and are available at nurseries. I also have two big lavender plants that are perennial and smell like heaven. A few sprigs of lavender can really spruce up a bathroom or bedroom. Scented geraniums are also a "must". They come in so many scents from chocolate to rose fragrance. Try lining a layer cake pan with the rose or lemon geranium leaves and pour in your yellow cake batter. It really infuses the flavor through the cake. Then peel off the leaves before frosting! A pot or two of lemon balm is also a nice addition to the herb garden and is so easy to grow. I use these leaves in my ice cubes for lemonade. A side benefit to this little herb garden of mine is the delightful fragrance as we brush against the plants. Everyone pauses to enjoy!

It is about time now to start all those preparations for Valentine's Day. We are a family of sentimentalists so the first thing I do is prepare Roy's "Happiness Jar". We have been doing this for years, and the holiday wouldn't be complete without it. I promise it will bring happiness to your loved one and to you, also. Remember, giving of ourselves is the best gift of all. We use a little apothecary-type jar (or any container) with a ribbon around it and a label saying:

Roy's Happiness Jar– From, Bev
These notes are guaranteed to uplift, encourage, and please you.
To be drawn at the rate of one per week.

The jar is filled with slips that read:

- Good for an evening attending any sports event you'd like together.
- Good for one special moonlight walk together.
- Good for a dessert of your choice.
- Good for a movie of your choice.
- Good for one extra-special back rub.
- Good for writing two letters for you. (He hates to write letters.)
- Good for a quiet evening reading your favorite book. (I promise not to bother you.)
- Good for a nice polish on all your shoes.
- Good for a special big kiss.
- Good for an evening at the symphony.
- Good for a nice big hug and an "I love you" from the heart.

Neither of us will ever forget the time I was sharing my marriage ideas with a host on a syndicated talk show, and he pulled out a slip from the jar which read, "Good for a romantic evening — if I'm not in the mood, put it back and draw again!" Roy says we have no secrets from anyone! The list can go on and on. Give one to your someone special. Just remember to give him the things that make him happiest. Sometimes we get carried away with our own creative ideas that we forget the gift is for someone else. Think of their needs, desires, and wishes so that the gift will be personally "for them". This, in turn, will give you the most joy.

Instead of a "Christmas" gingerbread house, why not a "Valentine" house? Make it lacy and frilly, trimmed with red licorice, red hots, heart shaped candies and red gum drops, with lots of white icing!

Every house should have a valentine tree. These are so easy to make. Just go out and find a small, sturdy branch with lots of tiny little branches on it. Then spray it with white paint. (Be sure you do this in a well-ventilated room.) When the paint is completely dry, "plant" it in a clay flowerpot filled with sand or pebbles. You can tie a bow around the pot or cover it with foil or wrapping paper. Then the kids can attach their valentines with a little transparent tape, and it makes such a pretty decoration in the house. Everyone loves to trim a tree, and you'll find that you can use it over and over again.

Since we were talking about birds, did you know birds and flowers are an integral part of Valentine's Day? Long ago in England, it was believed that birds chose their mates on February 14th. It was, therefore, a good time for men and women to become sweethearts, too. Some birds keep the same mate all their lives, and birds in general have come to stand for love and faithfulness. Here is where we get our phrase "lovebirds". The English have a tradition that the first bird a young lady sees on Valentine's Day determines the kind of marriage she will have.

- If she sees a robin, she will marry a sailor.
- If she sees a goldfinch, she will marry a millionaire.
- If she sees a sparrow, she will marry a poor man, but will be happy.
- If she sees a flock of doves, it is a sign of good fortune in marriage.
- If she sees a single white dove flying overhead, it is a sign of good luck.
- If she dreams of a dove, it is a promise of happiness.

Valentine's Day was also the start of the saying "Rich man, poor man, beggar man, thief, doctor, lawyer, merchant, chief". The number of buttons on a girl's clothing on Valentine's Day determines her future husband.

The first flower to be associated with Valentine's Day was the violet. The legend goes that these grew outside St. Valentine's jail window. He spelled messages on the petals and the birds delivered them. If a man wears Bachelor's Buttons on Valentine's Day, he will wed his sweetheart within a year. During Civil War time, tomatoes grew only in flower gardens. Considered unfit to eat, they were admired for their beauty and referred to as "love apples". Many flowers have meanings associated with them from centuries ago.

- Red rose – I love you
- Yellow rose – I am jealous
- White rose – I am worthy of you
- Four-leaf clover – Be mine
- Gardenia – I love in secret
- Lily of the valley – Let us make up
- Ribbons – You are tied up (as my sweetheart)
- Lace – (the Latin word for net!) You have caught my heart in a net
- Fan – Open up your heart.

Food and decorations for this holiday always follow the basic theme – red, pink and white, hearts, cupids, flowers, birds, ribbon, and lace. Heart-shaped French toast with apple rings on the side and cranberry juice make a nice breakfast. Pink lemonade is a favorite at parties. Instead of red gelatin salad for dinner, cut jellied cranberry sauce with a heart-shaped cookie cutter. A white lace cloth with a red underlay makes a pretty table. Add a vase of red carnations, baby's breath, and fern. Red ribbon streamers with hearts strung along them, or just on the ends, make the final touch.

In this cold wintry month, Valentine's Day provides a perfect "excuse" for a party. There are lots of games that are fun to play and can be adapted to any age group.

Make two pairs of large cardboard hearts (a little larger than the foot size of the group) for each team. Split each team in half and put half on each side of the room. Then begin the race. The first person on each team places one heart on the floor and steps on it. Then he places the other heart in front of the first and steps on it with the other foot. Balancing on one foot, he moves the first heart forward, re-steps on it, carefully making his way across the room without ever letting a foot touch the floor. At the other side, he gives the hearts to the next teammate who takes his turn going across the room. The first team finished wins.

Or play a variation of "stone, paper, scissors." Divide into two teams. The three choices will be:

1. A maiden (looks sweet and puts finger under chin)
2. Her sweetheart (one hand on heart and one hand outstretched).
3. Disapproving father (scowling with arms folded across chest).

On the count of three the first two display their choice of characters. The maiden beats the sweetheart, the sweetheart beats the father and the father beats the maiden. The team with the most wins gets the prize.

A game that my kids loved as teenagers was called "If You Love Me, Smile!" Everyone would sit in a circle with one in the middle. The person who is "it" goes up to another, kneels down, and says, "If you love me, smile!" That person has to answer, without smiling, "I love you but I won't smile." If he smiles, he becomes "it". "It" has three tries to make the person smile (and they both have to say the complete sentence each time) before he has to move on to someone else. "It" can spice the game up a little but no tickling etc. is allowed. Everyone will be roaring with laughter!

Someone once said that February is the smallest month with the biggest heart. And isn't it true? The love that Valentine's Day brings out really creates a season of affection in our homes — relatives, friends, and especially our sweethearts.

Many of you have heard me talk about our weekly "Family Night". Maybe you would like to start one in your family during this month of caring. Set aside one night each week and devote it just to your family. This is a great way to bring everyone closer together whether there are just the two of you or a whole house-full. Even if you're alone — start a little group of friends!

There are lots of things you can do on Family Night. We always like to start out singing a song. It starts us on the right foot and really sets the mood for whatever we're doing that evening. We also have a few minutes right at the beginning to quickly go over the week's calendar so everyone knows a rough schedule and we don't plan conflicting activities. After the activity period, we close with another song and prayer and then refreshments.

During the activity period, do things that are suited to your family's interests. You can all go somewhere together or stay home and have a family talent show, or a lesson (given by any family member on any topic), or play games, or watch family slides or home movies, or do anything you enjoy doing together.

With Valentine's Day and President's Day this month, there are different ways to plan Family Night. The first week of the month, you could have a lesson on love, appreciation, and affection. Sometimes the most effective lessons are taught by the youngest family members. Remember, too, that the person who prepares the lesson usually learns most about the topic. Get everyone involved!

The second week is the week before Valentine's Day. Spend the evening making valentines for each other and the special people in your lives. It's fun to set out a pretty covered box filled with cards, pens, and stamped envelopes for the full week before Valentine's Day. Encourage each family member to write one note or card each day to a faraway relative or friend who otherwise may be overlooked.

The third week have each member of the family be prepared to give a short "love-line" about what he likes best about each of the other family members. Tape record these love-lines for memories everyone will treasure. You could also plan specific ways to keep this love in your home all year. Set up a pixie system – this was always our favorite. We drew names and were secret pixies for this person for a certain length of time. Everyone had a good time doing small, nice things for others. It was so much fun to sneak in and turn that person's bed down at night, pin an "I love you" to his or her pillow, empty the garbage when it was his turn, drop a stick of gum into his lunch sack for a surprise, or put a little note or treat somewhere for them. The most fun was in trying to keep it a secret and still doing as many things as possible.

The last week of February center your Family Night on the presidents of the United States. Perhaps everyone could tell a story about his favorite president, or fix dinner that night with each dish being a different president's favorite food. Abraham Lincoln's favorite dish was a potato casserole. Washington's favorite vegetable was onions. Some creamed onions and peas or onion rings would be fun to serve on "his" day. Thomas Jefferson loved fresh grown vegetables and crisp salads. For an activity why not visit a historical museum and visit the section on the United States.

Most of all, have fun with your family and grow closer together. By having a specific "family night," everyone feels secure in each other's love and everything runs more smoothly. Families are love, and love is "a relationship where each can grow together better than any could individually."

Speaking of families, during these last few weeks of wintry weather as our hearts are turned to hope and love, why not get to work on those scrapbooks. Pictures and memories are what keep our hopes alive.

When it comes to scrapbooks, there are so many options it's hard to know where to start. Roy prefers 35mm slides, and he has them chronologically by trays from the beginning of our life together. He also has them labeled on a large card in each tray box so he knows what, where and when each slide is. If you do this, on going, as you develop film, it really doesn't take much time. We have great evenings of slide shows (complete with popcorn), and it's one of the favorite activities when families or grandchildren come to visit.

I love photo albums so I have volumes collected on my library shelf. They also start with our courtship and have continued through our family life. I'm now working on Volume 7. It's so fun to leaf through and see the progression of the grand babies, the changing hairstyles, etc. In these albums I also keep special awards, programs, etc. of the family members. We then have a separate album labeled "Friends". Any pictures, newspaper articles, or Christmas photo cards are included in this book. Then, there's the special wedding album from our children's weddings. Soon I'll be starting another wedding album for grandchildren.

Roy and I each have a family history album that contains our genealogy, family group charts and pictures and stories of all our ancestors. What a fun project this is! Writing letters and visiting older family members can reap a wealth of information as well as searching city records, cemeteries and church records. This undertaking can certainly be time consuming but how satisfying to find out who you really are and where you came from. We are each currently working on writing our own "personal" histories. This is a real eye-opener, also. We've shared many laughs and tears as we recall happenings in our earlier years. The secret with any of these projects is to keep them current. Don't let pictures or news items accumulate for months or even years. Add them to the books as you get them. It really doesn't take that much time.

A friend of mine keeps all her current pictures and clippings in a pretty dish on the coffee table to share with family and visitors. Then the first Sunday of each month she counts her blessings as she reviews the pictures and places them in the books where they belong. Fun idea, huh?

Whether your interests and hobbies include birding, herbs and gardening, scrapbooking or whatever, there is much in life to bring love and hope! Spring and busier times are nearly upon us, so enjoy the last few days of quiet Winter and have fun catching up on those projects.

February Food for Fun
Recipes that say "I Love You."

On a cold winter day while we're working on projects, we love a big steaming bowl of this unique chowder with some crusty rye bread.

Bavarian Chicken Chowder

Cover 2 chicken breasts with 6 cups of water and add 1 small chopped onion.

Then add:
- 1 carrot
- 1 celery stalk
- ½ tsp. salt
- dash of pepper

Cover and simmer 1 hour.

Strain broth and remove meat from bones. Reserve 1 cup broth.

To 5 cups broth add:
- 1 c. chopped celery
- 1 c. chopped onion
- 1 c. chopped carrots

Bring to a boil and simmer until tender (10 minutes).

Meanwhile, melt ½ c. margarine in saucepan. Stir in ¼ c. flour. Cook a minute or two and stir in the 1 cup reserved broth. Cook until thick.

Add sauce to vegetables, then stir in:
- 1 ½ cups half and half
- 1 cup chopped drained sauerkraut
- chicken meat
- ¼ tsp. nutmeg

Heat thoroughly and serve.

¤ ¤ ¤ ¤ ¤

If the weather keeps us homebound, there are always ingredients handy to make one of Roy's favorites.

Cabbage Patch Soup

Brown 1 beef shank (or piece of beef with bone).

Cover with 5 cups water. Season with salt and pepper.

Simmer for 2 3 hours to make rich broth.

Then sauté: 2 T. butter
            1 chopped onion
            1 chopped celery stalk with leaves

Stir and cook until transparent.

Add to broth: Cooked onions & celery
            2 diced tomatoes
            I diced potato
            1 sliced carrot
            ½ head cabbage, shredded
            1 T. brown sugar
            Beef picked from bone.

Cover and let simmer for 1 hour.
Check seasonings.

¤ ¤ ¤ ¤ ¤

Anyone that has enjoyed a trip to Historic Williamsburg, Virginia, will agree with me that a bowl of peanut soup is mighty delicious. Now don't laugh, I know it sounds unusual but give it a try. It's terrific!

Southern Peanut Soup

Sauté (until soft but not brown):   ¼ c. margarine
1 medium chopped onion
3 stalks chopped celery

Stir in 4 T. flour until well blended. Let cook for a minute or two.

Add 2 qts. chicken stock, stirring constantly. Bring to a boil. Remove from heat and strain.

Add: 2 c. smooth peanut butter
2 c. half and half

Blend thoroughly and heat through to serve.

¤ ¤ ¤ ¤ ¤

The first soup I made, years ago, was this delicious recipe. It has been an all-time favorite with family and friends ever since. I promise it will be on your permanent list also. Ooh, it is so good with bread fresh from the oven, and a fresh vegetable relish tray. A piece of apple pie for dessert couldn't hurt!

Potato Soup

In saucepan, combine: 6 diced potatoes
½ c. chopped onion
2 stalks chopped celery
1 tsp. salt
1 tsp. celery salt
2/3 tsp. pepper

Cover all with water and cook until tender.

Fry 8 slices bacon; drain and set aside. Save 6 T. drippings.

Make a white sauce of: 6 T. drippings
2 T. flour
2 c. milk

Add white sauce and crumbled bacon to soup. Heat thoroughly and serve.

¤ ¤ ¤ ¤ ¤

A fun casserole to break the monotony and spice up your meal time — served with a spinach-orange salad and fortune cookies, everyone will have a good time.

Chinese Chili

Brown: 1 lb. ground beef
1 large chopped onion

Add: 1 can cream of mushroom soup
1 can cream of chicken soup
1 ½ c. warm water
½ c. uncooked rice
1 T. soy sauce
1 can sliced, drained water chestnuts
1 can drained bean sprouts

Mix together, cover and bake at 350 degrees for 30 minutes.

Add 1 pkg. snow pea pods and stir in. Bake for another 30 minutes uncovered.

Sprinkle with chow mein noodles. Set back in oven for 3 - 4 minutes. Serve.

¤ ¤ ¤ ¤ ¤

There are so many spices, herbs and seasonings that many people overlook. Be inventive and try something new!

Dutchman's Pizza

In mixing bowl, combine: 2 ¼ c. flour
    2 tsp. baking powder
    dash of salt

Cut in (as for pastry): 1 c. small curd cottage cheese

Then stir in: 1 beaten egg
    4 T. milk
    4 T. oil

Mix well and pat out to fit 14 inch greased pizza pan.

Brush top of crust with 1 heaping tsp. table mustard.

Cover with: sliced tomatoes
    1 tsp. caraway seeds
    1 small can sauerkraut, well drained
    ½ c. chopped corned beef
    2 ½ c. shredded Swiss cheese

Bake at 400* for 40 minutes.

¤ ¤ ¤ ¤ ¤

Now try this variety!

Mexican Pizza

Mix up one recipe of corn bread/muffins. Grease a 14 inch pizza pan and 6 muffin cups.

Fill muffin cups 1/2 full of batter and spread remaining batter in the pizza pan.

Bake at 425* for 8-10 minutes. Set aside to cool.

Combine: 2 c. refried beans
                1 c. leftover roast beef
                2 T. green chilies
                2 T. finely chopped onion

Spread mixture on cooled pizza dough.

Top with: 1 c. sour cream
                2 large, thinly sliced tomatoes
                1 chopped avocado, if desired
                2 c. shredded Swiss or Monterey Jack cheese

Bake at 400* for 15 minutes.

Cut into wedges and serve with hot pepper sauce, if desired, and the corn muffins.

This is a family-pleaser I make often. It's great because you don't have to precook the noodles. I love it!

Noodles Mexicano

Brown: 1 lb. ground beef

Add and cook until tender: 1 large chopped onion
2 cloves minced garlic
½ chopped green pepper
1 tsp. salt

Add: 1 can (17 oz.) corn and liquid
6 oz. pitted sliced olives and liquid
½ lb. dry noodles
1 large can (or 1 quart) tomatoes
1 tsp. chili powder

Mix well, then cover and cook on low heat for ½ hour.

Remove cover and sprinkle ½ lb. grated cheese on top. Cover and return to low heat for 5 more minutes.

Makes 6 servings.

¤ ¤ ¤ ¤ ¤

For those cold "stay-at-home" days, this is a super recipe and combines some nice old-world seasonings.

Roy's Country Supper

In a large, heavy pan brown a small beef roast (any kind; I usually use a round bone type). Brown the roast well on all sides and remove from pan.

Combine: 1 T. cornstarch
           ¼ c. water

Stir into pan drippings.

Then stir in: 1 c. water (approx.)
               1 small, finely chopped onion
               1 T. horseradish
               1 bay leaf
               salt and pepper to taste

Add the roast to the sauce, cover and cook over low heat for 2 3 hours.

Then add: several cut up carrots
            potatoes
            rutabagas
            cabbage wedges

Stir sauce over vegetables. Cover and cook for one more hour, stirring occasionally.

¤ ¤ ¤ ¤ ¤

Be sure you try this potato recipe. Kristen could eat a whole pan all by herself! It's a good reminder of Abraham Lincoln's favorite dish. He would like it, too.

Kristen's Yummy Potatoes

Cook 8 medium red potatoes in salted water with a bay leaf. Cool.
When cold, peel and grate coarsely. Put potatoes in a greased 9x13 inch pan.

Mix together: 1 can cream of chicken soup
¼ c. melted margarine
1 ½ c. sour cream
1 ½ tsp. salt
pepper to taste
1 finely chopped small onion
1 ½ c. grated cheese

Combine with potatoes. Cover and bake at 350* for 30-35 minutes.

Sprinkle top with mixture of: ½ c. grated cheese
½ c. crushed potato chips

Bake a few more minutes to melt cheese.

¤ ¤ ¤ ¤ ¤

When fresh garden tomatoes are not available, I always use this recipe for Salsa. We like it on baked potatoes, omelets, and most kinds of meats.

Salsa

Combine: 1 quart chopped tomatoes (fresh or canned)
1 chopped medium onion
1 can (4 oz.) chopped green chilies
½ tsp. salt
¼ tsp. coarse black pepper
1 can (8 oz.) tomato sauce
½ chopped green pepper
¼ c. fresh cilantro
dash of cumin
juice of 1 lime

Blend in the blender for just a second — it should still be a little chunky, not smooth.

Keep covered and refrigerated.

¤ ¤ ¤ ¤ ¤

Some soups and casseroles simply call out for a square of cornbread. When they do, stir up a pan of this tender, fluffy variety. Ooh, a hot piece of cornbread dripping with butter and honey will make your meal complete!

Bev's Fluffy Cornbread

Cream well: 1/3 c. Crisco
 ½ c. sugar

Add: 2 eggs and beat well until light and fluffy.

Stir in: 1 cup milk

Gently stir in: 1 ¼ c. flour
 ½ c. cornmeal
 ¾ tsp. salt
 2 ¾ tsp. baking powder

Pour into a greased 8 inch square baking pan. Bake at 350* for 35 minutes.

¤ ¤ ¤ ¤ ¤

The BEST biscuits — I promise you!

Southern High Rise Biscuits

Dissolve 2 T. yeast in ¼ c. warm water.

In large mixing bowl, combine: 5 ½ c. flour
 1/3 c. sugar
 3 tsp. baking powder
 1 tsp. soda

Cut in 1 c. Crisco, as you would for pie crust, until mixture forms coarse crumbs.

Stir in 2 c. buttermilk and yeast mixture. Mix well with a fork. Knead lightly a few times on a floured board.

Pat dough out to about ½ inch thickness and cut out biscuits with a small round cutter (I use a juice glass). Place on a lightly greased cookie sheet.

Bake at 425* until nicely browned (about 10-12 minutes). This will make about 48 biscuits. Dough will keep in refrigerator nicely or freeze extra biscuits.

¤ ¤ ¤ ¤ ¤

Don't be afraid to try a sourdough starter. It's so simple and really delicious.

Sourdough Starter

In glass or plastic bowl (never use metal for sourdough), dissolve 1 pkg. dry yeast in 2 c. warm water. Stir in 2 c. flour.

Let stand, covered, on your counter overnight (don't refrigerate).

In the morning, remove ½ c. of the starter and store it in the refrigerator in a glass jar. Use the rest of the "sponge" to make your recipe.

The Next Time you want to make something:

The night before, take out your ½ c. starter and add: 2 c. milk
                                                       2 c. flour

Mix well and let stand overnight as before.

¤ ¤ ¤ ¤ ¤

Sourdough Pancakes

To sourdough sponge, add: 1 tsp. salt
                            1 tsp. soda
                            1 T. sugar
                            3 T. oil
                            2 beaten eggs

Mix well, then fry on griddle.

¤ ¤ ¤ ¤ ¤

Sourdough Muffins

Mix together: 1 ½ c. whole wheat flour
½ c. sugar
1 tsp. soda
1 tsp. salt

Make a well in the center and add: ½ c. oil
2 beaten eggs
sourdough sponge

Stir only to moisten. Add ½ c. raisins or currants if desired.

Bake in muffin pans at 375* for about 30 minutes or until done. Makes 16 muffins.

¤ ¤ ¤ ¤ ¤

Sourdough Chocolate Cake

Mix together: ½ c. sourdough sponge
1 c. milk
1 ½ c. flour

Stir well and let stand for 2 hours or so until foamy and bubbly.

Cream together: ½ c. shortening
3 T. butter or margarine
1 c. sugar
1 tsp. vanilla
½ tsp. salt
1 ½ tsp. soda
1 tsp. cinnamon
½ c. cocoa

Add: 2 eggs, beating after each one.

Then stir in the sourdough mixture. Mix just until blended.

Bake in a greased 9x13 inch glass pan or 2 layer pans at 350* for about 30 minutes or until well done. Frost as desired.

¤ ¤ ¤ ¤ ¤

It's hard to beat these tender, light cookies. They really melt in your mouth.

Grandma Scheel's Butter Cookies

Beat together: 2 sticks margarine
1 c. sugar

Add: 2 egg yolks
pinch of salt

Then add: 1 ½ tsp. soda
1 ½ tsp. lemon extract
2 ½ c. flour

Beat well. Form balls the size of walnuts. Dip top side in sugar. Press flat with fork.

Bake at 350* for 8-10 minutes.

¤ ¤ ¤ ¤ ¤

This is the easiest cutout cookie recipe I have ever worked with. Super for Valentine's Day!

Heidi's Sugar Cookies

Combine: 1 tsp. soda
1 c. sugar
1 egg
1 tsp. vanilla
½ tsp. salt
½ c. margarine
½ c. sour cream

Beat for 2 minutes, then add: 3 ¼ c. flour.

Mix well, chill dough, then roll out and cut with cookie cutters.

Bake at 375* for 8-10 minutes.

Frost with powdered sugar frosting, or try mixing egg yolk, water and food coloring, and then painting on the unbaked cookies.

If you like chocolate sugar cookies, add ¼ c. cocoa to the dough.

February Grocery Bag

February is a good month to stretch those budget dollars. There will be lots of good buys on dairy products, so plan some meatless meals – macaroni and cheese, lasagna, and omelets. There will be some specials on the less tender cuts of beef, so work them into your budget, also.

There will still be plenty of chilly mornings ahead, and nothing starts the day better, helps the purse strings more, or makes you feel as fit, as a steaming bowl of hot, home-cooked cereal. Give all those grains a try!

The items in the grocery store that are most overlooked this month and are really a wealth of nutrition for pennies are the root vegetables — rutabagas, turnips, parsnips, and carrots. Please give them an honored spot in your menus.

Rutabagas are really a "yellow turnip" and require a little longer cooking than turnips. I usually cut mine in pieces and steam them about 30 minutes. They contain a lot of vitamin C and only about 30 calories per cup, cooked. Try peeling and cutting them in strips to eat raw. They are really yummy with a sandwich. Cooked, you can mash them or fix them almost any way you would potatoes. They are even good fried. Roy likes them especially well cut in slices, raw, and then marinated overnight in an Italian-type dressing. When buying rutabagas, look for smooth skin, ones that are uncracked, and those that are heavy for their size. They are usually waxed to preserve them, so it is necessary to peel them before using.

Turnips are a real winner because you can eat the root and also the tops as a green vegetable. When buying turnips, choose the small ones. The older, larger ones can be coarse textured and quite strong in flavor. Cook the turnip before peeling it for a nice, sweet taste. They cook tender in about 20 minutes. I like to serve turnips with pork, and both turnips and rutabagas are great in stews and soups.

Parsnips are almost always waxed to preserve them. Avoid the large ones — they will be woody and extra dry. Peel them thinly, cut in pieces and steam for about 20 minutes. Our favorite treat is to serve them buttered with a sprinkle of nutmeg — boy, are they good!

February is also a great month for those of us who love **avocados**, but feel we can only afford them for special occasions. During these winter months, when prices are low and the supply is good, avocados can liven up any sandwich or salad, and they are so good by themselves! We like them best halved, pitted, and sprinkled with a little salt and pepper. When shopping for avocados, remember that it's best to buy them when they're solid and not quite ripe. Then let them sit out in your fruit bowl and in just a few days, they'll ripen. An avocado is ripe when it yields to gentle pressure under your fingertips. To speed up the ripening process just a little, place the avocados in a little brown bag or in foil. Choose avocados with skins of uniform color and free of cracks. Irregular brown markings don't have any affect on the fruit inside. The skin should feel "velvety" and be dull in texture. If the skin is shiny and hard, the avocado is not yet ripe. Avoid avocados with dark soft spots — these indicate decay.

To remove the skin of an avocado, use a sharp knife and pull the skin away. The skin from a ripe avocado should peel almost as easily as a banana. Be gentle or you'll bruise the inside. If you only need half of the avocado, use the half without the pit first. The other half will store so much better if the pit is left in, leaving the meat unexposed. To keep avocados from darkening, sprinkle them with a little lemon juice. This will also add an extra little "tang" to your salad or sandwich! Ripe avocado should be used immediately or stored in the lower part of the refrigerator where it is a bit warmer. Chilling sometimes prevents ripening, so let them grace your fruit bowl until they're ripe.

There are so many fun ways to use avocados. Besides just eating them plain, we love them "on the half-shell," filled with a scoop of tuna or chicken salad or cottage cheese. Peeled and sliced, they add an "exotic" touch to any green salad, and you'll just love them on whole wheat bread with mayonnaise, sliced tomato and lettuce or sprouts. Their flavor blends well with many foods, so have fun creating your own new sandwich ideas.

Be sure to save the pits and — with patience — you can grow pretty little plants. Peel off the brown coating on the pit (this will speed sprouting) and insert 3 toothpicks around the pit. Then put in water, big end down, and place on your windowsill. Be sure not to let the water level go below the end of the pit or it will dry out. This is a fun project for your little ones!

This month, as cold wintry weather still prevails, avocados will add color, flair and flavor to lots of your meals, not to mention nutrition. Avocados remind me of sunshine and exotic places — a feeling we can all enjoy in February as we begin to anticipate springtime!

With food prices as they are and our budgets becoming ever more tightly stretched, it's a real challenge to prepare creative as well as nourishing meals day after day. By knowing how to use **spices** to the fullest, we can have more fun making distinct, better-tasting dishes from even the most ordinary foods. A little pinch of spice is the quickest and least expensive way to add individuality to our cooking. Here are some important facts about buying and using spices to help you get the most for your money.

Strength, quality of flavor and good color are the most important considerations in buying spices. To judge the quality, first look for deep, rich color. Color is indicative of fresh flavor — the more intense the color, the more flavor you can expect. Next check for fragrance — the stronger the better! Obviously, if the fragrance is gone, the spice is not worth much.

I've always recommended buying spices in bulk quantities because of the enormous savings, but it's vital to store them properly when buying larger amounts. Under the proper storage conditions, spices will retain their flavor and aroma for a long, long time. For best results, spices should be stored in a cool, dry place. Heat, light and moisture can all rob the flavor from spices, and moisture will cause caking. Many people make the mistake of hanging their spice rack directly over the stove. This might be convenient, but it's probably the worst place to keep spices because of the excessive heat and moisture (steam) from cooking. I even keep my "red" spices such as chili powder, paprika, etc. in the freezer. This helps them retain their vitamin C and keeps them from getting buggy. It is never wise to store any dried or powdered food items above or near the stove. The heat combined with the steam that is created from cooking is harmful. Not only does it harden things, but the heat will destroy the nutritional value. Even though it seems like a handy place for storage, I would recommend keeping something other than food above a range.

In most cases whole spices can be stored longer than ground ones, so the little hand spice grinders on the market now are a good value. These allow you to grind just the amount you want.

Herbs will lose their flavor a little faster than spices, so when buying herbs such as oregano and basil, keep in mind that the "leaf" form will keep its flavor longer. If you're fortunate enough to be able to grow your own herbs, store the leaves whole and crumble them as you need them to release all that flavor!

Spices should be used to enhance natural flavors, not hide or mask them. Ground spices will flavor your dishes quickly, so in recipes that cook for a long time, add ground spices near the end of the cooking time. Uncooked recipes such as salad dressings should be mixed and allowed to stand for several hours to bring out all the flavors. Whole spices are especially useful in long-cooking dishes and should be added at the beginning of the cooking time. If you wrap whole spices in a small piece of muslin or cheesecloth they can be easily removed from the pot.

Learning to use herbs and spices creatively as flavor enhancers will enable you to use much less salt, an important factor!

Here's a description of some of the more common spices and some ways to use them:

Allspice tastes like a mixture of cinnamon, nutmeg and cloves. Use it whole in pickling meats, for gravies, soups and stews; or ground in baking, relishes, preserves and tomato sauces.

Basil is an important seasoning in tomato dishes. Use in cooked peas, beans, carrots and squash, or sprinkle over lamb before cooking.

Bay Leaves are the dried leaves of an evergreen tree. Use for pickling, in stews and soups. Excellent with a variety of meats.

Chili Powder is a ground blend of chili peppers, oregano, cumin seed, garlic salt, sometimes cloves, red pepper and allspice. It's a basic seasoning for chili and Mexican dishes.

Cinnamon comes from the bark of an evergreen tree. Use whole sticks in pickling, preserving, stewed fruits and for flavor in hot drinks and punches. Use ground in baking, mincemeat, applesauce, cooked cereals and sprinkled on sweet potatoes.

Cloves can be used whole for pork and ham roasts, pickling and soups. For a tasty stew add a small onion studded with three or four cloves. Use ground in baking. Try a dash in chocolate pudding or on vegetables.

Cumin is an important ingredient in curry and chili powder. It gives enchiladas their characteristic flavor.

Ginger is the root of a plant. Use ground in gingerbread cakes, pumpkin pie, canned fruits, pot roasts and other meats.

Mace is the fleshy growth between the nutmeg shell and the outer husk. The flavor resembles nutmeg. Ground, it is essential in good pound cakes and contributes a golden color and exotic flavor to all yellow cakes. Great in all chocolate dishes; for variety try 1 tsp. in 1 pint whipped cream.

Marjoram is a relative of mint. Good in stews, soups, sausage and with poultry, fish and lamb.

Nutmeg is the kernel of the nutmeg fruit. Grate whole or use ground in baked goods, on eggnog, custard, whipped cream or pudding. Good on cauliflower and spinach. Delicious for flavoring doughnuts and pie crusts.

Oregano is also known as Mexican sage. It's great in any tomato dish.

Paprika is a sweet red pepper, ground. It is prized for its brilliant red color. Pretty as a colorful garnish sprinkled on foods. Important in Chicken Paprika and Hungarian Goulash.

Pepper is the small dried berry of a vine. Known as the world's most popular spice. White pepper is black pepper with the outer covering removed.

Sage is especially good with pork. Use it in sausage, meat stuffings, poultry and salads.

Thyme has a strong, distinctive flavor. Use it in soups, stews, poultry stuffings, clam and fish chowders. Thyme and fresh tomatoes are a must together.

Turmeric is a root of the ginger family. Good in combination with mustard, in flavoring meats, dressings and salads. Use in pickling and relishes. Also good on yellow corn.

Have fun and be adventurous with spices!

It seems like everyone loves pasta! **Pasta** can be divided into two general groups. These are macaroni (including spaghetti, lasagna, macaroni, and all the other Italian-type pastas), and noodles (such as egg noodles and vegetable noodles). The reason they are divided like this is because of the difference in ingredients. They are both made out of one or more of several types of flour, but noodles also have eggs in them.

The common types of flour used in making macaronis are:

Durum flour and semolina— both of these varieties are made from durum wheat which contains a "tougher" protein. This is preferred, and durum wheat is the most commonly used in making macaroni. Semolina is a coarse, granular product from the endosperm of durum wheat.

High protein flour— pasta made with this type of flour will have a slightly higher food value.

Regular flour and farina— these are made from soft wheat, and although the physical aspects of the product are a little different, the nutritional value is not changed.

Any of these flours can be bleached, so be sure to watch product labels for unbleached flours. The government permits the manufacturer to decide how much he tells on the label about the flour(s) used. Although most macaroni is enriched with B vitamins, calcium and iron, the label only has to say "enriched." Be aware, too, that the flour is what is enriched, not the complete product. Occasionally, a manufacturer will also enrich the actual product with wheat germ or food yeast.

All pasta products should have natural coloring only, so don't be swayed by brands advertising "no artificial color added." Manufacturers are allowed to add seasonings or disodium phosphate (to make it quick cooking), but both of these must be noted on the label.

Noodles are different from macaroni in that eggs are added. The eggs can be fresh or dried, whole eggs or just yolks. Of course, the ones that use fresh whole eggs are best. These have a slightly higher protein content. The brands that use egg yolks are just a little higher in vitamins, but also contain a lot more fat. Even though the eggs add to the nutritional value of noodles, the quality of flour used is lower, making noodles lower in protein than macaroni. Again with noodles, federal regulations prevent artificial coloring and preservatives, and any other added chemicals must be listed on the label.

Flat egg noodles are the most common. However, noodles come in lots of other shapes, so try them. They're especially fun for children. Of the vegetable noodles, spinach noodles are the most widely available. Any vegetable puree can be added. This really adds an interesting and different taste (usually not too much like the actual vegetable, though). The color also adds a special touch to your dishes.

Don't overcook pasta or you will get a sticky product, and you will lose most of your water-soluble B vitamins. You might try adding a little touch of sugar or honey to the water. It adds a great taste, especially to the whole wheat varieties.

Why not have some pasta tonight! Happy Shopping!

February Why Didn't I Think of That?

Remember, as soon as you remove food from any pan, fill it with hot water. That little step will save you lots of scrubbing later.

¤ ¤ ¤ ¤ ¤

The principle of letting lost oxygen return is true with canned vegetables. They should be opened and allowed to stand in the saucepan at least 15-20 minutes before heating to regain the oxygen they lost in canning. I always open them and let them sit on the stove while I make my other meal preparations, and then heat them through at the last minute. It really improves the flavor.

¤ ¤ ¤ ¤ ¤

Be sure and develop the habit of turning the pan handles in or to the side when cooking at the range. Doing so will eliminate lots of spills and accidents.

¤ ¤ ¤ ¤ ¤

Meat stocks are one of the most valuable items you can keep in your freezer. Then delicious soups, casseroles, and main dishes are a snap to make. Never throw a bone away. Cover that turkey carcass, pork roast bones, or whatever with water, onion, a little celery and carrots, salt and pepper, and let it simmer for a couple of hours. Then freeze broth in containers. You can make a rich beef stock by browning beef bones (the smaller the better — saw them up if you need to) on a cookie sheet in a 400* oven until dark brown and then proceed to make stock.

¤ ¤ ¤ ¤ ¤

Instant potato flakes are a quick, last minute thickener for soups or stews. Just be sure and add them a little at a time!

¤ ¤ ¤ ¤ ¤

For a fantastic quick dessert, split purchased croissants, fill with raspberry pie filling, drizzle with a little chocolate sauce and top with a dollop of whipped cream. A chocolate "leaf" and a raspberry on top make it extra special.

¤ ¤ ¤ ¤ ¤

Small custard cups filled with water and a few fresh sprigs of herbs make nice little finger bowls when serving fried chicken or ribs.

¤ ¤ ¤ ¤ ¤

To make fresh herb butters, use: 1 T. fresh chopped herbs OR 1 ½ tsp. dried herbs to 1 stick of butter. Mix well and roll in parchment paper. Tie rolls with gold cord or string.

¤ ¤ ¤ ¤ ¤

Add a few sage leaves when frying chicken, pork chops, or browning a pork roast.

¤ ¤ ¤ ¤ ¤

For herb teas, use 3 tsp. of fresh leaves to 1 c. water and steep for 5-10 minutes.

¤ ¤ ¤ ¤ ¤

For a great egg salad add celery seed, dried onion and dill weed.

¤ ¤ ¤ ¤ ¤

Be sure and grow lots of thyme in your herb garden. It's an excellent substitute for salt in a salt-free diet. It is even good on popcorn or french fries!

¤ ¤ ¤ ¤ ¤

A few brightly colored marbles in your bird bath will really attract the birds.

¤ ¤ ¤ ¤ ¤

Remember, as your lavender begins to bloom, cut a few sprigs occasionally to lay across your pillow. Free but luxurious!!

¤ ¤ ¤ ¤ ¤

As you are planting your herb and garden seeds, use some of your plastic egg halves filled with potting soil. They'll be growing by Easter, and you can fix some pretty baskets for your friends.

¤ ¤ ¤ ¤ ¤

We all keep photos of our families and friends, but it is also a good idea to keep photos of furniture and household valuable items. Put them in a safe place for insurance purposes in case of theft or fire. We also keep photocopies of our credit cards, etc.

¤ ¤ ¤ ¤ ¤

Words of comfort are the best tonic!

¤ ¤ ¤ ¤ ¤

The more you carry the past around, the less likely it is that the future will improve.

March

March

By golly, I believe Spring is on the way! At least, when I took my walk this morning, the wind in the air seemed to be telling me something! It seems March brings with it a renewed enthusiasm for life. I get excited thinking about Easter, Spring parties, and doing some sewing for that spring and summer wardrobe. I hope you'll have a happy and satisfying March. Remember Spring is just around the corner, so let's get those muscles moving and our blood stirring. We've got good things to accomplish!

Food for Thought

"Life is like a quilt." My project for this past winter was to learn everything I could about quilting — many trips to the library, afternoons and evenings studying, hours browsing in fabric stores, and then many long days of practical application. It was exciting, challenging, enjoyable; but the most enlightening discovery I made was that while learning about quilts, I was learning about life!

A quilt starts with pieces, every one different. Some bright, some subdued, strong or gentle, delicate or fragile. Just like you and I, different right down to our individual fingerprints. We can each be our best and not compete with anyone else. Someone once said, "It's not what you are that holds you back, it's what you think you are not". Remember what my Grandma Benson always said, "You can't chew with someone else's teeth!" Be the best "you!"

"Don't be a life collector, be a life celebrator." We all have a tendency to collect pieces of our lives like fabrics and are afraid to use or celebrate them. Go ahead and have those friends over for dinner, throw a birthday party, learn a new craft or skill, have a family get-together or try a new style. I have a sister who still has tablecloths, etc. in her cedar chest, waiting for that "special" occasion! Golly, she's older than I am. Let's use those pretty things, have a party or just enjoy them with our families (who better do we invite to our tables!) Each "piece" of our lives is as important as each piece in a quilt. One strengthens the other.

Every quilt must have a BATTING or filler. The true purpose of a quilt is to give warmth to others. Isn't that true in each of our lives? Only when we lose ourselves serving others do we really find the happiness we all search for. Whether it's a loaf of fresh bread from the oven, tending a neighbor's children, a hand-made gift or just a hug or smile for someone in need, we are adding the "batting" or warmth to life and fulfilling our purpose.

Each individual STITCH taken in our quilt is like our daily activities, each working together creating an end result. Some stitches may seem boring or like drudgery but are necessary and are as important as the fun or more decorative stitches (or activities). Nothing we do should be considered just "busy work." That's like quilting with a needle and no thread! Abraham Lincoln once said, "I want it said of me by those who knew me best that I always plucked a thistle and planted a flower where I thought a flower would grow." Let's share compliments instead of gossip, and hugs and smiles where we can. Make every "stitch" of life count!

March being a month of new beginnings is a great time to start making our "life quilt" even better. Do you enjoy holidays at your house, including everyone, and really have a good time? We all remember the morning Heidi made green pancakes for Saint Patrick's Day! Celebrate each day and make all holidays special!

Why not start Easter morning by serving your hard-cooked eggs as "little chicks". Cut the white of the egg in half, being careful not to cut the yolk. Then with the whole yolk sitting in half of the white, it becomes the "head" of a little chick. Use two bits of raisin or currants for his eyes and a carrot tip for a beak. They look so cute sitting on a plate, served with a slice of ham, a fruit cup and a hot cross bun. You'll please the family for sure!

Our children never cared for all the commercial candies, so our Easter morning consisted of a treasure hunt, complete with notes to finally find their "nest". A book, musical tape, game, etc. was usually their big "find." Attitude is the key to any holiday or party. If everyone is involved, the enthusiasm is high, and it's done within your means and physical limitations, it's bound to be a success!

Nothing says "I love you" and "I care" more than a gift you create yourself, whether it's a flower arrangement from your garden or an item lovingly stitched with your own hands. The most important thing to remember in gift-giving is to give what the person would like and not what you want them to have! This is especially true with older people (and I am getting there). After all, how many handkerchiefs can we use? How about a pretty night light, a box of stationary and cards complete with stamps, some homemade soups and " TV" dinners for the freezer, a magazine subscription, gift certificates for a nearby restaurant, some new soft fluffy towels, or a scrapbook or photo album for all the pictures we accumulate!

Every day we each are literally "STITCHING" the "quilt" of our life. None of us want to end up as a harried, worn, faded, flannel blanket or an irritating, coarse, scratchy army blanket (don't we all know a few people like that?) Let us be a beautiful, colorful, warm, loving creation so that our Heavenly Father can say "This is My child in whom I am well pleased!"

March Food for Fun
Recipes to Usher in the Springtime

Nothing says "SPRING" like this smooth, rich and creamy mixture of asparagus, chicken and cream. You'll love it! My daughter Heidi's family loves this so much, she makes it all year long and substitutes broccoli for asparagus.

Velvety Chicken Asparagus Soup

In a 3-qt. saucepan, melt: 1 stick of margarine

Stir in: ¼ cup of flour.

Let it cook a minute or two, then gradually add: 2 c. chicken broth
2 c. half & half
4 T. minced onion

Continue to stir until thickened, then add:
1 tsp. salt
½ tsp. pepper
3 tsp. minced fresh parsley
2 c. diced cooked chicken
1 can asparagus, diced
OR 2 c. cooked asparagus

Heat thoroughly and serve.

¤ ¤ ¤ ¤ ¤

One of the nice things about baking ham for Easter is the wonderful soup you'll have to look forward to. We love this soup any time of the year, and it freezes well. I keep extra jars of it frozen to enjoy later.

Ham and Bean Soup

Cover 1 lb. great northern beans with 2 ½ qts. cold water. Soak overnight.

The next day, drain and add:
- 1 ham bone (or 2 ham hocks) with meat
- 2 chopped onions
- ½ tsp. coarse black pepper
- 1 bay leaf

Cover all well with water. Simmer for 3-4 hours until beans are tender.

Remove ham bone and pick meat from bone.

Add to soup:
- Several sliced carrots
- 2 sliced celery ribs
- 1 large potato, diced
- 2 T. brown sugar
- 1 T. vinegar
- ½ tsp. chili powder
- 1 can (8 oz.) tomato sauce

Simmer for 30-45 minutes until vegetables are tender, add meat, heat through and serve.

¤ ¤ ¤ ¤ ¤

If you're doing a buffet for Easter, you will want to include this rice dish. It's so pretty on the table and absolutely delicious. It goes so well with ham, and there won't be any leftovers!

Country Rice

In 2-qt. casserole, combine:
    3 c. cooked rice
    ½ c. chopped parsley
    ½ c. grated cheddar cheese
    ½ c. chopped onion
    2 T. chopped green pepper
    1 clove minced garlic

Blend: 1 can (14 ½ oz.) evaporated milk
    2 beaten eggs
    ½ c. vegetable oil
    1 T. salt
    dash of celery salt
    ½ tsp. pepper
    3 T. lemon juice

Mix rice and sauce together in casserole dish, then sprinkle with paprika.

Bake at 350* for 45 minutes or until set.

¤ ¤ ¤ ¤ ¤

This is super served with that baked ham for Easter.

Raisin Sauce

In saucepan, melt: 2 T. butter

Stir in: 2 T. flour

Cook for a minute, then add:
    2 c. apple cider
    ½ c. raisins

Bring to a boil, stirring constantly. Simmer for 2 minutes. Serve hot!

¤ ¤ ¤ ¤ ¤

This is so tender and light. It's nice to serve for a spring get-together.

Grandma's Lemon Pecan Bread

Cream together: 2/3 c. sugar
½ stick butter

Beat in: 2 eggs
2 tsp. fresh lemon peel

Then add: ¾ cup milk

Gently stir in: 2 c. flour
2 ½ tsp. baking powder
dash of salt

Then add: ½ c. chopped pecans
½ c. chopped golden raisins

Bake in 2 nut bread pans (7 ½" by 3 ½" inches) at 350* for about 50-55 minutes.

While warm, glaze with ½ c. powdered sugar and enough fresh lemon juice to make thin glaze.

This freezes well.

¤ ¤ ¤ ¤ ¤

Everyone needs a good cream puff recipe. You'll find yourself being so creative in serving these wonderful shells.

Cream Puffs

In heavy saucepan, combine: 1 c. water
                             1 stick margarine
                             ½ tsp. salt

Bring to a boil to melt margarine. Stir in 1 c. flour (all at once). Cook and continue to stir until mixture forms a ball, then remove from heat.

Add 4 eggs – I at a time, and beat well after each addition.

Drop by tablespoonful onto greased cookie sheet (4 per sheet). Recipe makes 8 nice-sized ones. Bake at 400* for about 30 minutes or until well done. Cool.

Cut off tops, pull out any soft dough, fill with whipped cream or pudding, replace tops, and sprinkle lightly with powdered sugar. Serve immediately or refrigerate.

Shells freeze well to fill later. Fill with chicken salad for a nice luncheon or fill tiny ones with various types of salads for appetizers.

¤ ¤ ¤ ¤ ¤

After a hard day's work, it's hard to beat the comfort of a big bowl of freshly baked bread pudding, topped with warm lemon sauce. Ooh, I think I'll make some right now.

Bread Pudding

Combine in baking dish: 6 c. day-old bread cubes
                         4 c. scalded milk with 1 stick margarine melted in it
                         1 c. sugar
                         4 beaten eggs
                         ½ tsp. salt
                         1 tsp. cinnamon
                         1 tsp. nutmeg
                         ½ c. currants or chopped raisins

Stir well. Set dish in a pan of water, having water one inch up on side of casserole dish.

Bake at 350* for one hour or until knife comes out clean.

Serve warm with lemon or chocolate sauce.

◘ ◘ ◘ ◘ ◘

Mom's Lemon Sauce

In saucepan, mix together: 1 T. cornstarch
　　　　　　　　　　　　½ c. sugar
　　　　　　　　　　　　¼ tsp. salt

Add:　1 c. hot water

Cook until thick, then add:

　　　1 tsp. lemon peel (I like to use fresh lemon; it really is better)
　　　3 T. lemon juice (here again, fresh is better)
　　　2 T. butter or margarine (I always use butter)

Serve warm. Especially yummy over bread pudding.

March Grocery Bag

It's that time again to grab our grocery carts and head for the store. I hope you're adopting my philosophy of making it an exciting challenge instead of drudgery. If you'll continue to avoid the convenience foods and those empty-calorie snacks and then use those extra pennies to stock up on the sale items you use and need, you will soon find yourself on the way to having a nice food supply. I can't stress how much this will save you by never having to go to the store but going only for specials to keep your stock up.

This is the time of year we all enjoy meal-in-a-bowl type soups and stews, and the ingredients are exactly what the best buys are right now. It's still a little early for many fresh things in the green family, so try a Jello mold with fruit or coleslaw. Pork prices will be inching up, but it is still a good buy, so consider some ham and beans, pork and sauerkraut, split pea soup, lentil soup, potato soup with bacon or some tamale balls. You still can't go wrong economically with a turkey (have it cut in quarters) and then you're all set for chicken (turkey) and noodles or rice or dumplings or meat pies or casseroles.

Remember also that meat isn't always necessary. There will be some good cheese buys this month; and macaroni and cheese, cheese soup or some of the seafood and cheese chowders really hit the spot.

We will be seeing the last of the good California navel oranges this month and the other citrus fruits have reached their peak, so enjoy some of these before they are gone.

For desserts this month stick to the hearty, wholesome type you can bake in the oven right along with the casserole, stew or hot bread for supper. Try bread pudding with lemon sauce, fudge pudding, fruit cobbler, rice pudding, or how about good old-fashioned tapioca.

Artichokes and asparagus are starting to appear at the markets but both will be at their peak with better prices in April. Look for compact, tightly closed artichokes that are plump and nicely green on every side. This vegetable is high in food value, especially potassium, and low in calories. They have a nice, mild flavor and are delicious with butter sauce (of course, that adds the calories.) Keep them unwashed and well-wrapped in the fridge. They will keep well for about 4-5 days.

Asparagus stalks should have firm stems and tightly closed tips. The stalk will automatically snap at the right place to remove the woody end. Asparagus loses its sugar very quickly so use it right away. If you must keep it a day or two, store it in a plastic bag; or I stand mine on end in a pitcher half filled with water and a plastic bag over the top. Asparagus is a great source of vitamin A & C, and is also low in calories. It is so tasty in stir-fry or steam it in a small amount of water.

This is also the peak month for **bananas**. There are many kinds of bananas all over the world, including long, green ones (green when they're ripe); short, square ones (even the banana inside the peel is square) that are used only for cooking and frying; long, red ones; and short, yellow, very thin-skinned ones that are the sweetest of all; besides the "normal" bananas we receive. Most of these varieties are not shipped because of the thin peeling, which makes them difficult to handle, and because of low demand. Bananas are rich in carbohydrates, phosphorous, potassium, and vitamins A and C. They are also very easy to digest. They are at their best when the skins are yellow flecked with brown.

The vegetable of the month is **cabbage**. This vegetable is so versatile, delicious and good for us. The consumption of cabbage has declined in the last 30 years by 50% and that is really a shame. I guess it's underrated because it is considered a poor man's food, but it's really so rich in iron, potassium and vitamin C, and it's great for providing body roughage. I always keep a head or two in the refrigerator because I can use it for a fast salad of coleslaw, in stews, soups or casseroles, or just steam it and add a little butter or cheese sauce for a yummy vegetable dish. When you shop for cabbage, look for solid, heavy heads that are deep green. Avoid too many loose leaves or a white head. This usually means it's been in storage a long time. Don't buy heads that have wilted or yellowish leaves and watch for worm holes. Be sure and try the red cabbage, too. It's just as tasty and so pretty. When you get it home, don't wash it, just wrap it tightly in a plastic bag and store it in the refrigerator. In cooking your cabbage, don't boil it to death. This is why many people don't like cabbage. Serve it while it still has a little crunch, and ENJOY!

March Why Didn't I Think of That?

When giving money or some financial gift, why not wrap it in the financial page of the newspaper and tie with a gold or silver cord.

¤ ¤ ¤ ¤ ¤

For newlyweds a big box of laundry detergent and a cute container of quarters for the Laundromat makes a welcome gift.

¤ ¤ ¤ ¤ ¤

For an Easter Bunny salad, place shredded lettuce on each salad plate, topped with one pear half – cut side down. Add apple slices for ears, currants for eyes, shredded cheese for whiskers and a little spoonful of cottage cheese for his tail. Viola! A bunny!!

¤ ¤ ¤ ¤ ¤

To properly boil those eggs, check the July Why Didn't I Think of That? Section.

¤ ¤ ¤ ¤ ¤

For coloring eggs just use food coloring in a bowl of water and add a few drops of vinegar to "set" the color.

¤ ¤ ¤ ¤ ¤

Always keep boiled eggs refrigerated!!

¤ ¤ ¤ ¤ ¤

To remove an egg that is stuck in the carton, simply wet the carton and the egg will slip out easily.

¤ ¤ ¤ ¤ ¤

Use older eggs for hard boiling; they peel easily.

¤ ¤ ¤ ¤ ¤

To test if an egg is fresh, float it in a bowl of cold water. If it SINKS it is fresh, if it floats — get rid of it!

¤ ¤ ¤ ¤ ¤

A hard cooked egg will spin, an uncooked one won't.

¤ ¤ ¤ ¤ ¤

When beating egg whites be sure and never get a speck of yolk in the bowl, and never use a bowl that could be slightly greasy.

¤ ¤ ¤ ¤ ¤

A few good ways to use up all those colored eggs –
    Slice into a chef salad.
    Make an egg salad sandwich.
    Slice into a white sauce, and serve over toast points sprinkled with crumbled bacon.
    Stir up a potato salad.

¤ ¤ ¤ ¤ ¤

Some "green" dishes for St. Patrick's Day –
    Broccoli with cheese sauce
    Spinach
    Split pea soup with ham
    Lime Jello with cottage cheese and crushed pineapple.
    Country Rice.

¤ ¤ ¤ ¤ ¤

Keep candles in the freezer. They will burn longer and won't drip.

¤ ¤ ¤ ¤. ¤

Lifesavers make great little candle holders on a birthday cake.

¤ ¤ ¤ ¤ ¤

Why not start a tradition of inviting the number of guests to coincide with the year of the child (such as 3 guests at age 3.)

¤ ¤ ¤ ¤ ¤

Balloons tied to a chair are fun "place cards."

¤ ¤ ¤ ¤ ¤

For those pretty spring bouquets, stick them in the refrigerator each night while you sleep, and they'll last much longer.

¤ ¤ ¤ ¤ ¤

For containers at parties, I cut off liter pop containers to different heights, surround them with asparagus stalks, celery stalks, carrot sticks, green onions, pasta or bread sticks and tie with raffia. These are great filled with relishes and other "finger foods."

¤ ¤ ¤ ¤ ¤

To make fascinating marble eggs for Easter, hard cook eggs, then tap and crackle the shell all over, but DO NOT PEEL!! Dissolve 1 pkg. unsweetened Koolaid in 3 c. cold water. Soak eggs in mixture, covered, overnight in the refrigerator. When they are peeled in the morning, they are BEAUTIFUL! Any color will work, and the eggs do not take on the Koolaid flavor.

¤ ¤ ¤ ¤ ¤

With those "first of the season" strawberries try these fun, quick treats —

In a parfait dish, layer whipped cream (flavored with a little rum extract), grated chocolate, and sliced, sweetened strawberries. Repeat layers, ending with a dollop of whipped cream and a chocolate curl. Gosh! Is that good!

Another absolutely delicious combination is to whip a carton of cream, flavored with a little powered sugar and almond extract. Then fold in sliced berries and silvered almonds. Serve in dessert dishes with a simple cookie. It's super!

An unusual taste treat that everyone loves is a mixture of 2 tablespoons sour cream and 2 teaspoons real maple syrup. Fold in sliced strawberries or use as a dip for fresh berries. You'll be surprised how good it is! Try it, you'll like it!!

¤ ¤ ¤ ¤ ¤

Frozen peas make a great snack for toddlers and will tide them over until mealtime while you're busy cooking.

¤ ¤ ¤ ¤ ¤

To dust my cake tops, puddings or cream puffs with powdered sugar, I just put a little powdered sugar in my strainer and shake it over the tops. It works beautifully.

¤ ¤ ¤ ¤ ¤

Salt toughens eggs, so never add it until they are cooked.

¤ ¤ ¤ ¤ ¤

I'm surprised that so many people don't know how to fry sausage properly. If you just try to "fry" it until it's done, you may have awfully crisp patties. Just put about ½ cup water along with your sausage in a skillet, cover, and steam it for about 15 minutes. Then remove the cover, drain off the liquid (not down the drain), and fry until lightly browned on each side. That way it will be well done without being overcooked and will be much better for you, also.

¤ ¤ ¤ ¤ ¤

A little baby powder dusted on your hands makes it easier when doing needle work.

¤ ¤ ¤ ¤ ¤

When sewing and making crafts, don't forget the handicapped. Anyone with a physical impairment would appreciate an apron made from a strip of fabric with a casing on top. Run a plastic waist hoop through the top and add some pockets. These are so easy to just clip on — no ties, buttons, or strings.

¤ ¤ ¤ ¤ ¤

Begin now building a "gift drawer" or cupboard. In it, store gift-wrap you buy after the holidays and used paper and ribbon you "iron" to use over. Pick up those little gifts when you see something "just right" on special and keep these tucked away. It sure saves time and money later when you would run all over to find something like what you once saw!

¤ ¤ ¤ ¤ ¤

Use an old empty ball-point pen to trace a pattern with tracing paper. It works so slick and leaves no ink marks.

¤ ¤ ¤ ¤ ¤

A wallpaper sample book will provide many, many pretty placemats for a child or invalid. Just cut the edges with pinking shears.

¤ ¤ ¤ ¤ ¤

I purchase a newspaper on each birthday of my grandchildren and am keeping them in separate files to give them on their eighteenth birthday. Won't they be fun to read?

¤ ¤ ¤ ¤ ¤

If you're stumped for a gift idea, why not give a class as a gift? Maybe your mother would like to learn how to paint, or your hubby might be interested in a foreign language. It will be a cherished gift, I'm sure.

¤ ¤ ¤ ¤ ¤

How about making a little grandma's comfort quilt for them — flannel on one side for warmth and coziness and tricot on the other for a cool feeling on a hot or "trying" day. Using a layer of batting between, you could tie the quilt in an evening.

¤ ¤ ¤ ¤ ¤

If your grandchildren come for a week or two to visit you, why not make them a scrapbook of activities, food you ate, things you saw, and record happenings and funny experiences. They will read and reread it, and it will be treasured as a special memory builder.

¤ ¤ ¤ ¤ ¤

It is also fun to keep a grandmother's book on each child. Use it to collect their art work, letters, and pictures and add your feelings and thoughts occasionally. It will be a treasure for them to have someday.

¤ ¤ ¤ ¤ ¤

Many fun and teaching toys can be made to give to children for just pennies; and they'll love them –

Finish a square of wood and pound in several rows of finishing nails part way. Accompanied by a box of colored rubber bands, give it to the child and he'll play for hours.

A roll of discontinued wallpaper and a box of crayons is a treat any little one will love.

A square of pegboard and a bunch of colored golf tees can also keep little hands busy.

A magnifying glass or a magnet will be a gift any child will treasure.

A jar of big buttons and string to thread them on is fun. A cardboard picture and a shoestring make a nice sewing card.

¤ ¤ ¤ ¤ ¤

Learning, as well as entertainment, does not have to be costly. Children are such a joy. Let's take advantage of every minute. I'll always remember a picture of a little boy that I saw. He had on tattered pants and jam on his face, and hanging around is neck was a sign that read, "Please recognize me for what I am. My present appearance is deceiving!"

¤ ¤ ¤ ¤ ¤

Spend "one-on-one" time with your children; maybe a special hour each week with each child. Learn a new skill, sew, learn about nature, cook together, read aloud, or go to see something new and different.

¤ ¤ ¤ ¤ ¤

Spend time building memories with your family. Make a family scrapbook, learn a new skill together, have a pioneer evening pulling taffy, or tell stories about ancestors, write a group letter to someone far away, have a "hobby sharing" night or start a family project. Enjoy a special breakfast together, watch the sun rise. Do a good deed together now. Don't wait!

¤ ¤ ¤ ¤ ¤

Plan a fun evening by giving each family member an invitation at breakfast to a "surprise supper." When they meet at the table, which you have previously set with a pretty centerpiece, give each one a designated amount of money and then go together to the grocery store. Each one can buy what he'd like for supper. When you come home, each one prepares his dish, and you all have fun enjoying your surprise meal. This is a great way to get to know each other better and learn skills at the same time.

¤ ¤ ¤ ¤ ¤

Once a week, put a slip of paper under someone's plate with a subject listed on it and have them give an "after-dinner speech" about "My Happiest Day," "My Most Embarrassing Moment," "My Favorite Place," and so on. Or put a word on each person's plate and have them tell what they think about when they hear that word. Words might be wind, clouds, cat, music, airplane, and so on.

¤ ¤ ¤ ¤ ¤

Why not record conversations on the cassette player? We keep picture records; why not voices? Think how much fun it would be to hear a loved one relate an incident 10 or 20 years from now.

¤ ¤ ¤ ¤ ¤

With small children, when you are looking forward to an upcoming event, make a paper chain with links for the amount of days to wait. On each link, write a suggested activity or thought to do that day. This keeps them interested and involved without asking, "How many more days?"

¤ ¤ ¤ ¤ ¤

Put rubber bathtub decals on seats of swings outdoors. This will save lots of slips and accidents.

¤ ¤ ¤ ¤ ¤

It's fun to make personalized pillow cases for each young guest at a slumber party and have everyone autograph each other's with permanent marking pens.

¤ ¤ ¤ ¤ ¤

Next time it snows, mix up some food coloring and water in containers and let your youngsters paint pictures in the snow with a small paint brush. They'll have a ball.

¤ ¤ ¤ ¤ ¤

With toddlers, divide their toys in seven little boxes and get them a different box each day of the week. Everything will always seem new.

¤ ¤ ¤ ¤ ¤

Save the daily comic strips for your children to color.

¤ ¤ ¤ ¤ ¤

Let your children have the privilege of reading in bed for half an hour each night. It is a great relaxant, and they will develop a love of books.

¤ ¤ ¤ ¤ ¤

Attractive food goes a long way in stimulating a child's appetite. Make that hot dog into a hot rod using the bun as the car, carrot slices for wheels, olives for headlights, and cheese and catsup for trimming. They'll love it.

¤ ¤ ¤ ¤ ¤

As the kids and I used to travel a lot with Roy, we spent quite a bit of time sitting in the car waiting while he was at an appointment. I always tried to use this time as a learning experience. While we observed people walking by, we would discuss what kind of person he was — successful, happy, and so on. Through our little game, I hope the kids learned the value of a good image. How others see us does matter.

¤ ¤ ¤ ¤ ¤

One of our friends has a bean jar for each child; a white bean stands for a good deed or special behavior, a brown bean for bad behavior. If a child gets all white beans in a week, he gets a special day of no chores. This is a cute idea with lots of possibilities. Let's start a bean jar for everyone today!

¤ ¤ ¤ ¤ ¤

To keep a little one busy on a rainy day, give him various shapes of pasta and beans and let him divide and separate them in an egg carton or muffin tin.

¤ ¤ ¤ ¤ ¤

Whispering will nearly always get a child's attention if he is upset or noisy. (This works for adults, too.)

¤ ¤ ¤ ¤ ¤

With children or teenagers, if there seems to be a problem, why not go on a walk- or car-talk. It's so much easier to discuss a problem as you walk or ride along one to one.

¤ ¤ ¤ ¤ ¤

Daddy-daughter dates and mother-son dates can be real special occasions, teaching social skills, sharing time and experiences, and helping the child to feel important.

¤ ¤ ¤ ¤ ¤

Sincerely ask your children's opinions and then respect them. They are a somebody, too!

¤ ¤ ¤ ¤ ¤

Teach your children to see. Too many people go through life missing all the beauties and pleasant things around them. Point out a dewdrop on a fresh rose, a new bud just opening, the design of a snowflake, a baby's precious smile, or a gentle old man's loving eyes.

¤ ¤ ¤ ¤ ¤

Spend an evening dancing as a family. You might want to invite another family to join you. Roll back the rugs and try everything from the old waltz to disco and rock. One of our favorite evening activities when the kids were all home was exercising to the "Chicken Fat" record by Robert Preston. If you can find a copy, give it a try. It is really terrific.

¤ ¤ ¤ ¤ ¤

Read to your family. Even the youngest will gain from this. Help them to understand. Get them involved by making sounds or asking questions. Reading to the whole bunch doesn't take any longer. Choose things that are exciting and put yourself into it. Boredom and indifference will be just as catching as your enthusiasm!

¤ ¤ ¤ ¤ ¤

Encourage children in art. They remember what they do far more than what they see or hear. Have the young ones draw pictures of their day's activities or for a grandma or holiday. Their artwork can be slipped under a clear plastic tablecloth to be enjoyed at mealtime. Art can be done and enjoyed by all members of the family whether it's a "Welcome Home" sign strung across the front door for daddy, personalized Christmas and birthday cards, paintings, or needlework.

¤ ¤ ¤ ¤ ¤

Before leaving on a vacation, let the children draw "bingo" cards with various objects in each square. They can then be used to play the game as you travel. It's much more meaningful if they made the cards themselves.

¤ ¤ ¤ ¤ ¤

Sing together. You can even sing messages like "Put your toys away." Whistle, hum, or sing while you're working. It's contagious.

¤ ¤ ¤ ¤ ¤

Play charades and act out favorite stories for a family activity. This does wonders for a child's confidence and self-esteem.

¤ ¤ ¤ ¤ ¤

Encourage writing poetry, letters, stories, and so on, and have each family member keep a personal journal. Remember, you will be someone's ancestor someday, and how special it would be to have a handwritten journal of your life.

¤ ¤ ¤ ¤ ¤

A special friend of mine has a loose-leaf notebook in which she puts all the letters she receives from her family and friends. Her first one dates back many, many years. What a priceless possession! All of these things bring about activities and traditions that bind families together and help us each to build a better world with happy, well adjusted, and self-confident people.

¤ ¤ ¤ ¤ ¤

If you live alone, why not plan a week of sunshine? On the first day, give the "hand" of sunshine to someone by writing a letter or making something for someone by hand. On the second day, give the "voice" of sunshine with a cheery phone call or visit in person. On the third day, give the "heart" of sunshine by doing a kind deed for someone in need. On the fourth day, give the "mind" of sunshine by sharing a book or helping someone with a skill to develop their intellect. On the fifth day, give the "taste" of sunshine by sharing a special casserole or dessert with someone. On the sixth day, give the "rays" of sunshine by smiling at everyone you meet. On the seventh day, give the "warmth and soul" of sunshine by giving love to someone who needs it most.

¤ ¤ ¤ ¤ ¤

A most thoughtful gift, whether it's for the newlyweds, a wedding anniversary, a new baby, a birthday, or for a shut-in, is a bunch of bulbs, some mulch, and a planting tool. Many, many months of enjoyment will come from a gift like this. Why not twenty-five tulip bulbs for that twenty-fifth anniversary or fifty for a fiftieth birthday.

¤ ¤ ¤ ¤ ¤

Roy prefers pie over cake, so for his birthday I write his name or "Happy Birthday" by piping extra meringue on top of his lemon pie. It browns so nicely, and he is sure proud. You can also pipe "Happy Birthday" around the edge of the plate of a dessert with frosting or melted chocolate in a squeeze bottle.

¤ ¤ ¤ ¤ ¤

Instead of "tying" a quilt, use buttons and stitch in place using embroider floss or crochet thread.

April

April

I read once that "America is the only country where a homemaker hires a woman to clean her house so she can volunteer all day at the nursery where the cleaning lady leaves her child!" Ironic, but often sadly true. What happened to the old saying, "Home is where the heart is." The time has come in this world of ours to return to home values and truly make it a piece of Heaven on Earth. When life gets tough, I can't think of a place I'd rather be than in the comforting walls of my own home, surrounded by those I love.

Food for Thought

O.K. friends, let's roll up our sleeves, put on those aprons and get to work! We are going to have so much fun cleaning, organizing and decorating these special places where we live. When we finish, our houses will truly be homes!!

Let's stand back and take a hard look at each room. Does each space reflect your family life? Decorating can be such fun if we use our imaginations and let the things we do declare just who our family is!

There are so many ways we can get "extra mileage" out of items and save money. I had a large battenburg-type tablecloth I bought in Bermuda. It was beautiful, but I never used it because it was HORRIBLE to iron. I cut squares off each corner that had beautiful lace work and made four lovely doilies. Then I cut the large rectangle in the center where there was more pretty lace work. This became a wonderful doily for the top of my piano. I now have put to use all the "prettiness" of the tablecloth in manageable-sized pieces to launder and iron. I also purchased a huge Irish linen tablecloth with much white "handwork" on it for $2.00 at a yard sale because of several burn spots on it. I immediately cut it up and made some gorgeous pillows for my couch and bedroom and some darling little trims on clothes for my granddaughters. Who would ever know?

Nothing makes a house "your home" more than pictures. We have one wall for our grandchildren's pictures (there are 23 now.) We use 5"x7" black document frames. The children keep us up to date each year with their school pictures, so the wall is always current. Golly, they are so proud to see themselves "on display" at Grandma and Grandpa's house. Sarah always runs over and says, "There's me!"

On one hallway wall we have a collection of ancestor's photos. How interesting as we reflect on the hard life Grandma had, how tall Aunt Verna was, and even how many features we have like that favorite uncle. It gives our family a feeling of belonging and continuity! On running past the wall one day, our son Steve commented, "Gee, this wall is neat, Mom. When I get to heaven, I'll recognize all my family!"

As you will see in October's chapter, Roy and I have "tree friends" as well as "people friends". Roy has taken many outstanding slide pictures of these trees. We now have them blown up to 10"x12" and 11"x14" and framed on our stairway. Around the crown molding near the ceiling, we have written the words "Hurt not the Earth, nor the sea, neither the trees" from the Book of Revelations. Visitors to our home are so taken with this wall, and Roy and I enjoy it everyday!

When we left our large home and moved into our condo, I pressed some of the beautiful fern leaves we grew in our back yard. I now have them framed, also, and my heart floods with memories each time I look at them.

We have recently started a new fun practice with pictures in our family room. I have a bulletin board for all snap shots from the grandchildren. Each month I stick up a few "oldies" of Roy and I or other family members, and when the children come to visit they love to try and guess who that baby or cute little boy is. Of course, there is a prize for who ever gets them all right!

I have a collection of fun little clear antique bottles I set on a shelf, and they are a great place to "start" cuttings of ivy or other plants. Just fill with water and watch them root.

Naturally at our house Roy and I love to decorate with little bird houses. We have started collecting cute titles to put on them. Here are a few —

- Home Tweet Home
- For Wren't
- Duplex for Sale
- Gone South for the Winter
- Snow Drift Inn
- Cheep Housing
- Bird and Breakfast
- Seediest Place in Town

These are sure to bring a smile to every guest.

Nothing can bring sunshine into your heart and a rainbow over your roof like a little organization. Some folks are natural-born organizers, and system and order come automatically to them. Others, however, have not developed this knack and become a bit discouraged by their shortcomings. They might even feel so inadequate compared to those who seem to accomplish things so easily that they don't even have the time to begin. Of course, the media leads us to believe that everyone is a bundle of energy, never tiring and always coping with every problem. This can be very disheartening, especially when you don't feel or look like the person on TV.

When our chores go undone — dishes piled up, house a mess, paperwork never finished — we find that the worse the situation gets, the worse we feel and vice versa. Then, usually out of desperation, we try to turn over a new leaf and get totally overwhelmed, realizing there is no way we can do everything. Herein lies the key! We can't do everything, but we can do something, and that's exactly the way to start. We are only human, but we are a "special" human being with needs, talents, and abilities.

My old philosophy of a positive attitude and wearing a smile is never more important than when your life needs some organization.

Begin by making a list to rid your mind of the old cobwebs and start building some self-esteem:

    Column I — Things that really count in my life (If I had a week to live, how would I spend my time?)

    Column II — Things I love to do (Have you ever asked someone what they would do if they could do anything they wanted? Their eyes light up, and a zest for living suddenly becomes contagious.)

    Column III — What special talents and abilities I have

    Column IV — My weaknesses

    Column V — What goals I want to accomplish in one year, in five years

After spending some time pondering these things, it's amazing how much better you'll feel about yourself. Whether you're a wife, a bachelor, a single parent, or a widow, you must begin getting your life in order by liking yourself. I'm sure you know the feeling; when you like yourself, everything seems terrific, even scrubbing the dirty kitchen floor. You feel as if you could conquer the world, even pass up that delicious hot apple strudel for dessert! You feel like throwing your shoulders back and smiling at everyone you meet. When you don't like yourself, life is yucky! You'd rather eat an extra piece of chocolate cake or take a nap than work. You don't want to talk to anyone or do anything, and soon you start worrying about trivial things or become cynical.

I'll never forget a story my friend, Jonas, told me once. There was a man driving down a country road at night. As he drove along, he passed a house with a light on. A few miles down the road, he had a flat tire and realized he didn't have a jack in the trunk. Recalling the house with the burning light he'd passed down the road, he decided he would walk back and borrow a jack. However, as he began walking, he started thinking and talking to himself. "Golly! By now," he said, "they may have already turned out the light." Worrying about this for a few minutes, he thought, " Oh, then I may awaken them, and they will be upset." Farther down the road, he thought, "They will probably be very angry and not want me to borrow their jack." And a little later, "They may even shout and scream at me for bothering them." At this point, he reached the front door and hesitantly rang the bell. By the time someone answered the door, he was in such a state of mind he just stammered, "I don't want to borrow your old jack, anyway!" and stormed off the porch! Isn't this exactly what we do by letting our imaginations run away with us when our self-esteem is low?

Concentrate on having days when you like yourself. Give yourself a pat on the back once in a while. You're a pretty neat person! Read and reread that list. As you go to bed at night, don't itemize the things you didn't get done; think of the good things you did. You'll have a peaceful sleep and awake refreshed.

Getting up an extra half hour early to spend that time just on yourself will pay dividends all day long and is worth so much more than that 30 minutes' sleep. For me, an ounce of morning is worth a pound of afternoon. Use the time to go for a brisk walk, do some reading, or spend it on a hobby. Then take the time to make yourself look nice and you'll like you all day long. When you care for yourself, you can think of others. Have you ever gone to a party when your slip was showing or maybe your shirt collar wouldn't lie flat? You are forever tugging and pulling, and your mind is on you and not on your activities or responsibilities. If you first take care to put yourself in order, then you can relax and truly think of others!

In taking care of yourself, besides eating balanced meals and getting regular exercise, keep that list in mind and concentrate on being a happy individual, accomplishing your goals.

In your new daily schedule, take a "2 minute break" once during each heavy task. If that doesn't sound like much, watch the clock and see how many pleasant things you can think of for those 2 minutes. You'll feel so refreshed. Touch up your makeup or comb your hair. If you've been sitting, stand up, or vice versa. A two minute change really helps. Make a quick "I love you" phone call. Whistle or sing a favorite tune. Fertilize and "mist" a plant. The nurturing will make you feel good inside.

Most of all, don't be too hard on yourself. If there are things about you that make you unhappy, you can change! Do it and be happy with who you are. Make a conscious effort to love life, and it will be like that smile — soon it will be there automatically.

Now we're ready to tackle the business at hand, organizing and scheduling time. My bulletin board contains my pattern for life, and I couldn't get along without it.

If you find yourself jotting down notes on scraps of paper and misplacing them, making lists in notebooks and then losing the notebook, or having stacks of papers and clutter around or even trying to keep everything in your head, then I suggest it's time you get a bulletin board. Now everyone knows that before you can build a house or sew a dress, you need a pattern; so the bulletin board can do exactly that with structuring your life. You may want to have different types of paper or vari-colored cards for each list or item because you can tell at a glance what you need to refer to. Keep one card or list of:

Long-range goals —
- A craft you want to learn
- A foreign language to master
- Weight to lose or gain

Weekly goals (or monthly if necessary) —
- Errands to run
- Meetings and appointments
- Projects to finish
- Deadlines to meet

I use a calendar with large squares for this one.

Daily chores —
- Clean the bathroom
- Mend shirts
- Weed the garden
- Scrub the floor
- Attend the meeting

I love this list because of the satisfaction I get as I cross things off when they are completed. I never make my daily list the night before, as some recommend. I find that I lie down and worry about the list at night if I do, so I prefer to check my weekly or monthly schedule and then make my daily list first thing in the morning. Sometimes I even write down a few fun things for added incentive. (Smell the fresh lilacs in the back yard, or stop and listen to the birds singing.)

Fun things to do —
- Those books you'd like to read
- Scrapbooks to update
- A movie you'd like to see

Just having these things spelled out in front of you will give you a real "together" feeling. And remember, the lists will change, so be flexible and update them often.

When planning your routine or schedule, remember it takes just that — some planning and thinking. These things don't happen by accident, so allow yourself the planning time to sit down with a pencil and paper. This can be done while you're waiting at the doctor's office, in the morning before the family gets up, while the iron is heating, or while the cake is baking.

To get on the right track, a few steps are required:

1. Organize the necessary tasks. Some things must be routinely done — like the meals, housework, laundry, and so forth. Plan your meals by the week or month in order to save trips to the grocery store and time on extra busy days. To keep your housework at a minimum, have a place for everything and keep it there. If you need an extra blanket in the dark, you'll be able to find it; and little Mary's shoes will be there when it's time to dress for school. My publisher told me once that an efficient executive strives to only handle a piece of paper once. If this works for business, why not at home? When you finish with a dish, why not rinse it and put it in the dishwasher? When you take off your blouse, why not hang it in the closet immediately? It sure makes life simpler and frees up time in the long run. It takes much more energy and time to wipe up a spill that has dried and hardened. So do it now and save minutes for later!

2. Outline each morning what must be done in order of importance. They say work expands to fill the time available, and this is certainly true. It's surprising how two things on the list can take all day or an extra two or three things can be added and get finished, also. Remember how fast you cleaned through the house when you learned relatives were coming? By looking at your list of things to do, it will help you remember to stop at the cleaners on the way to the grocery store and save you an extra trip and valuable time. Those saved minutes become precious and treasured. The more careful we are with them, the more valuable and useful our time will be. These minutes actually make up our lives.

3. Keep in mind that many hands make light work. If you have a large family, laundry can be quite a chore. Why not have a box or basket for each person labeled with his name. These are kept in their rooms for dirty clothes. Then, on laundry day, all baskets are carried to the laundry area. After the clothes are washed and folded immediately from the dryer (this saves much ironing, keeps things looking nicer, and gives everyone more pride in their things), put the clothes back into each person's container for them to put away. Stuff from pockets can also go into their basket or box. If you do not have a table nearby, remember to keep the dryer top free from clutter so that this space is available to fold clothes. For those of you who are single or a couple, those stackable plastic vegetable bins are great to keep in the laundry area. I use them as load sorters, one basket for whites, one for darks, and one for coloreds. As I gather up laundry each morning, I just drop it into the appropriate basket, and I can easily see which load needs to be done. That way I can do a load every couple of days and always keep ahead of things.

All household members, no matter how small, can be a great help around the house. However, nothing is more important than making sure they know how to do a job well. Work along with them until they understand it. Once you teach them, you can delegate chores and feel comfortable knowing it will be done right. A small child can dust furniture, set the table, fold socks, and help put things away. If they grow up learning everything has its place, it will become a habit to put it there. If scattered toys are a frustration to you, why not make large drawstring bags out of fabric like denim or duck. Then use shortening cans or cottage cheese containers to hold the smaller pieces inside the bag. These bags are easy to fill and can be hung on a little hook in the playroom or bedroom. Of course, the one positive rule is that no second bag is opened until the first one is picked up and put away. This worked at our house.

After you teach the children how to do things, give them full responsibility. Give them specific instructions, answer all their questions, then don't take over! Relax, enjoy the help they give you, and be appreciative and flexible. Nothing deflates an ego and ruins incentive like criticism and lack of enthusiasm. (This goes for husbands and wives as well!)

Job charts are a terrific way to distribute work without fuss. One method is a chart with pockets (a pocket for each person). Jobs are then outlined (or pictures drawn for little ones) to inform each one of their responsibilities. Another idea is a rotating wheel made from two circles of cardboard, the inside one with each person's name and the outer circle listing jobs to do. Our kids each had a little "job jar" with slips of paper listing things to be done. On the list, they would often find "free day" or "time for an ice cream cone." Little incentives never hurt!

As part of learning responsibility, children should know that there are rules that everyone needs to obey if there is to be order in our homes. A friend of mine had a rule that if anyone left his bed unmade, the next day he had to make everyone else's beds. Be careful of too many rules and not enough love, though; and be sure that the "punishment fits the crime."

Above all, be consistent. Set up a routine and schedule with the whole family. You'll find everyone more willing to do their work if they have a voice in the plan.

You'll soon discover that by enlisting everyone's help at home, the burden will be lighter for you. It will help you to have more time for your hobbies and interests, as well as teach your family the proper use of time and money, learning skills, and most of all, pride in a job well done. Of course, the most beneficial underlying advantage is the sense of being needed, one of the most valuable gifts we can give our children!

4. Be realistic in your goals. Remember the little slogan above my kitchen sink. "You can only peel one potato at a time." Don't start several projects at once and finish none of them. Spread out big projects and pace your energies. Don't try to clean the oven and the refrigerator on the same day. Alternate big and small jobs. Plan tasks for appropriate times. Don't scrub the kitchen on Friday if the boys will be doing the yard work and tracking grass clippings in on Saturday. Don't clean your oven and cabinets the day before your girls have a slumber and cookie-baking party. Do the most difficult jobs or the ones you like the least when your energy level is the highest. Don't try to do things too fast. As Mom says, "Haste makes waste." Sit down when you can. You're not a machine, so rest while you work if you feel the need. Eliminate that nervous strain. Don't fight it. If the drippy faucet bothers you, do something about it. If the rug continually slips, put a piece of foam rubber under it. Many times, our work seems twice as difficult because of annoying little things we could eliminate. Dovetail your work. Curl your hair while the little ones are in the tub or clean the kitchen cupboard while supper is cooking.

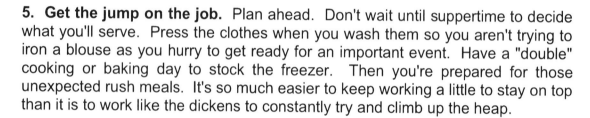

5. Get the jump on the job. Plan ahead. Don't wait until suppertime to decide what you'll serve. Press the clothes when you wash them so you aren't trying to iron a blouse as you hurry to get ready for an important event. Have a "double" cooking or baking day to stock the freezer. Then you're prepared for those unexpected rush meals. It's so much easier to keep working a little to stay on top than it is to work like the dickens to constantly try and climb up the heap.

To establish a daily and weekly schedule for your house, first remember, plan for your particular needs. Don't try to live by others' standards. Analyze your resources — number in family, budget, your energy and health, and your home and equipment. Ask yourself, "What is most important to accomplish for us?" and, "When do these things need to be done?" Then set up a simple schedule and follow it as closely as possible.

Here are some little tips that may help you on your daily routine.

Kitchen

As you clean up after the dinner hour, set the table and make any necessary preparations for breakfast. If you pack lunches, utilize any leftovers from dinner (roast beef, chicken) and prepare sandwiches or package food and refrigerate, ready to pack in the morning.

Arrange your cupboards so that dishes are closest to the dishwasher, baking supplies are all in one place, pans close to the stove, and so on.

Keep all your appliance cords together in a drawer with an elastic band around each one or cover toilet tissue tubes with contact paper and store one cord in each tube. (Covering or decorating these tubes is a great rainy-day project for youngsters and a nice help to you.)

If you use soap-filled scouring pads, cut them in quarters. They work just as well, you stretch your budget, and a small one makes a lot less mess.

If you have a self-cleaning oven, turn it on to clean right after you have finished cooking in it. This really saves on the electricity since it is already hot.

When you need extra counter space, just pull out a drawer and place a cookie sheet on it.

I hate to waste money on disposable paper cups for drinking. It's more economical to have a mug rack hung near the sink with personalized or color-coded mugs for each person.

Always peel vegetables, husk corn, or do any messy job on a newspaper. It's so much easier to clean up. I always grate my cheese on a piece of Handi-wrap for this reason, also.

Don't forget to clean all the crumbs out of the toaster every so often. It will work more efficiently, and you won't have those crumbs burning.

After a meal, we have a rule that each person is responsible for putting his dirty dishes in the dishwasher plus one other thing. That sure helps in clearing the table. (Guests don't mind this, either.)

Be sure you wipe off all bottles, jars, and containers before putting them away. That saves lots of hard cleaning and scrubbing later on.

Washable throw rugs are invaluable in helping to keep the floor clean. Keep them in front of the sinks and by each outside door especially. It's easier to throw a small rug in the washer than scrub a whole floor.

Each time you bake a cake, cookies, or whatever, wrap up a few single servings and freeze. They are great to grab for lunches.

To really save time and energy and boost your spirits, why not trade dinner with a friend once a week. This is terrific whether you have a family to feed or live alone. It's just as easy to fix a double batch of something. Maybe you can have a break on Thursdays and return the favor on Mondays!

Laundry

Anything with ties or sashes should be turned inside out to eliminate tangles.

Watch those laundry loads. If you are doing extra small loads, you may be wasting energy. However, if you fill the washer too full, the clothes will not be adequately cleaned and rinsed and may be covered with soap scum. Built-up soap is one of the biggest causes of dingy wash, so check your regular laundry loads occasionally to see if you are using too much detergent and not getting it all rinsed out. Also, be sure and clean the dryer vent regularly. It will save drying time and energy.

Keep your laundry area as attractive as possible. Your time there should be enjoyable, too. Make sure you have adequate hooks and lines to hang things from the dryer. They will only cost a few cents and will save many dollars worth of valuable time.

Bathroom

If you have more than one bathroom, it is just as economical, and saves much time, to have a supply of cleaning needs in each room.

Be sure you get everyone into the habit of wiping the shower down after each use. You may wash a few more towels, but you'll be absolutely amazed how much work you'll save cleaning that shower stall occasionally.

Before your shower curtain and rubber mat get too soiled or mildewed, toss them in the washer with a couple of old bath towels, a small amount of detergent, and ¼ cup vinegar. They are a breeze to keep clean. To keep the hooks clean, tie them in an old nylon sock and put them in the washer, too.

If keeping the towel hung up is a problem with your young children, simply use a couple of larger pins and pin the towel, from the back, over the rod. Be sure towels are within their reach.

Living Room

Be sure and vacuum rugs and drapes often. It will eliminate lots of cleaning bills or elbow grease later on.

Don't be tempted to use carpet scraps as throw rugs over your carpeting; the coarse backing will wear on your carpeting. Use regular throw rugs where necessary. The best use for carpet scraps is to cover the basement steps. Boy, does that save a lot of tracking, and it looks nice, too.

My kids tell me that the thing they remember best when being taught about cleaning is that as you dust, work your way around the room in a circle and work from the top to the bottom. Dust and then vacuum the floor, and so on. This eliminates doing things twice.

Bedrooms

Line children's drawers with white shelf paper and then draw pictures or write "socks," "underwear," "shirts," and so on, so they can keep things in the right places. For young ones, you might even want to put pictures on the outside of each drawer. Children enjoy being neat, and if they have a proper place, they can manage easily.

I line my dresser drawers with leftover wallpaper to match the room. It looks so pretty.

Never throw away those old pillowcases. They sure make neat covers to slip over hangers storing out-of-season clothes. It just requires a small hole at the top.

I've found that my luggage also makes a great place to store out-of-season clothes when I'm short on drawer space.

Don't get in a rut and use the same sheets each week. As you launder them, put them at the bottom of the stack so you rotate the wear.

Use a quilt or comforter on beds to speed up bed making. This is especially easy for young children, although adults also appreciate the convenience. Roy and I bought a feather comforter in Europe and really enjoy saving time each morning. All it requires to make the bed is to flip it back and fold it over. (Feels great at night, too!)

Never store your blankets or comforters in a plastic bag unless you make a few small holes or slits in it. They need air.

A neat way to store baby blankets is to fold them over a hanger and hang them in a closet.

Remember to turn all mattresses often. This will prolong their life considerably.

Always have hooks and rods within reach of children to motivate neatness. And supply a wastebasket in each room!

In general, the two rules that will help the most are: (1) Use each room for its purpose (eat in the kitchen, dress in the bedrooms, etc.). This can soon become a family habit if the proper facilities are arranged. (2) Eliminate clutter. Don't hesitate to throw things away that are useless and dust collectors.

I truly believe an organized home is a happy home. I get so much mail asking for formulas to accomplish this, and it certainly isn't as complicated as many believe. Too often we play catch-up all day instead of doing the necessary things when they are needed so that we have free time later on. Try it, it really works.

Isn't it a super feeling to make your house a home? Take off that apron, sit back and enjoy!

April Food for Fun
True "Comfort" Food

I like to have a pot of this tasty Oriental soup on the stove while I'm cleaning. It's so satisfying and light. Really hits the spot for lunch or supper. I'll always be grateful to a viewer of my television show for sharing it with me.

Delicious Hot and Sour Soup

In a large pot combine:
- 10 c. chicken broth
- 1 head napa cabbage, shredded
- 3 c. shredded carrots
- 3 c. sliced mushrooms
- 2 T. soy sauce
- 4 T. regular rice

Cook together 20-30 minutes.

Stir in:
- 3 c. diced chicken
- ½ c. rice vinegar
- ¾ tsp. black pepper
- a few red pepper flakes

Mix 1/3 c. cornstarch and 1/3 c. water

Stir into soup. Heat until thickened. Serve with sliced green onions sprinkled on top. This freezes really well and we love it!

¤ ¤ ¤ ¤ ¤

Don't you love the aroma in your kitchen when a pot of mouth-watering chicken soup is simmering on the stove? I'm sure this one will have the neighbors knocking on your door. Why not invite them over? It makes plenty. These velvet dumplings will live on in your dreams (if they don't float right out of the pot first!) They are so tender and literally "melt" in your mouth!

Roy's All-Time-Favorite Chicken Soup with Velvet Dumplings

Cover several pieces of chicken with 2 ½ quarts cold water.

Add: 1 carrot
1 stalk celery
1 small onion
salt and pepper as desired

Cover and simmer for 2 hours. Remove chicken and strain broth.

To broth add: ½ c. peas
2 medium sliced zucchini
1 sliced carrot
1 small diced onion
1 stalk diced celery
½ c. green beans
½ c. corn
¼ c. uncooked rice
1 bay leaf
1 T. parsley flakes
chicken picked from bones
salt and pepper to taste

Cover and simmer ½ hour until vegetables are tender.

Meanwhile stir up:

Grandma's Velvet Dumplings

In saucepan combine: ½ c. water
                       ½ stick margarine

Heat until boiling and the butter is melted, then stir in all at once:

½ c. flour
1 tsp. baking powder
dash of salt
pinch of sage
1 tsp. parsley flakes

Stir over heat until a ball is formed and all of flour mixture is well mixed. Remove from heat.

Stir in 2 eggs (1 at a time) until well beaten and the mixture is smooth.

Drop by teaspoonfuls on the top of bubbling chicken mixture, making about 12 dumplings. Cover immediately and simmer for 20 minutes. Do not lift lid during cooking time.

Serve immediately.

¤ ¤ ¤ ¤ ¤

Spring is the perfect time to serve spinach salads, when the greens are young and tender. What a taste treat!

Spinach Salads

1) Combine: fresh spinach leaves
            thinly sliced onion rings
            1 can drained mandarin orange slices (use the juice in Jello, add it to fruit punch, use it in fruit sauce, etc.)

Top with dressing (below); sprinkle with chow mein noodles.

2) Combine: fresh spinach leaves
             fresh sliced mushrooms

Top with dressing (below); sprinkle with bacon crisps.

Dressing — Combine: 6 T. olive oil
                                4 T. wine vinegar
                                1/3 tsp. table mustard
                                ¼ tsp. minced garlic
                                salt and coarse ground pepper to taste

Shake well. Great for any spinach salad.

¤ ¤ ¤ ¤ ¤

No family dinner is complete without this salad! It's delicious!

Mandarin Orange Salad

Prepare 2 pkgs. (3 oz. each) orange Jell-o as directed in a 9x13 inch glass pan.

When partially set, add: 1 can (11 oz.) drained mandarin oranges
                                      1 can (16 oz.) drained crushed pineapple
                                              (retain juice from both fruits for topping)
                                      2 sliced bananas
                                      8-9 chopped maraschino cherries
                                      2 c. miniature marshmallows

Stir together and then let set.

Topping — Combine: 2 T. flour
                                ½ c. sugar
                                1 beaten egg
                                1 c. juice (retained from fruit)

Cook until thick. Cool thoroughly.

Whip 1 c. whipping cream and fold into cold sauce. Spread topping on Jell-o and sprinkle with grated cheddar cheese.

Makes 12-15 nice squares.

¤ ¤ ¤ ¤ ¤

Our son first tasted this dish at a girl friend's house. He was so taken with it, he requested I make it every week for a long time. It is also the most requested recipe I got during my television shows. (We received over 10,000 requests in one week!)

Chicken Magnifico

Combine: 2 cans tomato soup
2 cans golden mushroom soup
2 cans water
1 bunch chopped green onions
1 clove minced garlic

Pour ½ of sauce into greased 9x13 inch pan. Cover sauce with ½ lb. uncooked noodles.

Lay 6 chicken breasts or 1 cut-up chicken on top of noodles. Cover with the rest of the sauce.

Bake at 350* for 1 ½ hours.

¤ ¤ ¤ ¤ ¤

We really enjoy a comforting meal of Salmon loaf, baked potatoes, peas and a salad! Why not cobbler for dessert?

Mom's Salmon Loaf

Mash 1 can pink or red salmon well with a fork. (Do not drain.)

Add: 1 beaten egg
2 T. grated onion
2 T. lemon juice
¼ tsp. salt
dash of pepper
2 T. chopped parsley
½ c. fine bread crumbs
2 T. flour

Mix well and then pack lightly in a small (7x3 1/2 inch) greased loaf pan. Top with buttered crumbs.

Bake at 350* for 1 hour.

¤ ¤ ¤ ¤ ¤

Here's a super lunch box cookie. Makes lots, and they're nice and chewy.

Donna's Everyday Cookies

Cream together: 1 c. margarine
                         1 c. vegetable oil
                         1 c. brown sugar
                         2 eggs
                         1 tsp. vanilla

Add: 3 ½ c. flour
         1 tsp. soda
         1 tsp. cream of tartar
         1 tsp. salt

Add: 1 c. quick oats
         1 c. coconut
         2 c. crisp rice cereal
         chopped nuts

Drop by spoonfuls onto cookie sheet. Flatten.

Bake at 350* for about 8 minutes.

April Grocery Bag

April is a good time to take a refreshing new look at your shopping habits. Most freezers and pantry shelves are getting a little bare since we've nearly used up our supply from last summer. I like to get my freezer defrosted now. It will soon be time to start with the rhubarb, strawberries, peas and other spring crops.

Pineapple is a good buy this month. Don't buy them too green. They should be tinged with yellow (but not brown). They should feel heavy and have no soft spots. Pineapples are always mature when picked, but not ripe. Leave them out at room temperature to ripen and then refrigerate. To test for ripeness, the green spikes on the top should pull out easily. Then just peel them, cut out the core and serve for dessert. (Remember you can't add fresh pineapple to Jell-o. It won't "set up.")

At the meat counter, ham is featured this month. See September's chapter for lots of good ideas about ham. Chicken and pork are good buys this month, also. So clean out your freezer, dust off your shelves and start today to economize and stock up on specials. You'll be glad you did.

It's such a shame that in this wonderful land of plenty so many people overeat and are still undernourished and feel they need to take lots of vitamins to be healthy. The secret is to shop wisely, store the foods properly and then cook them to retain as many nutrients as possible.

Here are a few things to remember to get the most for your food dollar:

1. Never presoak vegetables and then boil them until they are soft. Steam them quickly and serve them while they are still a little crunchy.

2. Never thaw frozen fruits, vegetables, juice etc., before cooking or mixing them, or you'll lose lots of vitamin C and B.

3. Never dice, chop or cut up your foods very much ahead of time because all the exposed surfaces begin losing valuable vitamins.

4. Air, heat and light all destroy vitamins and minerals, so always store things in tightly covered containers in the refrigerator.

Let's not find ourselves overweight but undernourished. There will be lots of sales on fresh garden greens during April and new peas as well as strawberries will begin to appear at the supermarket. Dairy products and eggs will be good buys, too.

There should be lots of the small "new" potatoes available this year. Why not cream some with a few fresh peas for supper. That's a real husband-pleaser at our house.

Avoid all the empty-calorie snacks and sweets and bake up a batch of cinnamon rolls (see January's recipes).

Shop well, eat right and feel terrific!

With Spring in the air we are starting to see a few new things on the market again which will give our budgets a boost as well as break the monotony of winter foods. Spring and Fall are fun times to prepare meals because there are different things to choose from, and it always seems like a new beginning.

As you shop for these products keep in mind: **Spinach**— don't hesitate to take the time to pick out a bunch of fresh spinach leaves. It may look like a time-consuming task to stand and pick over the leaves to put in plastic bags, but there is no comparison to that old canned spinach in taste or nutrition. Besides, there is nothing like a fresh spinach salad. Just take it home and store it in the refrigerator right in the same plastic bag (leaving the end of the bag open!) Only wash what you need as you use it. I usually let it stand in cold water just a few minutes, then rinse well. If you plan to cook the spinach, remember it cooks down. One pound of fresh leaves will end up about 1 c. cooked. I never add extra water when I cook it. The water that clings to the leaves will be enough. Put a tight lid on your pan and bring it to a simmer, then turn the heat to low and cook for only about 6-8 minutes. If you lift the lid a couple times while it's cooking the spinach will stay pretty green. Salt and butter it after it is cooked. Roy likes a little vinegar on his. A hard-boiled egg sliced on top looks pretty too. Don't cook your spinach in cast iron or aluminum pots, or it will have a metallic taste. Spinach is also good creamed. Then I like to add a dash of nutmeg.

Try adding it to your lettuce and other greens in a tossed salad. This goes great with my oven fried chicken, baked potatoes and buttered corn. It makes a "springy," colorful and nutritious meal.

Don't forget that spinach is rich in vitamin A, iron and adds that needed bulk or fiber to the diet. I even enjoy it on sandwiches instead of a lettuce leaf. It's so pretty and green, you feel healthy just looking at it.

Parsley— one of the most nutritious greens we can buy, and yet many use it only to decorate plates and then end up discarding it. Did you realize that it is very high in protein value and also iron, as well as being packed with vitamin A and C?

I cut up lots of parsley in our fresh, tossed salads as well as using it in abundance in soups and casseroles, even snipped into muffin batters and of course, sprinkled over cooked vegetables like carrots or peas.

When I bring a bunch of parsley home, I wash it well (don't leave it in water too long or it loses some vitamin C). I pick it over to remove any wilted or yellowed stems, then I pat it dry with a paper towel and pack it tightly into a glass jar. Screw the lid on and refrigerate. You'll be surprised how long it stays nice and fresh. Buy some parsley next time you shop, and then use it!

HAPPY, HEALTHY EATING!!!

April Why Didn't I Think of That?

Some items I feel are invaluable in your kitchen drawer are scissors (for bacon, herbs, paper, string, etc.), sharp knives, and a timer. I couldn't get along without these things. I think you'll find they are a big help to you, too.

¤ ¤ ¤ ¤ ¤

That extra iced-tea spoon works great in the jelly jar.

¤ ¤ ¤ ¤ ¤

A cookie sheet covered with a finger-tip towel makes a handy TV or lap tray.

¤ ¤ ¤ ¤ ¤

Keep a red and green magnet handy to indicate the status of your dishwasher — red for dirty, green for clean.

¤ ¤ ¤ ¤ ¤

Running your hot iron over a dryer sheet sure keeps the iron moving smoothly.

¤ ¤ ¤ ¤ ¤

Remember never to wash your windows in direct sunlight. They will streak every time.

¤ ¤ ¤ ¤ ¤

We recently had our furnace ducts cleaned and the fellow suggested putting a piece of nylon net over each vent under the vent cover. It really works great and sure cuts down on the dust.

¤ ¤ ¤ ¤ ¤

A few drops of shampoo in a sink full of warm water is super for washing those combs and brushes.

¤ ¤ ¤ ¤ ¤

Housework is something you do that no one notices until you don't do it!

¤ ¤ ¤ ¤ ¤

For a super clothes whitener try this: ½ c. automatic dishwasher soap
½ c. Clorox
1 gal. water

Soak items in this mixture then run through a normal cycle without soap.

¤ ¤ ¤ ¤ ¤

I like to tuck a tiny doily into my candle holder and then add a candle. It gives a nice touch in the bed or bathroom.

¤ ¤ ¤ ¤ ¤

A few sprigs of fresh eucalyptus in the bathroom sure gives a nice refreshing scent. The steam and moisture keeps it smelling nice for a long time.

¤ ¤ ¤ ¤ ¤

As your lavender bushes become prolific with buds, collect a bunch, cover small Styrofoam balls with glue and then roll in the lavender. I keep a basket of these on my end table, tied with a big "wired" ribbon bow, all summer. Um!

¤ ¤ ¤ ¤ ¤

In the sewing room, antique "mason" jars make nice holders for buttons, embroidery floss, etc. and they look pretty on your shelf.

¤ ¤ ¤ ¤ ¤

For those pretty decorative bottles on your kitchen counter, simply layer fruits or vegetables and cover with white rice vinegar. I especially like to do this with lemon slices. They look so colorful and refreshing.

¤ ¤ ¤ ¤ ¤

For some very inexpensive fresh greenery in your home, just plant some plain old grass seed in a cute flower pot or plastic lined basket. Spray with a squirt bottle for a few days until it starts to grow, then water lightly every several days. Add a colorful little bird, a few artificial bird eggs or a pretty ribbon and you'll have a fun plant.

¤ ¤ ¤ ¤ ¤

I always collect pretty small rocks and pebbles to add to the tops of my flower pots.

¤ ¤ ¤ ¤ ¤

For a rich, antiqued look, rub a white or cream colored candle with dark stain. Add a gold monogram or gold cord for a very elegant look for pennies.

¤ ¤ ¤ ¤ ¤

Polar fleece pillows are really a nice (and comfortable) addition to any room. Just cut 2 squares of fabric about 7 inches bigger than your pillow. "Pink" all the edges. Stitch a square in the center for your pillow, leaving one side open to insert pillow and leaving a 3-inch flange around the edge. Quick, easy and fun!

¤ ¤ ¤ ¤ ¤

A few bay leaves painted gold make a pretty addition to a bowl of dried white roses or hydrangeas.

¤ ¤ ¤ ¤ ¤

To remove odors from your plastic containers, stuff the item tightly with crumpled newspapers. Put on the lid and let it sit for several days. The paper will absorb the odor.

¤ ¤ ¤ ¤ ¤

Don't forget to wipe off your light bulbs with a damp cloth periodically. They'll last longer.

¤ ¤ ¤ ¤ ¤

Occasionally wash a load of towels without any detergent. You'll be surprised how much soap buildup there is.

¤ ¤ ¤ ¤ ¤

Remember nothing is lost, it's just not where it belongs.

¤ ¤ ¤ ¤ ¤

You can't have everything. Where would you put it?

¤ ¤ ¤ ¤ ¤

Dig the well before you are thirsty. – -Chinese Proverb

May

May

That saying "April showers bring May flowers" is certainly true in our neighborhood. The bulbs and blooms are beautiful! I love the scent of the iris and lilacs, and those peony buds are "bursting at the seams." As Roy and I enjoy our breakfast, it's so fun to watch the mother birds tending their nests, and down the road the baby calves and ponies are having great fun! I get such a feeling that "all is right with the world" when I see these new "families" getting started.

We have a saying at our house that "Families are Forever." I hope you have the same feeling in your home. As we celebrate Mother's Day this month, may we all count our blessings for families!

Food for Thought

Life is happening right now! Today is part of our lives, whether it's dull, exciting, challenging, miserable, or happy. What are we waiting for? Do you realize what a unique, original and beautiful person you are? No one is just like you; you are a special ONE!

My Dad died when I was 2 months old, and being the Depression years, I lived or stayed with grandmothers, relatives and sometimes my mother as I was growing up. Without a family structure, I often felt like a lost little lamb. One day, walking to school with a neighbor in a Nebraska snow storm, we ran and caught snow flakes on our tongues. My friend said, "Aren't they fun. Every single one is different, just like people." Whoa! What a profound thought for a little girl! As I lay in my bed that night, contemplating the thought, I realized I could be as unique as I chose! A true turning point in my life!

We don't have to struggle in life trying to be a good cook like Helen, a seamstress like Betty, or a mother like Sue. We can just be the best US! I love the quote from Robert Browning, "My business is not to remake myself, but make the absolute best of what God made." Life is good, and there is fulfillment at every turn if we just live the moment. My friend, Carma, always said, "Be where you are, when you're there!" Terrific food for thought!

When I was traveling, doing media tours to promote my other books, TV hosts often asked me after our discussions of motherhood and homes — "Yes, but Mrs. Nye, are you really fulfilled, just being a homemaker?" My answer to them was always, "When my husband walks in that door and gives me a hug, my daughter calls to say how much she loves me, or that little grandson crawls on my lap and gives me a squeeze, you bet! I know I am fulfilled!" What can bring us more joy and happiness than the little day-to-day things that make up our lives?

One day I was wiping up some spilled juice on the counter and squeezed it out in the sink. Since I was having a "low" day, I thought, "I'm just like this sponge. I soak up every negative thought and comment, and then just when I think I'm doing good, I squeeze out a thought or two and it brings me down again. It's time to rinse out the sponge in fresh, clean water and clear my mind." Now when you start to think negative thoughts, just visualize rinsing that sponge in sparkling, clear water. It really works!

Self-esteem is something we all need to work on every day. It can elude us quickly. We can't love others until we feel good about ourselves. Those who feel good about themselves can be more supportive of others, happy, and enjoy more growth and progression in life.

We need not be perfect to love and be loved. Nothing creates stress more than thinking we must be perfect. Perfectionism is a trait that can become a handicap. Do you know someone who won't try something new because they wouldn't do it perfectly? How crippling! And how much joy is missed in life from not trying. We are all in this world to learn and grow. Enjoy the journey!

Stress and worry are such deterrents to happiness. I remember seeing a sign that said, "Worry is like a rocking chair. It gives you something to do, but doesn't get you anywhere." Let's concentrate on building our self-esteem, which in turn will tear down our stress.

1. Always remember that those around you who seem to have it all together have doubts and fears, too. Be supportive of them. Lift others, and you will soon lift yourself.

2. Do what it takes to make yourself feel more confident. Study a new subject; exercise; learn a language (or just improve the one you use); try a new make-up; improve your posture; stand up and look the world in the eye.

3. Avoid people that make you feel "down." This is your life! Keep it upbeat!

4. Find your "specialty" and use it every day. Whether it's smiling, singing, or just a friendly word for someone, USE your talents!

5. Stop putting yourself down. Listen to compliments when you receive them. Maybe even write them down to cheer you up later.

6. Use positive words when thinking of yourself. Don't advertise your shortcomings!

7. Realize you have up and down times. If your health is not good right now, it's not time to tackle a big project. If your office or job is at a peak busy period, it's not time to start that new diet. Learn to roll with the "waves" of life. You'll always reach the shore.

8. Enjoy the things you do. Everyone does a better job at something with which they are having fun.

9. Practice relaxing and keep things in perspective! Find what works for you — music, walking, reading, prayer or just a few deep breaths. Face the moment and deal with it. Don't worry about things in the future and borrow trouble. None of us can control everything! Don't even try.

10. Most of all, remember things are more likely to be good if we expect they will! If you can't change things, you can always smile, or better yet — laugh! It's the best remedy to relieve your stress and give you a new attitude. Focus on that beautiful laughter and you'll soon think things must be OK. It's really not the problems or stress that get us down, it's how we handle them. To not laugh or cry is blocking our emotions and puts us at risk. And it's a boring way to live — tell a joke, see a funny movie, sing — take charge of your own happiness!

As each of our lives progress, we fill many roles. Since this is the month of May, my thoughts turn to mothers.

You young mothers, what an awesome but wonderful role you have ahead of you. Everyone has heard, "These are the happiest years of your life." Yes, I remember the cookie crumbs and spilled milk on the floor, the muddy foot tracks in the kitchen, the constant ringing of the telephone and the tears and frustration. But I also remember those tiny fingers curling around mine, sweet little Kristen singing me a song, the clean, fresh smell of Heidi after her bath, the look of pride on the boys' faces as they gave me a picture they drew "just for me", and that overwhelming feeling as I look at my grown-up son Mark thinking how much he looks like his Dad. Young mothers, relax and enjoy the time. It is one of the best times of your life!

However, as we move from phase to phase in our lives, each one seems "the best." No longer do I rock my little Kristen on my lap, but I can still hug her and tell her what a great "mommy" she is! Heidi and I no longer make mud pies together, but we share recipes and have a good laugh over a dud! I don't comfort Mark anymore on that first day at school, but I can be there to encourage as he undertakes a new project. Stephen no longer needs my help in training his puppy, but I can be there to love him through being a father. And now there's grandchildren! It just keeps getting better!

I feel so fortunate to have had two grandmothers that taught me how to live. They were as different as night and day, but I gleaned so much from each of them.

My German Grandma Scheel was a strong woman of true pioneer stock. Coming from Schleswig, Germany she fell in love at the age of 16 and married my Grandpa. He had headed west in the "Gold Rush," but got as far as the Dakotas, missed his sweetheart, and returned to Nebraska with just enough gold to make her wedding ring. Homesteading on a farm, Grandma made all her furniture, some very decorative, using a comb to pattern the stain on the wood. She raised 12 children and one grandchild, had lots of chickens, did all her own sewing for the family, had a huge garden and made the most delicious food. She dug a cellar under her porch where she could climb down and always come up with cold milk and rich, fresh-churned butter.

Grandma's life wasn't easy, but she had learned early on to accept the commitments of her life by loving and caring with dignity. She constantly was learning new things and always felt there was nothing you couldn't do with God's help. She was never lonesome. She surrounded herself with those she loved. Grandma had tragedy and pain in her life, but she understood pain is part of life and it doesn't last forever. Her solution was to pick someone else up that was in need. She made a difference in so many peoples' lives, and that's what kept her going!

Grandma Scheel died when I was 8 years old, but whenever I face a challenge, I think of her and know she would advise me, "Just do it with all your might, and God's help!"

Grandma Benson, of true Danish ancestry, really knew how to live. Her life wasn't easy and she sacrificed so much for her family and friends, but Wow! did she have a super attitude. Her philosophy was "sing a little, smile a lot and never take your teeth out in public!" She never wanted anyone to remember her as "old what's-her-name," so she worked hard remembering others. There was a "magic" in her laughter and the twinkle in her eyes. She could tell stories and keep you mesmerized for hours with her actions and antics and yet, she always had a listening ear. How often I observed her talking with someone about their problems or adventures. Grandma knew that people love to talk about themselves and to hear their names. I always marveled at her memory but realize now how she must have worked at that. Grandma knew everyone had talent, and she found ways for everybody to use them. She had us all perform in every program that came along, and if there wasn't any program available, she and I would entertain each other.

This special lady took care of herself. She walked nearly everywhere she went and stood straight and tall. She often said, "When some people get old, they wear a sour face and walk with their knees bent and heads sticking out. Why, they look like TURTLES! We need to get out and MOVE!" She took pride in her clothing even though she had little. She sewed everything she wore and kept up with the latest styles. No house dresses and "comfortable" shoes for this lady! She lived in the present, knowing all the latest news, events and even music. We loved her for that. Whenever I had friends over, we could roll up that huge rug she had crocheted from rags, and dance to the newest songs. She knew the dance steps as well as we did!

I think Grandma truly knew that "the past is to learn from, not to live in." I'm sure her life was full of struggles, hardships and disappointments, but she always seemed to learn and move on. Like the batteries, she just "kept going!" Grandma Benson lived for today and realized nothing was "too good" for the moment. We used that pretty tablecloth, lit that little candle, and enjoyed that box of chocolates. We often left the dishes to enjoy a favorite radio program and went back to them later. We walked and splashed in the puddles when it rained; we walked to the store for a pint of ice cream just to celebrate a sunny day. We sampled perfumes in the store and laughed all the way home about the different scents, and we smiled at everyone along the way. Every day was different. Grandma was never too old to change. She said when you're through changing, you're through! My wonderful Grandma Benson lived until she died.

I loved her so much, and I pray that I have learned these lessons well. My grand-daughter, Jessica, and I have a standing joke — I want her to write my obituary, and I don't want her to say I died peacefully. I want people to know I left flailing my arms with spirit!

May Food for Fun
Recipes — Good and good for you!

This is a great "keeper" to have handy in the refrigerator for a quick lunch.

Oriental Salad

Combine:
- 1 head shredded cabbage (I use part red cabbage)
- 1 pkg. broken up ramen noodles
- 2 shredded carrots
- 1 chopped green pepper
- ½ chopped red pepper
- ½ c. slivered almonds
- 2 T. toasted sesame seeds
- 2 c. chopped chicken, if desired

Mix with dressing:
- ½ c. rice vinegar
- ¼ c. sugar (you can substitute honey)
- 1/3 c. peanut oil
- ¾ tsp. ginger
- a little garlic
- a dash of soy sauce
- 1 tsp. sesame oil (a must! This oil seems expensive, but it lasts forever. A teaspoon does wonders for Chinese flavor!)

¤ ¤ ¤ ¤ ¤

It doesn't get any better than this recipe. I've even served it by candlelight for a romantic dinner. A loaf of crusty Italian bread and cheese cake or chocolate mousse for dessert, and you've got a winner.

Bev's Pasta Primavera

In a non-stick skillet, melt 2 T. butter.

Add ¼ to ½ cup each of cut up: Broccoli
Zucchini
Radishes
Green onions
Snow peas
Mushrooms
Green beans
Tomato
(Just use what you have)

Sauté for just a few minutes, until cooked but still crispy.

Add: 2 c. pre-cooked spaghetti
1 ½ c. half & half
1/3 c. Parmesan cheese

Heat together over low temperature.

¤ ¤ ¤ ¤ ¤

This is a tasty spring dish that keeps well in the refrigerator. You can serve it cold as shown here, marinated and cool, or serve it hot by heating it after sprinkling liberally with grated mozzarella cheese.

Hot and Cold Chicken Salad

Combine: 1 c. diced cooked chicken
2 c. sliced mushrooms
¾ c. cooked macaroni or spaghetti
½ c. sliced celery

Make dressing of: ¼ c. lemon juice
¼ c. salad oil
½ tsp. basil
½ tsp. oregano
dash of garlic powder
salt & pepper to taste

Shake all together in a jar, then pour liberally over chicken mixture. Marinate for at least one hour.

Just before serving, add 1 ½ c. diced tomatoes.

¤ ¤ ¤ ¤ ¤

This "different" salad really keeps everyone going back for more. It's so refreshing!

Springtime Tomato Aspic Salad

Dissolve: 6 oz. pkg. lemon Jell-o
1 c. hot water

Add: 1 c. cold water

Set aside to cool.

Heat 1 can tomato soup.

Add: 8 oz. cream cheese to soften

Whip in blender and add: 1 c. Miracle Whip

Blend again, then cool.

When cool, combine mixtures and add: 1 small finely chopped onion
1 small finely chopped green pepper
1 ½ c. chopped celery
1 c. chopped pecans

Let set until firm. Cut in squares.

¤ ¤ ¤ ¤ ¤

Here's a super accompaniment for that springtime supper.

Aunt Viola's Cucumbers

Combine: 1 c. sour cream
1 T. sugar
2 T. vinegar
¼ c. dill
¼ tsp. pepper
½ tsp. salt
1 tsp. celery seed

Then add: 2 sliced cucumbers
1 sliced onion

Keep refrigerated overnight for flavors to meld.

¤ ¤ ¤ ¤ ¤

This one's a winner — guaranteed to please! Be sure to serve it with the sauce.

Virginia's Ham Loaf and Mustard Sauce

Combine: 1 lb. ground ham
            1 lb. ground pork
            ¾ c. soda cracker crumbs
            ¼ c. chopped onion
            2 beaten eggs
            ½ tsp. salt
            1 T. parsley

Shape into loaf. Bake at 325* for 30 minutes.

Combine: ¼ lb. brown sugar
            ¼ c. vinegar
            ¾ T. dry mustard

Boil together, then pour over partially baked ham loaf.

Bake for 1 more hour and serve with mustard sauce.

Mustard Sauce — combine: 2 T. horseradish
                                ½ c. mayonnaise
                                1 T. minced onion
                                ½ c. sour cream
                                ¼ tsp. table mustard

¤ ¤ ¤ ¤ ¤

You'll want to try this for a quick and healthy summer supper.

Zucchini Monterey

Brown: 1 lb. ground beef
         1 small chopped onion

Add: 4 diced zucchini

Cook until tender, and add: 3 c. cooked rice
                              1 can chopped green chilies
                              1 tsp. salt
                              2 cloves minced garlic
                              ½ tsp. chili powder
                              2 diced tomatoes
                              2 c. grated cheese (Monterey Jack is best)
                              1 c. sour cream

Mix and put into a 9x13 inch pan. Cover with crushed corn chips.

Bake at 350* for 20 minutes.

This is sooo good served with a tossed salad and will serve 6 nicely. It can also be frozen before baking and cooked later.

¤ ¤ ¤ ¤ ¤

We first tasted this in a restaurant in Phoenix and have been making it for Jenny ever since. It's so refreshing. You'll love the flavor.

Jennifer's Springtime Parfait

Mix 1 large package peach Jell-o as directed in a 9x13 inch pan.

When firm, cut in tiny squares.

Whip 1 c. whipping cream.

Gently stir tiny Jell-o squares into bowl of whipped cream. Keep refrigerated.

May Grocery Bag

This is the month I like to check my pantry and freezer. The gardens will soon be producing, and it will be time to replenish our stock.

There are usually specials on **sugar** this month to prepare for the summer preserving season. I always empty my sugar sacks into a large plastic clean garbage container. This prevents the sugar from turning into a hard "lump" in the sack.

Canned goods will also be on sale so the packing plants can prepare for the new crops. Stock up on things you use normally. Just remember to mark the purchase date on the can so you can rotate your inventory. I usually plan 1 year shelf life on canned goods, and it sure saves trips to the grocery store (and helps avoid that impulse buying).

Chickens are a good buy this month and, again, so versatile. I keep bags of several types of chicken parts — boneless breasts for quick meals, white meat and thighs for frying, legs & backs for making stock and wings for those snacks (Roy's favorite – see June recipes.)

This is another good month for that pot of soup. (I know, I sound like a broken record.) While you're out working in the garden, visiting with a neighbor, doing the laundry or at work, it will almost cook itself and how nice to enjoy for supper or share with a friend. I'll bet you have some leftover vegetables in the fridge and some spices and seasonings in the cupboard right now, right?

Speaking of those vegetables, I never cease to be amazed at the new variety we are being offered in the supermarket. Don't be afraid to give them a try. That large ugly "celery root" is absolutely delicious, peeled and shredded for a salad or even sautéed with a dab of butter.

Remember to keep **"greens"** in a plastic bag in the fridge, but don't wash them until you're ready to use them. Never soak fresh fruits and vegetables in water. Steam those greens and serve with a touch of butter, salt and pepper, and a little splash of vinegar. What a treat!

This is the month that fresh fish becomes plentiful in the markets. It is so simple to prepare and good for us. I try to have fish twice a week.

For you **lamb**-lovers, this is the time for you. Just remember that lamb chops should always be at least an inch thick or they will be dry and overdone when cooked. Broil them only until the centers are pink. A little lemon sprinkled on lamb adds a delicious touch and helps to tenderize it, also. Enjoy!

May Why Didn't I Think of That?

Concentrate on your potential, not your weakness.

¤ ¤ ¤ ¤ ¤

Plan for success.

¤ ¤ ¤ ¤ ¤

If you had a friend who talked to you the way you talk to yourself, how long would he be your friend?

¤ ¤ ¤ ¤ ¤

No matter what we achieve, we had a helper.

¤ ¤ ¤ ¤ ¤

An edible flower, or herb, berries or a cherry make a pretty addition in each ice cube when serving a cold drink. No trouble, but adds a nice touch.

¤ ¤ ¤ ¤ ¤

The man who removes a mountain begins by carrying away small stones — Chinese Proverb.

¤ ¤ ¤ ¤ ¤

Keep a little bag of potpourri in the drawer with your napkins. So pleasant at mealtime!

¤ ¤ ¤ ¤ ¤

"In seed time, learn. In harvest, teach. In winter, enjoy." William Blake

¤ ¤ ¤ ¤ ¤

Attitude begins with Gratitude.

¤ ¤ ¤ ¤ ¤

Treat yourself to a childhood desire.

¤ ¤ ¤ ¤ ¤

"To dream of the person you wish to be is to waste the person you are."

¤ ¤ ¤ ¤ ¤

Often we say "yes" too quickly and "no" not fast enough.

¤ ¤ ¤ ¤ ¤

"When you cease expecting, you have all things."   Buddha

¤ ¤ ¤ ¤ ¤

Only I can make me happy!

¤ ¤ ¤ ¤ ¤

The reason so many people never get anywhere in life is that when opportunity knocks, they are out in back looking for a four-leaf clover.

¤ ¤ ¤ ¤ ¤

A formula for failure — try to please everyone.

¤ ¤ ¤ ¤ ¤

Hard work is really the easy work you didn't do when it needed doing.

¤ ¤ ¤ ¤ ¤

No matter what, pin that smile on in the morning and by noon it will stay all by itself.

¤ ¤ ¤ ¤ ¤

Your body does what your face says. SMILE!

¤ ¤ ¤ ¤ ¤

Live life so you're too tired to worry at night, and too busy to worry during the day.

¤ ¤ ¤ ¤ ¤

"There are two kinds of people — those who enter a room and say 'Well, here I am' and those who come in and say 'Ah, there you are.'"   Fredrick L. Collins

¤ ¤ ¤ ¤ ¤

There's no bad weather, just inappropriate clothing!

¤ ¤ ¤ ¤ ¤

Successful people are those who are doing what the rest of us don't feel like doing.

¤ ¤ ¤ ¤ ¤

Just Do It!

¤ ¤ ¤ ¤ ¤

Windshield cleaner makes a great window washer in the house. It doesn't streak.

¤ ¤ ¤ ¤ ¤

When making Jello, put the boiling water in the bowl first. Start stirring and sprinkle in the Jello powder. No more globs in the bottom of the bowl.

¤ ¤ ¤ ¤ ¤

Freeze some of your homemade chicken and beef stock in ice cube trays. Great to add to gravy, etc.

June

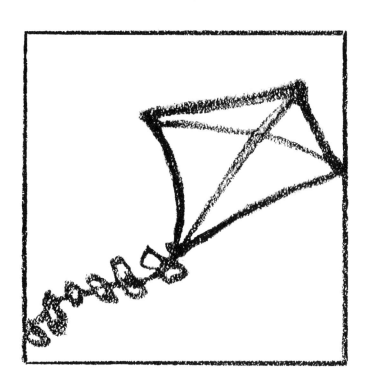

June

Summer is really here! Aren't these sunshiny days beautiful? Nothing brings sunshine into my life more than my sweetheart and mate. Let's spend a while talking about these special people in our lives. I think they placed "Father's Day" in this sunny month just for that purpose!

Food for Thought

Yes, the flower gardens are in bloom all around us, and aren't they beautiful! Every color, variety and size! However, a lot of care and work went into these gardens. Today, one of the most overlooked and neglected "flower gardens" is marriage!

After giving a talk on marriage to a large group of women in Indiana, I had a little lady come rushing up to me and say, with her hands on her hips, "Well, Mrs. Nye, marriage is no bed of roses!" I thought about her statement on the long drive home. "Oh, yes," I thought, "marriage is like a bed of roses. It requires tender care, feeding, some pruning, weeding, and sunlight. It takes work and effort, and there are some thorns along the way. But, oh, when those blooms come, it is worth it all!"

Like the flowers, one of the things we enjoy most in our marriage is that we are different. We each bring many things to our home and can grow together as long as we think "we" not "I." I remember growing up on a farm in Nebraska. As I observed the horses, a pair would always stand head to tail. One hot summer day I suddenly realized that way they could each swat the flies from the other's face! How thoughtful! A small gesture, but it came naturally. Isn't it nice to hear a husband remark, "My wife taught me about orchids. She's really an expert." Or, "My husband has shared his love of classical music with me. I never appreciated it before." We can all enrich one another by sharing our unique personality, gifts and talents with each other. Instead of being threatened by each other, let's learn and grow together with enthusiasm.

I once read a quote from the psychologist, Carl Rogers, about accepting others, "When I walk on the beach to watch the sunset, I do not call out 'a little more orange over to the right, please' or 'would you mind giving us less purple in the back?' No, I enjoy always different sunsets as they are." We do well to do the same with people we love.

Roy and I have lived together nearly 50 years and are well aware of our differences. It took us awhile, but we finally realized we actually help each other more because we are different. Roy is slower and methodical; I tend to rush and be impulsive. He is a saver, and I like to clean and throw things out. He's quiet;

I'm talkative. And he enjoys the moment; I like to get things done. He's always teasing me that he can't get up to go to the bathroom or I have the bed made! Reminds me of Satchel Paige saying, "He's so fast he could turn out the light and get in bed before the room gets dark."

I used to tease Roy about "frittering," but I have come to appreciate how helpful and therapeutic that can be. It is not wasted time, but healing time — cleaning a drawer, looking at old pictures, walking through the garden or even just sitting.

Doesn't it make life interesting? Think how boring life would be if you agreed on everything. Neither would grow. We have never been afraid of disagreements. I think the only people who never argue are those who don't care or are dead! Just don't develop hardening of the attitudes. Our goal has always been not to think alike but to think together! We know we are different, and we're happy about it. In the things that matter most, we do think alike. We have the same eternal and family goals!

Many times this requires change. Remember Grandma Benson — "When you're through changing, you're through!" Like these beautiful plants and flowers we talked about, sometimes we get root bound. It's difficult to remove the plant from that "comfortable" pot, shake off the stagnant soil, trim the scraggly roots and start fresh. It can be a scary and hard thing to do, but we will flourish and blossom even more.

To paraphrase Shakespeare, "If a trait you desire, assume it." It really works!

Learn to be a good listener and really listen to your spouse. Truly listen; listen thoroughly until he has emptied his heart. You'll find he will share his worries, frustrations, feelings and joys! Be happy for him, care about him — don't interrupt — listen with your ears, eyes and heart. What a blessing in both your lives! And nothing will make him more interesting than your enthusiasm.

If you are the partner in your relationship that has the most enthusiasm and creativity, don't worry, nag and complain for your mate to do more. You are blessed with this gift, and you owe it to your marriage to use it. Each partner contributes in their own way. It just may not be the same way!

It's true. We have some weeds and trials along the way in our marriage garden. Only through trials do we become stronger.

Irritating habits can get in the way. Little annoying things get out of control. Think of the oyster. It takes the little grains of irritating sand that get in its shell and makes a pearl. He can't change them or get rid of them, so he turns them into something beautiful. Don't be a fault-finder. Your mate can become so discouraged thinking it's impossible to please you, and after a while won't care whether they do or not. "Treat a man as he is and he will remain the same; treat a man as he may become and he will become that man." Goethe.

I have found if you expect people to be better than they are, they will keep trying. Don't let your ego get in the way. It's nice to be important, but it's more important to be nice.

As Roy and I drove across the country recently, we couldn't help noticing how the scenery changed — from the fields of flowers in Olympia, Washington, to the barren fields of tumbleweeds in Wyoming. This kept us on our toes and helped us appreciate each part more. Don't complain about your barren fields of life. Learn from them, observe and grow. Nothing lasts forever!

Even though at times our budgets can be strained, remember — how rich we are has to do with our attitude. Many couples say they were happiest when they had little. That ice cream cone or splurge on a bunch of daisies can make all the difference. Live rich, not beyond your means! The greatest thing you can spend on your mate is your time.

Add some spice to your life. Don't be predictable. If you are bored, you may be boring. It can be something as simple as changing your places at the table. You'll see things in a whole new way! We love to take "penny walks" — flipping a penny at each corner to see which way to go. Gosh, you'll discover a whole new neighborhood.

Recently we took a jar along on our car trip filled with subjects to talk about and took turns drawing. We learned so much about one another. Even after 50 years! Some of the subjects were: Favorite dessert & why, My biggest scare in life, My best childhood friend & why, What I admire most about you, Our favorite vacation, My favorite childhood toy, If I could be any profession I'd like…, My best feature is, How I am most like my mother or father, The happiest moment as a child, etc. What a wonderful sharing time this was. We picked one every hour or so and had some of the most tender, sharing moments of our years together. Try it!

It's interesting that what means the most and builds our relationships the greatest is what takes the least amount of money. It's back to that little word "time" again. Why do we have to hurry through life at the expense of really living? We hurry up in the morning to get going on our work, so we can hurry home to bed to get up again. We are always trying to get ahead or do something for tomorrow. What about today! I don't know about you, but I'm old-fashioned enough to say, "Wait a minute! I don't need that instant breakfast. I want to see my husband's smiling face as we sip our juice, enjoy our toast and listen to the birds singing 'Good Morning.'"

Look for the good things in your mate. Praise them, applaud their efforts, thank them for being there. Every one wants to be appreciated, and it sure makes the rough times smoother. Instead of listing their faults, think of the traits you admire in them. If you haven't said anything nice for a while, try it!

Learn how to deal with hurt and anger. Some friends of ours have a rule that they can't be upset at the same time. They take turns airing their problems. At our house, if I'm out of sorts, I just put my apron on backwards, and Roy understands I need a cooling off period. Then we can discuss it! A "peaceful" relationship is not always a healthy one. The most important part is to listen to each other without interruption. Both are allowed time and opinions. No one can be married and right all the time. Winning is beside the point!

Don't become so over-efficient that you sacrifice precious time together. If he runs errands and she goes grocery shopping, they may save time, but they miss out on a choice closeness. One of the joys of being retired is our ability to do things together. This includes cleaning house, creating meals and gardening. Creating order in our little corner of the world makes us feel so good. There's something very therapeutic about climbing into a crisp, clean bed, putting on a freshly ironed shirt, walking on a shiny clean floor, or sitting down to a colorful, healthy salad. It perks us up whether we have a problem to solve, a dreary day, or just a down mood. Find what works for you and enjoy it. The key is to have FUN. If you're happy, tell your faces and get busy.

Everyone makes appointments to take care of the "important" things, but do we make appointments with our spouses? Every week Roy and I have a "Date" night. We take turns planning, and the other one must go along with the idea. We've done simple things like movies and a hamburger, or quiet talks by the fire with some popcorn, to roller-skating and a "White Castle." (Our muscles and stomachs felt that for several days.) We've experienced a contemporary dance theatre, making spaghetti sauce together, visits to the library, walks in the rain, and once I called him at work, as a stranger, said I had admired him from a distance and would love to have a secret meeting with him to get acquainted. I picked him up from work; he came out in his trench coat, looking both ways and slipped into the car. We drove to a nearby park and enjoyed a picnic in the car (it was January in Ohio) having a fun conversation as if we were strangers. Then I dropped him back off at work. What a fun memory! I keep a journal of our dates, and we have as much fun reading about past ones as we do planning the next.

Do you give fun little gifts when it's not necessary? How about notes hidden around the house, in a lunch box or freshly done laundry? Do you share special winks, hand squeezing or bear hugs? Don't sacrifice the fun of today either worrying about tomorrow or saying you're too old today. Give each other plants and flowers while you can still smell them. Share your dreams and work toward them, enjoying the journey along the way.

Roy may not buy me a huge corsage for our anniversary, but he picks an early morning rose, covered with dew drops, and brings it to me with a kiss, and occasionally throws a cold glass of water when I'm in a nice warm shower! Is it any wonder love him?

Before we move on, let me just share a few thoughts on dads for this Father's Day. A wise person once said, "More children are punished for imitating their parents than for disobeying them." What a truth! Example is so important in being a parent. In our homes we teach the importance of work and learn how to cope with life. Fathers play such an important part in this. What children see at home determines how they act and re-act toward things in the world.

Fathers, make that child a priority. Be there to share the little things. They are BIG things to them. Be the head of the family and lead them, nurture them, and let them see your emotions. Don't be afraid to say, "I was wrong, forgive me." Be generous with your praise and enthusiasm. Be their hero by giving them your time.

I don't remember where I got this letter, but I have carried it around for a long time. What a tribute!

    October 19
    Dear Sir,

    A great man died today. He wasn't a world leader or a famous doctor or a business tycoon. But he was a great man. He was my father.

    He didn't get his picture in the paper for heading up committees. I guess you might say he was a person who never cared for credits or honors. He did corny things like paying bills on time, going to church and working in the PTA. He helped his kids with homework, went grocery shopping with his wife, enjoyed hauling us kids and our friends to and from football games. He liked simple things like picnics, country music, and running with the dog.

    Tonight is the first night of my life without him. I don't know what to do with myself, so I am writing to you. I am sorry for the times I didn't show him proper respect. But I'm thankful for many things.

    I am thankful that God let me have him for 15 years. And I am thankful I was able to let him know how much I loved him. He died with a smile on his face. He knew he was a success as a husband, father, son, brother and friend. I wonder how many millionaires can say that? Thanks for listening. You've been a great help.

    His daughter.

Know the value of your role as father. A child never forgets the principals, teachings and examples they receive from you — good or bad! Cherish your role. Realize how lucky you are. Chose happiness, and help your child develop this trait. True, everyone can't be happy all the time. There's the lost ball game, a scraped knee, or an unpleasant chore to do, but we can develop the trait of happiness. The "predisposition of feeling of well-being." This gives us an attitude of optimism and hopefulness.

Being "happy" all the time can lead to frustration when things don't go right, but maintaining a happy disposition helps us deal with life. A child can learn that happiness is his responsibility. A parent can help him learn this by letting him make choices, promoting good relationships with people, and teaching empathy with others by example.

Most important is to build a happy home. Love their mother, and be a happy, fulfilled person. Not someday when…but now! Love the role you're living.

One of our family's richest blessings is the patient, kind and loving example Roy has set in our home. To be loved and needed by this great man is a special thing to us, and we will do all we can to make his life easier and love him in return.

June Food for Fun
Some Sure-fire Husband Pleasers

Roy always asks me why we have to call this Monday Salad. He could eat it any day of the week (but it is such a great use for left-over Sunday roast).

Monday Salad

Combine: 2 c. leftover roast beef
1 ½ -2 c. leftover vegetables (green beans, zucchini, or asparagus)
1/3 c. salad oil
4 T. cider vinegar
1 tsp. salt
½ tsp. coarse ground pepper
1 T. chopped onion
1 clove minced garlic

Place in refrigerator and marinate overnight. Stir occasionally.

Serve on chopped lettuce.

Makes 3-4 servings.

¤ ¤ ¤ ¤ ¤

Roy will promise to do just about anything if I'll make him a pan of wings. He loves them as a hot and spicy snack!

Roy's Hot Buffalo Wings

In a 9x13 inch pan in a 400* oven, melt: 1 stick of margarine
1/3 c. Tabasco sauce (that's right!)

Place about 2 ½ lbs. chicken wings in pan and bake for 30 minutes.

Turn and bake another 30 minutes.

Serve with blue cheese or ranch dressing and celery sticks. These are "lick your fingers" good!!!

¤ ¤ ¤ ¤ ¤

I can be sure of a smile on Roy's face if I tell him we're having this stew for supper.

Yummy Beef Stew

Cut in cubes about 2 ½ lbs. of beef (roast or thick round steak works well). Shake in a bag with flour.

Then brown meat in 4 T. olive oil in a medium-hot pan. Make sure meat is well browned.

Then add:	1 large can (28 oz.) diced tomatoes
2 ¼ c. water
1 bay leaf
2 large cloves of garlic

Simmer, covered, for about 2 hours.

Then add:	2 c. small carrots
4 diced potatoes
2 medium onions
2 cans green beans

Continue simmering until vegetables are done — about 45 minutes.

Add salt and coarse pepper to taste and serve.

¤ ¤ ¤ ¤ ¤

For a meal of "pure heaven" I'll take this dish any time. The pork gets so tender it literally falls off the bone, and the sauerkraut becomes so mellow, you can't believe it. The Pennsylvania Dutch prefer this served over mashed potatoes; the Nebraska Germans opt for a good, hot, buttered baked potato!

Pork and Sauerkraut

Brown a pork loin roast well on all sides.

Add:	1 large can (29 oz.) sauerkraut with juice
2 heaping T. brown sugar
1 bay leaf

Cover tightly and simmer for 4-6 hours.

¤ ¤ ¤ ¤ ¤

Since we're talking about sweethearts and husbands this month, I have to share this pie recipe. It will get me about anything I want! Roy is a push-over for pie (especially this one!) The pie crust is so simple and tender and flaky every time!

Roy's Lemon Meringue Pie

Easy Pie Crust

Mix together: 1 c. flour
½ tsp. salt

Stir in with a fork: 1/3 c. Crisco oil

Sprinkle with 2 T. cold water. Mix thoroughly with a fork.

Roll out between 2 sheets of plastic wrap. Peel off top sheet of plastic wrap, flip into pie plate, shape to fit. Then peel off the other piece of plastic wrap.

Prick crust all over with a fork and bake at 450* until nicely browned. Cool.

To make **filling:**

In a saucepan, combine: 1/3 c. cornstarch
1 c. sugar
dash of salt

Add: 1 ½ c. boiling water

Mix well and cook over heat until thick and clear.

Add a little hot mixture to 3 beaten egg yolks. Then add egg yolks to pan and cook 2 minutes longer, stirring constantly.

Remove from heat and add: 1/3 c. lemon juice
½ tsp. grated lemon peel
2 T. butter

Cool slightly and pour into pie shell.

Top with this:

Perfect Meringue

Dissolve 1 T. cornstarch and 1 T. cold water.

Add ½ cup water and cook until thick and clear. Cool thoroughly.

Beat 3 egg whites until foamy.

Add 6 T. sugar and beat until stiff.

Add cooled mixture to beaten egg whites and spread over pie.

Bake at 350* for 12-15 minutes or until browned.

¤ ¤ ¤ ¤ ¤

Keep a batch of these muffins in the freezer to make a special treat of breakfast. Your husband will love you for it! They are absolutely "the best."

Breakfast Sunshine Muffins

Beat 2 eggs at high speed in large mixing bowl.

Add 2/3 c. oil and beat until well blended.

Stir in: ½ c. drained crushed pineapple
       1 c. finely shredded carrots

Combine: 2/3 c. sugar
               1 ½ c. flour
               1 tsp. baking powder
               1 tsp. soda
               1 tsp. cinnamon
               ¼ tsp. salt

Combine two mixtures and mix well.

Add: ½ c. coconut
       ½ c. currants
       ½ c. chopped nuts

Spoon into greased or paper-lined muffin pans.

Bake at 350* for 25 minutes. Serve warm. Freezes well. Makes 2 dozen muffins.

¤ ¤ ¤ ¤ ¤

When I think of sharing recipes with you that make a husband happy, this is one of the first that comes to mind. Roy is happy if his granola jar is full!

Delicious Granola

Spread 4 c. rolled oats on ungreased sheet cake pan and bake at 350* for 10 minutes.

Stir in: 1 c. flaked coconut 1 c. coarsely chopped peanuts (or other type nuts)
     3/4 c. wheat germ

Then add: ½ c. honey
             1/3 c. vegetable oil
             1 tsp. vanilla

Mix until dry ingredients are well-coated.

Bake at 350* for 20-25 minutes, stirring occasionally to brown evenly.

Stir in: 1 pkg. (8 oz.) dried chopped apricots
     1 c. raisins

Other dried fruit may be substituted for apricots or raisins.

Store in tightly covered container.

June Grocery Bag

June is the beginning of the hustle and bustle of weddings, showers, graduations and family vacations and reunions. It seems like we celebrate all of these occasions with delicious food. With a little planning, it can be tempting and pretty as well as economical and nutritious.

There will be plenty of fresh produce at your grocer's at reasonable prices, or you may be fortunate to have a garden or nearby produce stand. Be sure to treat your family to lots of fresh green peas. Nothing compares with the flavor and satisfaction of a dish full of peas you and your family have just shelled together. With a dab of butter on top, they're delicious! Remember never to salt the vegetables until after they are cooked. Green beans, mushrooms, apricots, summer onions and some tomatoes should start appearing again. Won't it be terrific to sink your teeth into a fresh tomato after those "winter-time" tasteless varieties?

My suggestion for menu planning and grocery shopping this month is to simplify. People have been buying things in boxes, cans, and cartons, then saucing and topping them to death for so long that they've forgotten how delicious simple, plain, basic food can be. Try steaming your vegetables and serving them with just a dab of butter and salt and pepper. Boil up some new potatoes in their skins, or just broil a piece of fish or chicken and enjoy the yummy flavor of the natural juices. Raw fruits and vegetables are bursting with flavor and make a great snack or dessert. There's an endless abundance of whole grains and beans that make mighty tasty soups, cereals and breads. A cold glass of milk is more refreshing than any fancy expensive punch. A glass of milk with a wedge of cheese, some homemade bread and a salad or piece of fruit is a feast for anyone.

June is also the time to fill our grocery bags and baskets with strawberries and rhubarb. There are Strawberry Festivals going on all over the country, and I think Roy waits all year just so he can declare his own festival and eat his fill of strawberries and cream. Nothing fancy for him — just give him the biggest bowl in the kitchen and a pitcher of cool cream, and he's in heaven.

Actually, **strawberries** are very rich in vitamin C, and the nice part is they retain their vitamin content even after being picked, as long as their little caps are left on. Once you remove the caps and clean them, they not only lose their vitamin C quickly, but they also start to deteriorate in a hurry. So clean them as you use them. We like them cut up on our cereal in the morning or tossed in the blender with some fresh, cold milk for an afternoon "pick-me-up."

Mix some with a little sugar or honey and freeze in containers. (I always slice the ones I freeze like this.) Then I always lay out a bunch of nice, whole ones on a cookie sheet and freeze. Then toss them in a plastic bag and keep frozen. They are fun to have to "top" a special salad or dessert. Of course, every freezer needs some freezer jam, also.

When buying strawberries, look for a full, red color and medium-sized berries. Large ones may look impressive, but they are usually tasteless and pithy inside. Avoid the ones with uncolored spots and lots of surface seeds. Keep them refrigerated and enjoy to your heart's content.

Mother Nature really knew what she was doing when she arranged to have strawberries and rhubarb in season at the same time. No two fruits could be more compatible. **Rhubarb** is so plentiful and inexpensive, and when combined with the berries you get twice as much sauce or jam. Of course, there's a lot to say about rhubarb on its own. Many people have never eaten it, and as you drive down the street or road there are always oodles of "hills" of rhubarb just going to waste in people's yards. I really feel bad about this. We love it in so many forms — sauces, pies, cobblers, combined with strawberries or pineapple for jam, and Roy and the boys love to peel and eat the stalks fresh with a little salt, like a green apple. Just remember to discard the leaves as they are poisonous.

Use honey instead of sugar as a sweetener in the sauce for a real taste treat. Look for firm, crisp stalks, and by the way, these should be pulled and not cut. (Just grasp the stalk firmly and pull.) Avoid the real thin stalks. Promise me you'll try some this season.

Lettuce is beautiful right now. In choosing a head of lettuce, look for a big head that has a lot of green and feels light and springy. That way you will get a tender, sweet young head. Those heavy ones that have a lot of white will be old and bitter and often full of rust. I hope you all are trying the other varieties. Most of them — romaine, red and curly endive — are the same price as head lettuce but watch the Boston, bibb, and butter types. Some will be the same in price, and others sold by the pound may be very expensive. You may want to remember that the "leaf" varieties have much more vitamins A and C than head lettuce (or iceberg).

Instead of serving your family only chopped lettuce as a salad, add a shredded carrot, some radishes, chopped green pepper and some parsley. You'll be surprised at the added nutrition you'll be getting.

With **fresh peas and corn** keep in mind that both these vegetables start to lose their natural sugars as soon as they are picked, so use them as soon as possible. Once they are shelled or husked, they should be used immediately. Don't buy corn that has already been husked at the store. It will be tough, starchy, and unflavorful. Peas are very high in iron so, you young mothers, enjoy them with your children. Be sure to also pick up some of those little, new potatoes while you're shopping. Scrub them well (don't peel), cook until tender and then combine them with fresh peas in a medium white sauce. We wait all year long to enjoy this dish in the early summer. Keep the peas and corn in plastic bags in the refrigerator to retain their moisture, but use as soon as possible.

Also watch for the seafood specials this month. The shrimp and fish fit right in with the plentiful salad time. Eat healthily and enjoy!

June Why Didn't I Think of That?

Never salt steaks, chops or hamburgers until they are thoroughly cooked. Salt leaches out the juices.

¤ ¤ ¤ ¤ ¤

Always use your kitchen shears to cut little slits around your steak or chop. It will keep it from curling.

¤ ¤ ¤ ¤ ¤

Handle those hamburgers gently when forming "patties". Too much handling will make them heavy and compact. I also wet my hands. It makes the raw meat easier to handle.

¤ ¤ ¤ ¤ ¤

When buying meats think in terms of how many servings or meals, not how many pounds, for the price.

¤ ¤ ¤ ¤ ¤

Often a round steak (cut it up yourself) is a better buy than stew meat. Think creatively!

¤ ¤ ¤ ¤ ¤

Keep raisins, currants, and other dried fruits in an air-tight container in the freezer.

¤ ¤ ¤ ¤ ¤

Save your little plastic berry boxes. They are so nice for a serving of potato chips or a nibbling snack.

¤ ¤ ¤ ¤ ¤

If you haven't tried the cultured buttermilk powder in cans at the grocery store, I highly recommend it. It sure comes in handy for baking.

¤ ¤ ¤ ¤ ¤

Husbands, don't work so hard earning your salt that you forget your sugar!

¤ ¤ ¤ ¤ ¤

Ropes don't hold a marriage together. It's the threads, the tiny little threads of every day.

¤ ¤ ¤ ¤ ¤

"Nothing is as hard to do gracefully as getting down off your high horse." Franklin P. Jones

¤ ¤ ¤ ¤ ¤

It's always the best time to do your best.

¤ ¤ ¤ ¤ ¤

A man convinced against his will is of the same opinion still.

¤ ¤ ¤ ¤ ¤

"In marriage, being the right person is as important as finding the right person." Wilbert Donald Gough

¤ ¤ ¤ ¤ ¤

No camel route is long with good company.   Turkish Proverb

¤ ¤ ¤ ¤ ¤

Some flower tips to remember —

Use unique and different containers — teacups, pretty pitchers, soup bowls, fancy jars, or candy dishes.

Flowers will open more quickly if placed in warm water.

Never place flower arrangements in direct sun.

Always strip all leaves that will be below the water line.

Change water regularly.

Pick flowers in the morning for longer blooms.

If you'd like to "color" that bunch of fresh daisies, just put them in a vase of cold water with food coloring added and let them sit overnight.

¤ ¤ ¤ ¤ ¤

I always keep a "tear" jar in my cupboard. Ours is just a little decorated mustard jar. Then when the grandchildren are visiting and the tears start to flow, we run and get the jar to "catch" the tears. As I struggle with the lid, the laughter starts and…it works every time. I even remember little Jacob bringing it to me once. It worked then, too!

July

July

Summer is well under way. Families are gathering and the earth is colored in all its glory. Aren't you glad to be alive? It's a great time of year to be able to celebrate the birth of our nation. We have all experienced that lump that comes in our throats as we sing "The Star-Spangled Banner" or the feeling of pride that we have as we see that beautiful flag unfurled. However, patriotism is more than a feeling. It is doing the things that show our love for our country. It is voting, obeying the laws and signs, respecting public property, learning about the history and beauty of our land, and expressing to those around us the love and pride that we feel.

Every year to celebrate the Fourth of July, our family looks forward to our traditional picnic and attending the community fireworks display. As I sit and observe the children and Roy enjoy the fireworks, I always think how much like life this celebration is. There are dark periods and then a sudden jolting flash of bright light or maybe a great burst of color. Occasionally the silence is broken by a loud bang which brings us up short and back to reality. Everyone has a dark period of life at times, but with a little patience and even some hope and anticipation a brilliant light will come, or colorful blessings and opportunities appear. Then as we get lulled away in boredom and routine again, the loud bang comes, shakes us up, and we're ready to begin living again with enthusiasm and determination.

May we each realize how blessed we are to live in this beautiful America and learn to enjoy and make the most of the fireworks display in each of our lives. Hooray for the 4th of July!

Food for Thought

Mention the word "picnic" to anyone and I guarantee you will prompt a flood of memories. Since this is the month we celebrate our wonderful, free country, what better way to see and enjoy the beauties around us than with a picnic basket in hand.

One of the first picnics I remember was when I was four years old, and we all drove to a city park in Cozad, Nebraska for a family reunion. We grandchildren had our picture taken with my little Danish great grandmother. She was a tiny thing. We were nearly as tall as she. Great-grandma Benson was such a happy, cheerful lady, we loved being with her. The park seemed extra pretty and green that day because of the happy time we were experiencing.

Do you have a family reunion or get-together every year or two? It is such a perfect opportunity to get better acquainted, enjoy each other and see different parts of the country.

Mom was famous for her picnics on the farm, and the Fourth of July she went all out. I can remember being up until the wee hours of the night before, getting all the chickens butchered and ready for frying. We set up huge, long tables out under the Linden and Cottonwood trees, and Mom always had plenty of freshly laundered check tablecloths with which to cover them. We fixed lots of mason jars full of zinnias from the garden and then filled the table with potato salad, corn on the cob, baked beans, several salads, lots of homemade pickles and relishes, delicious fresh rolls, and oodles of pies and cakes. I don't know how she managed, but we sure had fun. There were games, visiting, and walks in the afternoon and fireworks at night.

Grandpa always had homemade root beer for everyone. We saved our catsup bottles all year and he had a capper to finish off the bottles. They were stored under the beds to "age" and more than once, one of us were awakened by the Bang! of a bottle exploding!!

There is something magic for a child to eat outdoors, and as an adult, what better way to keep the child in us! Break the rut, ignore those excuses — "It's too much work," "I don't like bugs," etc. — and see the world through the eyes of a child. Fix a simple sandwich and walk through a park; walk barefoot in the sand; splash in the puddles; breathe deeply; enjoy the silence, the breeze in the trees, the sun, the clouds, the moon and the stars. It's a big wonderful world out there. Don't let it get away.

It never ceases to amaze us to discover how many people have never visited some of the beautiful sights in their own cities. We travel across the world and don't realize what is in our own backyards. Why not go exploring? Share the wonder with your family. There are "pick your own" fruit and vegetable farms, libraries, museums, parks, interesting architecture, flower gardens, zoos, forests, mountains, water, unique shops to explore, and fun people to meet. How can we be bored in this land of plenty?

Set up a card table or end table in your home and have an ongoing "show and tell" display of the places you've been, the things you've done, and treasures you've collected — rocks that Johnny found, that bunch of dandelions Sarah picked, or that fun post card from the beach. It's a terrific memory builder and a fun conversation starter when visitors come.

Seeing new things in our neighborhoods or across the country may build hobbies that last a lifetime. Take sketch books along for new landscapes, a tape recorder, or binoculars and a bird book to learn about the many species in the area. Study the plants, the trees and flowers — they are fascinating! If you live in a city, the children may not realize the intensity of the stars at night when you're out in the country. Children, as well as adults, become intrigued with the patterns of stars in the sky as well as cloud shapes in the day. Relax, breathe deeply, and take time to appreciate these gifts of nature.

Everyone needs to eat and why not combine this pleasure with the great outdoors. One of the choicest ways our family has built "togetherness" has been through picnics.

Our first was with our first baby, Stephen, in Olympia, Washington, feeding the peacocks as we enjoyed our sandwiches. Stephen was in awe at the beautiful birds and the sound they made. As our family grew to four little ones, we had a favorite spot in Big Cottonwood Canyon in Utah where we had many wiener roasts while chilling a watermelon in the stream, breakfasts of pancakes and hot chocolate, and even wintertime cookouts. Our "spot" was always waiting for us — peaceful and inviting. It's a place we all still love to go. We have had picnics at historical sites, in the desert, under the pines, at ball games, in a tent (with the crickets), and even in our basement in Missouri when a tornado warning sounded.

Now that the family is grown, Roy and I thoroughly enjoy a leisurely breakfast in the back yard, a hot dog shared in the park, or chicken sandwiches while we "people-watch" on a busy city street.

Isn't it interesting how different things look from another vantage point? When I was about eight years old, I remember my mother packing me a special lunch of fried chicken, and I set out for the largest haystack I could find in the field. After climbing to the top, I surveyed my kingdom and felt like I had the whole world to myself!

We keep a picnic quilt and a basket packed with necessities in the trunk of the car, then we can simply add some take-out food or stop at a market and pick up some cheeses, rolls and fruit for a picnic anytime. Even a picnic in the car, in the pouring rain, singing with the radio can be romantic!

I guess I get extra excited about July because it's the time to enjoy two of my most favorite things — food and the terrific outdoors. Living in this abundant land, we all have the opportunity to make life fun, to play and to change our ruts and routines. Don't "busy" this summer away. Time flies by too quickly.

Roy and I recently went to our grandson Christian's ball game. It was a match between arch rivals, and the play was very intense. Basket after basket the score remained tied and my poor stomach was in knots. We were sitting on the edge of our seats, chewing popcorn frantically, when I heard a voice faintly from the sidelines say, "Time out!" Wouldn't it be great if we all carried a little tape recorder around with us that would periodically call "time out." Maybe then we would hear that bird sing, feel the sun on our backs and the breeze in our face, see the smile of a passerby, or really feel that hug from a little one.

I love the saying by Horace — "Whatever hour God has blessed you with, take it with a grateful hand, nor postpone your joys from year to year, so that in whatever place you have been, you may say that you have lived happily." Don't postpone that picnic! Pack up a sandwich and get out and see the world, even if it's only the front porch!

July Food for Fun
Recipes for Family-pleaser Picnic Fare Every Time!

Who doesn't like taco salad? It's a healthy quick meal that is sure to satisfy. It always calls for chocolate pudding for dessert at our house.

Bev's Taco Salad

Toss together:
- 1 head of lettuce, shredded or torn
- 1 can (15 oz.) kidney beans, drained and rinsed
- 1 c. sliced ripe olives
- 3 chopped green onions (include tops!)
- 1 T. canned green chilies
- 2 chopped tomatoes
- 1 chopped avocado
- 2 c. shredded cheese

Brown together:
- ¾ lb. ground beef
- 2 T. Mexican Taco Season Mix (see September recipes)

Just before serving, combine:
- ground beef mixture
- 2 c. Fritos
- salad mixture

Serve with a dollop of sour cream or yogurt. Makes 6 big servings.

¤ ¤ ¤ ¤ ¤

Potato salad recipes come and go, but this one has been in our family since I was a tiny girl. It can't be beat! Boy, the picnics we had on that Nebraska farm with fresh fried chicken and Mom's Potato Salad!

"The Best" Potato Salad

Boil 12 medium potatoes in their skins until tender (red potatoes are always best for potato salad — white potatoes get mealy).

Hard boil 12 large eggs.

Chop the cooled potatoes and eggs into a bowl along with 1 large onion and 1 green pepper.

Stir in: 1 qt. Miracle Whip salad dressing
      a good dash of salt, pepper, and cayenne! This is a must! Really makes it super.

Taste for seasoning. Feeds 10 nicely.

¤ ¤ ¤ ¤ ¤

Who can have a picnic without Baked Beans? And you'll never make another kind after these!

Opal's Baked Beans

Fry until crisp: ½ lb. bacon

Crumble bacon and combine with: ½ chopped green pepper
1 chopped onion
3 T. Worcestershire Sauce
1/3 c. catsup
½ c. brown sugar
3 cans (14 oz. each) pork and beans

Bake at 250* for 2 hours.

I bake them in my bean pot, removing the lid the last 30 minutes, but this isn't necessary.

¤ ¤ ¤ ¤ ¤

You can't beat this little casserole for a fast summer supper.

Mexican Vegetable Bake

In saucepan, melt: 2 T. butter

Sauté: 1 small finely chopped onion
       1 clove minced garlic

Stir in: 2 c. diced fresh tomatoes
         2 c. corn cut from the cob
         1 small can chopped green chilies

Bring to a boil, then stir in 1 ½ c. coarsely crushed corn chips.

Put mixture in a small casserole dish and top with shredded cheddar cheese.

Bake at 350* for ½ hour.

¤ ¤ ¤ ¤ ¤

A hamburger is a hamburger, but not when you serve one of these! If you're lucky enough to have a gas grill, these burgers are terrific anytime.

Pinata Burgers

Filling: 1 medium finely chopped onion
         2 fresh, finely chopped jalapeno peppers
         1/3 c. shredded Jack or cheddar cheese
         3 T. fresh, chopped cilantro
         2 cloves minced garlic
         1 tsp. cumin
         pinch of oregano

Make 8 thin patties of extra lean ground beef. Divide filling into 4 portions, and put filling on half of patties. Cover with other half of patties and seal edges. Grill until done.

I make a bunch of these ahead and freeze them before grilling.

¤ ¤ ¤ ¤ ¤

Tex-Mex Burgers

Mix: 1 beaten egg
1 can green chilies
minced green onion to taste
¼ c. salsa
salt and pepper
1 clove minced garlic
a pinch of cumin

Then add: ½ c. crushed corn chips
1 lb. lean ground beef

Mix well. Form into patties. Grill until done.

Serve with lettuce, cheese, salsa, and sour cream.

¤ ¤ ¤ ¤ ¤

For the "picnic of the year," this brisket is a must! But it's so easy and delicious you will find yourself serving it over and over. If you tire of beef, do the same thing with a turkey breast. Fantastic!

Barbecued Brisket of Beef and Sauce

Combine: 1 tsp. minced garlic
3 tsp. chili powder
1 tsp. paprika
1 tsp. brown sugar
½ tsp. cumin
½ tsp. sage
½ tsp. basil
½ tsp. oregano
dash of salt, pepper, and Tabasco sauce

Rub well into brisket (about 5 lbs. or so). Place on foil, fat side up. Wrap tightly and place on a cookie sheet.

Bake at 225* for 8 hours.

Slice thinly and serve with Barbecue Sauce.

Barbecue Sauce

Combine in saucepan: 14 oz. tomato sauce
 1/3 c. sugar
 1 ½ T. Worcestershire sauce
 1 ½ tsp. chili powder
 1 medium chopped onion
 ½ tsp. minced garlic
 ½ c. cider vinegar
 ½ tsp. tarragon

Simmer for 30 minutes. Store in jar in refrigerator.

¤ ¤ ¤ ¤ ¤

For an evening on the patio, there is nothing like this for a snack. Have lots of corn chips and vegetable sticks handy!

Chili con Queso

Melt: 3 T. butter

Stir in: 3 T. flour
 ¾ tsp. salt

Then slowly add (while stirring): 1 cup whipping cream.

Cook until thickened.

Then stir in: 1 small can chopped green chilies
 1 can tomatoes, drained (or 2 c. fresh chopped tomatoes)
 8 oz. shredded cheese (I use a mixture of Monterey or Jack/Colby)

Heat through until cheese is melted.

Serve hot as a dip with corn chips.

¤ ¤ ¤ ¤ ¤

For a sure-fire budget-pleaser, keep this recipe handy.

Mom's Lemonade

Stir together until dissolved:
- 2 T. fresh lemon rind
- ¾ c. lemon juice
- 2 ½ c. sugar
- 1 T. citric acid
- 2 c. boiling water

Store in a jar in the refrigerator. Use ¼ cup concentrate to ¾ cup water to make one glass.

July Grocery Bag

Now that summer is here in all its glory and abundance, we are serving meals that are lighter and easier to prepare. The nice parts, too, is that it's still possible to prepare nutritional, delicious meals that keep our calories to a minimum by using all the bargains in fresh fruits and vegetables.

Melons are really coming into their own now. To pick a good **cantaloupe**, look for one with a smooth stem end. The remains of a jagged stem mean it was picked green. It should also have a pleasant, sweet smell at the blossom end. Watch for soft spots. When you get your cantaloupe home, wrap it up in a brown bag or newspaper to store in the refrigerator or everything else will taste like cantaloupe. Serve wedges or halves filled with seafood, chicken or fruit salad. For a breakfast treat, cut halves in a zigzag pattern and garnish with some mint leaves from the garden. Our favorite treat on a hot summer night is a cantaloupe half with a scoop of vanilla ice cream in the center. Roy also loves it for breakfast on the patio along with sausage, scrambled eggs, toast and a glass of ice-cold milk. (Breakfast on the patio can be a real treat for your family. Don't use it only for guests in evenings.)

Honeydews are the creamy, white melons with green flesh. Their skin should be soft and leathery smooth. These are real pretty combined with cantaloupe because of their color. The flesh is very mild in flavor, so it is usually served with a wedge of lime or slice of proscuitto.

Watermelon, of course, is the all-time favorite. Do any of you remember when we went to the roadside stands to buy them and the farmer would "plug" a melon, cutting a triangle plug for you to sample for taste? Those were the days, huh? A watermelon should have a creamy to yellow underside and when you tap it with your knuckles it should sound hollow. If it sounds dull and hard, it's not ripe. You can hear a slight rattling inside, also, when you shake it. Keep watermelon in the refrigerator, and remember all melons keep best when they aren't cut. Always wrap them well after they are cut.

Use a watermelon as a fruit basket by scooping out a section on each side, leaving a center strip of rind to serve as a "handle." Cut the scooped-out sections into small pieces and combine with other types of melon balls, green grapes and berries. What a pretty fruit salad for family or guests!

This is also a good time to use **mushrooms**. They are really high in protein and phosphorus and also contain riboflavin, niacin, calcium and even some iron and copper, but you must not cook them to death! They are great raw and only contain 20 calories a cup. There are 6 cups (average) to a pound of mushrooms, so that's a lot of good eating. They will keep in the refrigerator for a week. Just wrap them in a damp paper towel and put them in a bag. Clean them as you use them. Just wash them quickly and pat them dry. They become waterlogged if you let them stand in water. They freeze very well, so if you find a bargain, stock up. Just wash, pat dry, slice, put in bags and freeze. Use them without defrosting. They'll taste just like fresh. They also dry beautifully.

If you want white mushrooms to keep their color, sprinkle a little lemon juice over them as they cook. If your recipe only calls for the caps, clean and freeze the stems to use in soups, stews or casseroles.

Fish — fresh, frozen or canned — is a good buy this month. It's quick and easy to prepare, low in calories and goes well with the vegetables we have so plentifully now. This is true of chicken also. Stock up on both. They're so much better for everyone than red meats.

Remember to use lots of **cheeses** as a meat substitute, also. The mild cheeses are less expensive than the sharp ones which have to be stored longer to develop their flavor. Watch the price per pound on the packages. You'll be surprised. If you want the best protein buy for your money, watch the label to make sure the last word is cheese and not cheese food, cheese spread, etc.

The gardens and fruit stands are an absolute picture this month. Stock up on these other beauties!

Zucchini — Try them sliced, dipped in a beaten egg, then crumbs, and fried crisp. Or stuff zucchini with a ground beef mixture and bake with cheese on top.

Cucumbers are at their peak now. Enjoy them in many ways. To make a pretty addition to a salad, take a fork and run the tines down the cucumber from top to bottom all the way around, creating a striped look. Then slice the cucumber sideways, and you'll have a pretty scalloped edge.

— Don't forget to try sautéing them in butter. Just scrub well, slice thin and sauté in a frying pan with a dab of butter until tender. They are absolutely delicious. This is a great time of year to serve these because you don't need to peel them now when the skins aren't waxed as they usually are in the grocery store in the winter.

— Large cucumbers can also be slit down the middle, the seeds removed with a spoon, sprinkled with salt and then left to stand for 45 minutes to an hour. Then rinse well, drain, and dice and cook with zucchini, tomatoes or onions as a vegetable dish. Or stuff the long halves with a meat loaf mixture and bake.

Cucumbers are very low in calories and the term "cool as a cucumber" is really true. Cucumbers in the garden are 15-20% cooler than the air that surrounds them. This is why a slice of cucumber laid over each eye while resting will remove that puffy look or bags under the eyes. Try it while you take a quick nap on a hot summer day!

July Why Didn't I Think of That?

A simple dip and fresh vegetable sticks are a great snack for children (and adults). They are nutritious and fun to eat.

¤ ¤ ¤ ¤ ¤

In the summer, never park your car in the sunshine if you can avoid it. The heat will cause your gas to evaporate, and the air conditioner will have to work lots harder to cool the car when you start driving.

¤ ¤ ¤ ¤ ¤

To really save energy in the summer, open your doors and windows to let in the cool, shady morning air; then close the blinds and shades to the sun later in the day. This works in the reverse in the winter. Draw your blinds and shades to block out the cold and dark, and open them to let in the sunshine. You'll be surprised what a difference this makes!

¤ ¤ ¤ ¤ ¤

Rubbing the slippery slide with waxed paper sure keeps it slick and slippery! The kids love this job!

¤ ¤ ¤ ¤ ¤

Before making a long distance call, I make a list of things I need to talk about and set my timer. Our phone bill is never small, but this sure helps.

¤ ¤ ¤ ¤ ¤

When I iron my tablecloths, I hang them over a pants hanger and hang them in my guest closet. They are easy to see, handy to use and never wrinkled. (My girls think that's so clever!)

¤ ¤ ¤ ¤ ¤

Setting up your ironing board and covering it with an oil-cloth cover provides added serving room for patio parties and picnics. It also makes a great bedside table for an invalid since it's adjustable. Very roomy and useful!

¤ ¤ ¤ ¤ ¤

Sew a pocket in each corner of your picnic tablecloth. Then when you set your table you can put a rock in each pocket and never have a cloth blowing all over.

¤ ¤ ¤ ¤ ¤

When planning a get-together, the first thing I do is pick a theme and then a type of food (Italian, B.B.Q., German, etc.), then the rest of the planning seems easier. Things to keep in mind are good color contrast, and ease of serving and eating. If you're having a buffet-type meal, arrange things in sequence so it's convenient for guests to fill their plates. Remember to "keep it simple," then everyone will enjoy it more. (Fruit and cheese make a nice dessert.)

¤ ¤ ¤ ¤ ¤

When it comes to inviting friends and family over, the ideas are limitless: from a fancy Italian meal complete with antipasto to Zabilone; to a southern "Pig-Pickin" barbeque with cole slaw and cobbler; to a Mexican "build your own" quesadilla; to a Halloween "Frank & Stein" (hot dog and root beer) party. Just relax and have fun!

¤ ¤ ¤ ¤ ¤

Why not have —

An old-fashioned ice cream party — make your own and have everyone bring toppings.

A pioneer taffy pull — assign each guest ingredients.

A sing along — everyone brings a favorite tape or CD.

A potluck dinner — be specific: a childhood favorite, family nationality dish, a dish beginning with the first letter of last name, and so on.

A game night — set up tables of old favorites: Chinese checkers, rook, dominoes, and maybe even a jigsaw puzzle. Every half-hour or so, guests switch tables.

A "You're the Star" night — have each guest bring his twenty-five favorite slides. Serve popcorn and cold drinks.

¤ ¤ ¤ ¤ ¤

A good mixer at any party is to have a "guest" scavenger hunt. As the guests arrive, give each person a list with questions like: Who is a skilled artist? Who once fell into the Pacific Ocean? Who was the class valedictorian? Then have them mingle and get acquainted. Whoever has the most questions answered correctly by a certain time wins a prize.

¤ ¤ ¤ ¤ ¤

Here are some more family and group games we have had fun playing over the years.

This is My Nose — Everyone sits in a circle, and the one who is "it" stands in the middle. He walks up to a player and, pointing to his ear, may say, "This is my eye," and quickly counts to ten. The player must then point to his eye and say, "This is my ear," before "it" counts to ten. If he goofs, he becomes "it." As this gets going fast, it can really be funny.

Chewing the Raisin — Tie a raisin exactly in the middle of a piece of string or thread 3 feet long. Then two people stand facing one another, and each puts one end of the string in his mouth. At the word "Go" they each chew as fast as they can, trying to get to the raisin first. Just warn them not to swallow the string!

Blow, Wind, Blow — Divide players into two groups. Have the teams sit on the floor facing each other with a bed sheet between them. Taking the sheet in their hands, they each hold it stretched tightly under their chins. Someone drops a feather into the middle of the sheet. At the signal, the object is for everyone to blow as hard as they can and get the feather to blow off the opposite side of the sheet.

My Cup Runneth Over — Divide group into partners; players line up at one end of the room with their partners across from them at the opposite end. Each couple is given a full glass of water and a spoon. The partner must run across the room and feed his partner the water with the spoon without spilling any. The first couple with an empty glass wins.

Upset the fruit basket — Everyone is seated on chairs in a circle. The player who is "it" stands in the middle. After whispering a different name of a fruit in each person's ear, he calls out two fruits. Those players must exchange chairs quickly without the person who is "it" getting a seat. The person who doesn't get a seat is "it." Occasionally, the person who is "it" may call out "upset the fruit basket," and everyone must change seats without "it" getting a chair.

Stack-Up — Each person is given twenty-five toothpicks; then, seated around a tall pop bottle, each person takes a turn laying one toothpick across the opening of the bottle. Continue in this manner until one person upsets the stack of toothpicks. He then must take all the toothpicks that fell. The object is to get rid of your toothpicks first.

Who Am I? – Sometimes in this busy world, our lives get so involved that we really don't know who our family members are and what they are all about. Set out a stack of old magazines, newspapers, and catalogs. Then give each person a sheet of construction paper, scissors, and glue. On the sheet of paper, list ten questions:

1. My favorite food
2. A type of place I like to go
3. My favorite color
4. A picture of my hobby
5. A job I would enjoy
6. Something I don't care for or am afraid of
7. Something I would like to own
8. Somebody I think is "special"
9. An animal I like
10. My favorite sound

Have family members paste corresponding pictures by the questions, and then try to discover whose page is whose. Then have each person explain his pictures and his reasons for choosing these. This is such a fun way to get reacquainted as a family and is an activity that can be adjusted to young or old members.

¤ ¤ ¤ ¤ ¤

Be sure to keep a file card on each get-together so you remember which guests, which games, and which food. You'll be having so much good, old-fashioned fun enjoying your friends, you won't want to duplicate. It's amazing how enjoyable a simple evening can be when we turn off the TV.

¤ ¤ ¤ ¤ ¤

I also keep a list of my menu pinned up in front of me while I'm preparing the meal for my guests. This serves as a constant reminder of what to do next and also helps me to remember a dish in the refrigerator that I made ahead and may forget to set out. (Guess I'm getting old; I need those lists!)

¤ ¤ ¤ ¤ ¤

If you're making an "ice bowl," add a little milk to the water when freezing, and it will have a pretty "frosty" look.

¤ ¤ ¤ ¤ ¤

Socializing should be just that — having a pleasant, sociable time with friends and family. Elaborate entertaining is real work, so concentrate on socializing and enjoy. Don't worry about the faded rug, worn upholstery, dishes that don't match, or spoon handles dented by the disposal. We're all human beings with problems, but the burdens will be lighter and the smiles broader if we share a little love with one another.

¤ ¤ ¤ ¤ ¤

A fun plan for a bridal shower is to have each guest bring her favorite recipe typed up and a package or can of the required spice. This gives the new bride a nice selection of spices to start out with. The hostess could supply a pretty recipe box.

¤ ¤ ¤ ¤ ¤

At a shower for Shelli, our daughter-in-law, the hostess assigned each of the guests a time of day on the invitation, and we each brought a gift to coincide with that time. The gifts were so clever. She got a toaster for one of the morning hours, a popcorn popper for the eight o'clock evening time, and for the ten P.M. hour, she received a canister full of beans and a saucepan so she could put her beans on to soak at night! Everyone got a chuckle out of that.

¤ ¤ ¤ ¤ ¤

Speaking of parties, we ran across the cutest idea and have started it for our grandchildren. We make a birthday banner each year on their birthdays from a 12-inch square of cream-colored canvas or duck-type fabric, hemmed, with a small dowel inserted across the top. This will resemble a child's building block. Then a large number (about 6 inches) is cut from bright-colored fabric and appliqued on, signifying the birthday — 1, 2, or 3, and so on. Each of the birthday guests signs the banner with a permanent magic marker, and a picture is taped along with the birthday child's height and weight on the back. These can be hung in his bedroom each year until he has a collection of every birthday past. Hung in a grouping, they form a stack of building blocks; later, they could even form a border around the room. What a treasure these will be as the child grows up.

¤ ¤ ¤ ¤ ¤

If you're serving ribs or something "messy" from the grill — dampen a small guest towel for each person and wrap them in foil. On a hot day keep them stacked on a bowl of ice. On chilly days, stack them on the grill so they're steamy and warm.

¤ ¤ ¤ ¤ ¤

"We do not remember days. We remember moments."   Cesare Pavere

¤ ¤ ¤ ¤ ¤

To hard-boil eggs for potato salad, remove from the refrigerator about ½ hour before cooking. When you are ready to cook them, cover the eggs with lukewarm water, put them on the stove, bring to a boil, turn down the heat a little so they just simmer, and simmer them for 10 minutes from the time the water started to boil. Immediately pour off the hot water, set the pan of eggs in the sink and let the cold water run on them. While the water is running, I "smoosh" the eggs against the sides of the pan so the shells crack all over. (Let the cold water continue to run until the eggs cool down.) Then while they are still sitting in the cold water, I peel them and the shells come right off in the water.

¤ ¤ ¤ ¤ ¤

When cantaloupe is plentiful, try dicing or cubing it, covering with orange juice or ginger ale, and freezing in containers. Makes a great appetizer or winter breakfast treat. Just remember to serve it while still "icy."

¤ ¤ ¤ ¤ ¤

I like to use a "nail" brush to scrub my vegetables instead of a regular vegetable brush. It's so handy to hold.

¤ ¤ ¤ ¤ ¤

To frost cupcakes in a hurry, just make your frosting a little softer and swirl the top of the cupcake in the frosting.

¤ ¤ ¤ ¤ ¤

Remember to keep all condiments (catsup, mustard, etc.) in the refrigerator.

¤ ¤ ¤ ¤ ¤

Watch for glasses, mugs, and goblets at yard sales. They make great containers for those homemade jams and jellies when you want to give a gift.

¤ ¤ ¤ ¤ ¤

A cupcake pan is a slick container for those toppings for hamburgers at your next picnic.

¤ ¤ ¤ ¤ ¤

Save your foil and plastic wrap boxes. They are great containers for cookies and fruit to take on a picnic. Stack cookies on their sides. This is also super for freezing. Just slip the box of cookies into a plastic bag and pop in the freezer.

¤ ¤ ¤ ¤ ¤

Roy's favorite treat to go with meat on the grill — thread boiled "new" potatoes and small onions on skewers, brush with Italian dressing, and grill, turning often, for about 10 minutes. Sprinkle with coarse salt!

August

August

Golly, summer is winding down. It's time to take inventory and be sure we covered all the things we hoped to do — most importantly, spending time with our families. I love the words to the song, "Sunrise, Sunset" from Fiddler on the Roof. These times certainly have a way of slipping by us, and time is something we never get back. Savor this month and the activities spent with those you love.

Food for Thought

In August a big share of the population is on the move. This seems to be the month for family vacations before the fall school sessions start or for families moving their residence to get settled for the school term. Since we have experienced eleven major moves in our marriage, let me share with you some tips we have learned.

It all starts with attitude. There will be so many new things to see and learn about, and there's always an exciting challenge to meet new people and learn new customs and ways of life. Every new place has something unique to offer to build a new "memory" every day. Books at the library and the internet will have pictures of the place you are going to — study them. Acquaint yourself and your family with landmarks, scenes, buildings, and the terrain and climate. Be proud of where you are going and never compare. No two places are alike and weren't meant to be. Nothing turns people off faster than to hear how great it was where you came from. One of the most valuable things you can take with you is your old telephone book. It will prove invaluable many times. We often subscribed to the "new" city's newspaper before moving. That is always fun as well as helpful.

Whether we're moving or just traveling on vacation, we'll all be in the car a lot this month. There are two things we carry in our car all the time — a dictionary and a cooler. You'd be surprised how much fun a dictionary can provide. There are so many word games you can play, and you all may learn a new word to add to your vocabulary each day. The cooler is always in our trunk because if we're traveling (even if it's a short trip) it is so much more economical (and healthy) to take along fresh fruits, vegetables, maybe some cheese cubes and juices and milk to drink. Then with a box of crackers in the car, you're never tempted to spend so much on fast-foods, and you feel better, too. I leave the cooler in the trunk all the time. It sure comes in handy when I go to the grocery store. I have them put my meat and frozen things in a separate sack. Then I can put it in the cooler on the way home. It's also great for those spur-of-the-moment stops at a roadside farmer's market.

As you travel with toddlers have them wear identification tags in case of accidents or little ones wandering off. One of the best thoughts we ever had traveling with our children cross-country was to put an alarm clock in the glove compartment. It seemed there was always a "discussion" about who could sit in the front. I set the alarm and when it rang, we traded seats. Worked perfectly!

Again, it's the attitude. Closeness and togetherness can be a reality if we work on it.

Since our family is grown now, they love to tell their children about "the good old days" when all six of us (most nearly 6 feet tall) climbed into our little Toyota and took a trip to Niagara Falls and Canada. Believe it or not we didn't have a cross word on that whole trip. Gas station attendants just stood and shook their heads as we all piled out like clowns at the circus.

Roy and I enjoy memory vacations now, seeing places that mean so much to us. We also have fun doing genealogy trips. It's amazing the stories you learn visiting older family members. Even trips to cemeteries can bring about interesting surprises. You'll find most people will be so helpful and accommodating. Put that smile on and you'll find friendly helpers everywhere you go. Our purses may not be full, but we hop in the car with our plastic goblets and take off on an adventure, sipping our cool drink in style and singing happy songs.

Now if your budget is tight, remember it's not always necessary to go thousands of miles from home to have a vacation. Children are just happy with your time and attention for a while. This can be an invaluable teaching time. I remember teaching the little ones how to dust the furniture while they learned to say "table," "leg," "under," "on top," "up high," etc. All children love to help and learn if you work with them and show them what is expected and then praise them for a job well done. A summer's worth of your time while they're little will provide a lifetime of pleasant helpers. Busy people (big and little) are happy people. While you're working in the yard or garden, get out a bucket of water and a paintbrush and your little ones can work for hours "painting" the house. Don't forget, also, the joy of making real mud pies. A little good clean dirt never hurt any one either!

Even though your kids think they are too old for a nap, these hot summer days we all need a pause in our routine. We used to gather on one of the beds after lunch and tell stories, share dreams, make plans, or sing songs; and it gave us all that needed rest. Try it, no matter what your age. It really makes the rest of the day happier.

Too often we work hard to give our families everything to live with but nothing to live for!

This month just seems to be made for children. A long time ago I had an experience that has stuck with me over the years, and I promised myself I would help some child to learn something special each summer for the rest of my life. I was standing at my kitchen sink, on Happiness Way in Cincinnati, Ohio, washing my dishes. I heard a loud squawking as I looked out to see a big mother black crow perched on our rail fence that went around the back yard. On the ground was a little bird looking up as the mother coaxed her to come up to the fence rail. This became a daily experience, and I could hardly wait for the next chapter each day. Eventually the little bird made it, only to have its mama jump to a tree close by and start calling again. I watched, encouraged, and prayed for that little bird every day until finally it was flying around confidently surveying our neighborhood. Each spring we had two or three crows that perched comfortably on our fence through the summer, and I just knew they were my friends coming back to their home where lessons were learned. There are so many ways we can teach our children. Love, patience and caring is the key.

All children are individuals, and we must treat them as such. Love them for their differences. Don't try to fit them in a mold. If we respect them for who and what they are, they will respect others. As they observe how we help one another, it will come natural to them. Criticism never gets anywhere. Build their self-esteem; and if they have problems or handicaps, help them learn to compensate (we all have them, don't we?) Help the child find his strengths and build his skills. He may not be a fast runner, but he can build the best birdhouse! By setting firm guidelines and then helping along the way, everyone can succeed. Just remember, everyone needs some rules and guidelines to show the way. These things give children a sense of security. How often I have heard our children say, "We just knew the rules and knew Mom or Dad would expect us to obey, so we did our best." Heavenly Father blessed us as a family, and we needed to do our part.

Teaching isn't always the easiest thing, but too often we say "grow up" and forget that is what they are trying to do but haven't gotten there yet. These children are not "finished" yet — like the building down the street, but we don't complain about it because the raw boards and cement still show. Be patient and remember that God loves every unfinished thing — even you and I.

Teach them honesty by being honest yourself. At our grandson, Cameron's, ball game on Saturday, the scoreboard keeper inadvertently gave our team one extra point. Cameron's dad went right over and told him to correct it. Since it was a "tight" game and we were all tense about the outcome, some of the kid's started asking, "Why did you do that?" He simply said, "Because it was the right thing to do," and sat down to watch the game again!

Give them a sense of direction. Set goals — big and little ones. As they work and achieve these things, they will try harder. Don't give up, and don't let them give up but encourage along the way.

Nurture your family — let them know it feels good to be in a family with them. Each member is a special person in his own right. Look at and listen to one another, consider their feelings, show affection. Let the quiet in your home be a "peaceful" quiet and the noise be a joyful noise. And most of all, remember we all change. Change is a vital part of life.

Our son, Stephen, has recently experienced change in his life and has married a new sweet wife with four children. Stephen also has four children, and it has been so interesting to watch the adjustments as they respect and learn from one another. Each family member contributes a unique characteristic that the others learn from. They have learned tolerance for girl or boy habits, shared camaraderie in sports, loved each other's pets, had new adventures in different foods, and most of all shared tears, laughter and zest for a new life.

Do we give our children responsibilities so they can learn to master challenges to prepare for adulthood?

Do we encourage their dreams and show them confidence so they can realize these dreams?

Teaching children is an awesome responsibility, but oh, so rewarding! Then comes the day that you realize they are gaining on you, and suddenly it's hard to understand the language of science or technology they are trying to explain. I think one of the things we parents often neglect to acknowledge is that, even though our responsibility is to teach our children, we are constantly learning from them!

I have learned from my children that life is too serious to be taken seriously. How could I pass up those chocolate covered peanuts to share with Heidi (even if my "diet" says no). I've learned to be brave — how could I show fear as Steve shared his bugs and nature interests with me. I've learned to broaden my intellectual interests as Mark has expounded on subjects that he was studying, and I've learned patience as I've watched Kristen experience trials and never complain. I've learned every day from them how to laugh, to cry, to share, to care, and to love. If only I can continue to live up to their great examples.

Learn to enjoy the books they share. Broaden your horizons. Appreciate their music. There is so much to gain by seeing things through "new" eyes. Support each other. Be there. Comfort in times of stress. Try a little exercise I once read about — "Breathe deeply through the holes in your feet!" Even the little ones can reduce stress this way!

Have fun with each other. Don't wait for a yearly vacation. Right now I'm having a great time just being a Grandma, which is why I love this poem.

Gran'ma

There is something 'bout a Gran'ma a boy can't help but like.
She's always glad to see you, and calls you "little tyke."
She says, "That boy's not naughty; he's only full of fun.
A child's a child — I know it, 'cause I myself was one."

That's how a Gran'ma argues, and when your stomach aches,
She doesn't call you piggy, and count what's left of cake.
No, that's a time, she tells you, a boy's in need of love,
And little candy pellets that have a taste of clove.

And if a playmate whistles and you get well and play,
She doesn't say, "I told you that would be the way!"
No, she's beside the window to smile and wave her hands,
And call, "Have lots of fun, dear." That's 'cause she understands.

She says the toughest children have tender kinds of skin,
And thinks a downright whipping is something of a sin.
A boy without a Gran'ma just misses half his life.
I'd rather have — I really would — a Gran'ma than a wife!

– Anonymous

August Food for Fun
Kids, Summer-time Traveling, & Good Recipes.
It can't get any better!

For a quick lunch or Sunday supper, this chowder is always a hit. I like to serve it with a crisp tossed salad and some freshly baked corn muffins — yum!

Country Style Corn Chowder

Dice and fry until brown and crisp: 4 slices of bacon.

Remove bacon from pan and sauté in drippings: 1 onion
2 large diced potatoes

Then add: Corn cut from 3 large ears
2 c. chicken broth
½ tsp. salt
dash of coarse pepper

Simmer until tender.

Then stir in: ½ c. whipping cream
crisp bacon

Heat through and serve.

¤ ¤ ¤ ¤ ¤

My fridge is never without a pasta salad of some sort through the summer, and this is one of our favorites.

Zucchini Pasta Salad

Sauté: 3 T. oil
      3 diced zucchini

Add: ¼ c. chopped green pepper
      1 c. green beans

Cover and steam until vegetables are tender.

Add: 1 tsp. salt
      2 c. cooked spaghetti

Heat through. Remove from burner and let cool to room temperature.

Stir in: 1/3 c. Parmesan cheese
      3 diced tomatoes
      ¼ c. chopped watercress or parsley (we like watercress best)
      salt and coarsely ground pepper to taste

Serve at room temperature with fresh, crunchy Italian bread.

¤ ¤ ¤ ¤ ¤

If you like spicy foods, be sure to try this! It's a winner on our table every time. (It's also good with other varieties of fish.)

Cajun Hot Halibut

In a glass 9 inch square baking dish, melt ½ stick butter or margarine in a 400* oven.

Then stir in: ½ T. coarse black pepper
a dash of dill weed
1 T. Worcestershire sauce
¼ tsp. Tabasco
1 clove minced garlic
¼ tsp. salt
½ lemon's juice and grated rind

Place 2 halibut steaks in butter sauce and turn so both sides are coated. Return to oven and bake until tender — about 20 to 25 minutes depending on fish size.

¤ ¤ ¤ ¤ ¤

If you know a bakery that makes a good crusty, Italian Hoagie bun, buy a supply for your freezer and mix up a batch of these Italian sandwiches. Your family will love you.

Italian Sloppy Joes

Crumble and brown 1 lb. of Italian sausage.

Add: 1 large sliced or diced green pepper
1 medium chopped onion

Sauté a few minutes then add: 1 c. diced tomatoes (fresh or canned)
a pinch of basil and oregano
coarse black pepper

Simmer 15-20 minutes.

Spoon into crusty hoagie buns, sprinkle the top generously with shredded Mozzarella cheese and pop into the oven a few minutes until cheese melts.

Sometimes I add a little shredded cheese in the bottom of the Hoagie bun before adding the meat.

¤ ¤ ¤ ¤ ¤

While the tomatoes and zucchini are still plentiful and tasty, you'll love this casserole.

Three Cheese Pasta and Zucchini

Brown: 1 lb. Italian sausage

Drain grease from pan and add: 1 small chopped onion
2 diced garlic cloves

Sauté until onion is transparent.

Stir in: 3 c. grated zucchini

Cook 8 oz. of Rotini pasta.

Beat 3 eggs in blender.

Stir in to eggs: 1 lb. cottage cheese
½ c. "Italian Blend" dry, grated cheese

Combine meat mixture, cooked pasta and cheese mixture.

Season with salt, pepper, and a sprinkling of oregano and basil (fresh if you have it).

Pour mixture into a buttered 9 x 13 inch pan, top with tomato slices and a generous layer of shredded Mozzarella cheese.

Bake at 350* about 40 minutes.

¤ ¤ ¤ ¤ ¤

Since Ohio is the Buckeye State and our home for so many years, these candies have become a tradition to serve at our house.

Ohio Buckeyes

Mix well:
- ¾ lb. powdered sugar
- ¾ c. peanut butter
- 1 stick softened margarine
- ¾ tsp. vanilla

Form into small balls about the size of a walnut.

Holding with a toothpick, dip ¾ of the ball into melted dipping (chunk) chocolate, leaving the top portion of the peanut butter mixture showing through to resemble a buckeye. Let cool and harden.

August Grocery Bag

This is the month to enjoy our land of plenty. Gardens are overflowing and roadside stands are bulging with beautiful, fresh produce. Plan your menus around this abundance, and your grocery bill will go down, your family's health will perk up, and it will be much less work for you also.

Salads are easy to prepare, which sure beats spending long hours over a hot stove — and the raw vegetables you toss into your salad contain lots more vitamins, minerals and enzymes than the same cooked ones. Most of the grocery stores use "specials" on fresh produce to get you inside their doors, so by taking advantage of the sale-priced items, in addition to stopping by your local farmers markets, you can create a magnificent salad very reasonably.

Since there are so many good salad vegetables in season now, you can choose the combination your family likes best. Once in a while experiment with some new ones, too. Of course, **tomatoes** are a standby and they should be plump, firm and uniform in color with no cracks or bruises. When you buy them at the grocery store, make sure they have been vine-ripened by smelling for that fresh tomato smell. Artificially ripened tomatoes are usually odorless and very inferior in flavor. In fact, they usually have no flavor at all. Your nose is a valuable guide in the produce section. The best clue to good taste is the rich flavorful smell they will have. Fresh tomatoes are loaded with vitamin C, so enjoy them often.

To peel a tomato easily, set it on a slotted spoon and lower it into a pan of boiling water. Leave it in the water about one minute. Then lift it out, and the skin will slip right off. Tomatoes are always at their flavor peak if they are served at room temperature. So if you have them stored in the refrigerator, remove them a while before mealtime. If a tomato is not quite ripe, it ripens best, like any fruit, in a brown paper bag at room temperature.

If you slice a tomato up and down instead of crosswise, you will have much less juice escaping and eliminate messy salads. Always add the tomatoes last when making a tossed salad.

With tomatoes in such abundance, serve them stuffed, either hot or cold. Before you stuff them, cut a thin slice from the top, scoop out the seeds, salt and pepper the insides and turn them upside down on a paper towel and refrigerate until ready to stuff. To serve them cold, I mix tuna, chicken, turkey, or shrimp with celery, nuts, a little onion and some diced or shredded zucchini (this is a great way to stretch your meat). Toss all these things together lightly with mayonnaise, and stuff each tomato shell and serve on a bed of lettuce. To serve tomatoes hot, I make my meat loaf mixture, sometimes adding some leftover cooked rice, stuff the tomato cups and set in a muffin pan and bake at 350* for about 45 minutes.

Fry up some red and green tomato slices that have been dipped in egg and cracker crumbs.

Combine tomato slices, cucumber slices, onion slices and green pepper slices in a glass dish and marinate in Italian dressing for an hour. Serve slices on a lettuce leaf.

Add chopped fresh tomatoes to your omelet or scrambled eggs.

One of Roy's favorite ways to have tomatoes is to slice 3-4 in an 8x8 inch glass baking dish, sprinkle with minced onion, a little garlic, basil, oregano and parsley and then lightly sprinkle just a little olive oil over the top. Cover with plastic wrap and refrigerate an hour or so, then set out to come to room temperature about half an hour before serving.

Now we can really enjoy that **corn on the cob** to our heart's content. Look for fresh green outer leaves and make sure the end is not shriveled and dried. The kernels should be just right, light yellow color and bursting with sweet liquid, never dented. Never overcook corn. As my mom always said, "You only need to cook the kernels, not the whole cob!" I place the ears into boiling water, cover and bring it back to a boil, and then immediately set the pan off the heat and let the corn stand in the water for 8-10 minutes. When cooking corn on the cob, add a teaspoon of honey to the boiling water, but never add salt until the corn is done. It will toughen it and leach out vitamins.

If you really want a taste treat and have your oven going anyway, carefully pull back the husks, remove the silk and replace the husks, fastening or twisting to secure the top (I use the little twistees). Sometimes I even slip some butter and salt and pepper in on the corn when I remove the silk. Lay the ears on a cookie sheet and bake at 325* about 45 minutes. Wow! Is it good.

Now is also the time to eat **bell peppers** They are just loaded with vitamin C and are very low in calories. The vitamin content and sweetness also increases as the pepper ripens, so don't avoid the red ones. Choose peppers that are firm, bright, and relatively heavy for their size, and avoid the ones that are flimsy or cracked. I like to dice up a bunch and keep them in a bag in the freezer for cooking and salads.

Two of our favorite fruits this month are **plums** and peaches. There are so many varieties of plums. Give them all a try; just avoid the soft or bruised ones. Our favorite is the Italian prune plum. It is so sweet! You get quite a few plums per pound, so they are a reasonable snack. Wash them just before eating. Store in the refrigerator in a covered dish (not a plastic bag). If they are not ripe when you bring them home, put them in a brown paper sack on the counter until they ripen, then refrigerate.

There is nothing like a fresh plum cobbler covered with "half-and-half" on a summer evening.

Georgia and California produce **peaches** a little earlier than Utah and the Midwest, which come in mid-August. There is nothing as sweet as a peach just picked off the tree, but if you are not that fortunate, be sure you choose the best at the market. Peaches that are picked when they are too hard and green will never ripen satisfactorily. Look for a golden color with a little red blush. The best test in buying peaches, as with tomatoes, is the "smell test." Peaches are very high in vitamins A and C and are low in sodium and calories. Store them in the refrigerator, but for maximum flavor, allow them to come to room temperature before eating.

Try adding some peaches to cole slaw for a different taste treat, and of course, there's nothing like fresh peach pie or peach fritters!

Right now while all the produce is so reasonable, buy it by the lug or crate. It never tastes as delicious as when it's fresh, no matter how you preserve it, so eat to your heart's content. We often have a meal of corn on the cob, sliced tomatoes, fresh baked bread and cheese — fresh fruit for dessert and you're living like a king!

August Why Didn't I Think of That?

Shredded carrots mixed with peanut butter makes a tasty sandwich spread.

¤ ¤ ¤ ¤ ¤

Add a little honey to peanut butter to make it spreading consistency and spread it over your chocolate cake before frosting it with chocolate frosting. Then sprinkle with some chopped peanuts. Delicious!

¤ ¤ ¤ ¤ ¤

Save your sweet pickle "juice." Drain a can of red beets and add them to the sweet pickle juice. Let the container set for a few days in the refrigerator and presto! Pickled beets!

¤ ¤ ¤ ¤ ¤

Save and dry your green pepper seeds. They make great seasoning.

¤ ¤ ¤ ¤ ¤

I like to use red, green, and yellow peppers cut in half vertically as nice little containers for dips and sauces.

¤ ¤ ¤ ¤ ¤

Just run a damp paper towel down the ears of corn to remove all those pesky "silks".

¤ ¤ ¤ ¤ ¤

When cutting corn off the cob, stand the "ear" in the tube of an angel food cake pan. Then as you cut the kernels off, they will fall into the pan.

¤ ¤ ¤ ¤ ¤

"Any child can tell you that the sole purpose of a middle name is so he can tell when he's really in trouble." Dennis Fakes

¤ ¤ ¤ ¤ ¤

Pack light and keep traveling.

¤ ¤ ¤ ¤ ¤

"If you want your children to improve, let them overhear the nice things you say about them to others." Haim Ginott

¤ ¤ ¤ ¤ ¤

Never tell a child he is hopeless. You are contradicting God.

¤ ¤ ¤ ¤ ¤

Family goals are great, just don't forget to enjoy the detours.

¤ ¤ ¤ ¤ ¤

You can't give a child a drink from an empty glass.

¤ ¤ ¤ ¤ ¤

Some good food ideas for little children —

　　Make mealtime a pleasant time! Don't make a big deal out of a child's "no." It will change.

　　Realize that children don't eat as fast as adults. Allow for this.

　　Keep the table and surroundings simple so that a spill or accident is not a catastrophe.

　　A few good finger foods for little ones 8-12 months are — dry toast pieces, crackers, small pieces of ripe banana (green tinted bananas are hard to digest). Foods to avoid until about 18-24 months because they could cause choking are — corn, bacon, nuts, popcorn, baked beans, uncooked onions, raw carrots and cabbage and lettuce.

　　A nourishing and good snack is a yogurt Popsicle — mix one carton of plain yogurt (any size) with one 6-oz. can frozen orange juice concentrate and put in molds and freeze.

　　Sometimes the best way to get children to try a new food is to treat it as an "adult food" and serve it only to the adults. When they want some, gradually feed them a little from your plate, then move some to theirs. A little psychology goes a long way!

¤ ¤ ¤ ¤ ¤

When we open a new package of bacon, we always roll it up (tube fashion) first. It sure makes the slices easier to separate.

¤ ¤ ¤ ¤ ¤

The next time you make a coconut cream pie, toast the coconut first in a 350* oven. We think it makes a much tastier pie.

¤ ¤ ¤ ¤ ¤

Some fun sandwich combinations that we enjoy are:

Monterey Jack cheese, sliced tomato, lettuce and mayonnaise topped with guacamole on a toasted English muffin.

Toasted French bread spread lightly with mustard, sliced tomatoes and a hot cheese sauce poured over all. Top this with minced green onions.

A club sandwich is one of Roy's first choices: Bacon, lettuce, tomato, mayonnaise, sliced turkey and cheese. We like to use two slices of whole wheat and the middle one white.

My all-time favorite is pumpernickel bread with Swiss cheese, mayonnaise, fresh spinach leaves, tomato and onion slices.

Nothing is more refreshing on a hot afternoon than fresh raisin bread with softened cream cheese, honey and walnuts. Serve this with some crisp apple slices. Ummm! Is it good.

Am I making you hungry? A variety of breads really makes the difference in making sandwiches. Make lunch time a pleasant, relaxing time and enjoy!

September

September

Roy and I enjoyed our morning walk today and were reflecting on what a nice summer it had been. The weather has been wonderful. Warm days and cool nights. Low humidity. Lots of sun, beautiful mountains, and especially, family close by. Grandchildren to play with, children to share with, lots of loving neighbors in our condos, and we even enjoyed a few picnics and short, relaxing trips. Life couldn't be better! Suddenly as we walked past the school grounds, the bell rang and we were surrounded with vibrant, happy children, eagerly running into classes to start a new and exciting year. As our walk progressed, we observed a few drying leaves on the trees, bright squash and pumpkins on the garden vines, and just as we turned into our backyard, a squirrel scampered across the fence and hurried up a tree with a mouth full of nuts!

That's all it took to get my "nesting" juices flowing. This time each year, I can hardly wait to take inventory from my pantry, make plans for the upcoming holidays, do some fall housecleaning, and just like the squirrel, get "settled in" for the winter.

Food for Thought

There is no better time than September when the children are back in school and the family has settled into a routine, to turn over a new leaf in our shopping and meal planning. Of all the speaking engagements I do, one of the most popular is my "Trip Through the Grocery Store." I have promised many of my friends I would include it here. Would you like to come along? I'd love to have you!

Before we leave for the store, will you do me a favor? Put two wide-mouth quart jars and two zip-lock bags in the freezer compartment of your refrigerator. These four items will save you lots of money and add some interest and fun to your menus. The one jar will be used to collect every little bit of vegetable you have left over from each meal (two peas, four carrot slices, one bean, etc.) Never waste a thing. Just pop it in the jar and back into the freezer. You'll be surprised how fast the jar fills up. Then you're ready to add the vegetables to a soup, stew, casserole or toss with some Italian dressing and add to a salad.

Your other jar will hold bits of fruits (that slice of peach, half a banana, a few grapes, etc.) When the jar is full, thicken the fruit with a little cornstarch and sugar, top with a simple crust, and you've got a super dessert. Or layer the thickened fruit with vanilla pudding, more fruit, then more pudding and top with a dollop of whipped cream. Serve the fruit over ice cream or a slice of plain cake. Yum!

The one zip-lock bag will hold all your leftover bread products (that half piece of toast after breakfast, a crust of bread, a leftover dinner roll, or hamburger bun.)

For super easy breadcrumbs, just put the contents of the bag in the blender and zip! Can you believe people actually BUY breadcrumbs? We also love to make bread pudding when our bread bag is full. Served with some hot lemon sauce, it is "food from heaven." (See March recipes) Of course, nothing pleases Roy more than some delicious bread stuffing with pork chops.

The other zip-lock bag will hold the leftover sweet things (that doughnut, the last piece of dried cake, or cookie crumbs.) When I have quite a collection in this "sweets" bag, I "blend" it in the blender and use it to top my thickened fruit! No need for a crust! These sweet crumbs are also tasty sprinkled over ice cream instead of nuts or layered in a parfait glass with chocolate pudding and whipped cream. Just imagine — you can make nearly a whole meal from what you would have thrown away!

As we head for the grocery store, just a few things to remember —

- The most expensive and tempting items will always be at eye level.

- The sights, sounds and smells make impulse buying very easy — be prepared.

- One rule about shopping I disagree with and that is not to take children with you. I think it's a great learning experience. Where better to point out good and bad values, how to choose a head of lettuce or a good melon! Take them and teach them.

Let's grab those carts and get started. (By the way, did you know shopping carts are 30% larger than they used to be because many people shop until they are full!)?

We'll start in the produce section. It's usually up front to tempt you with those delicious smells (right next to the bakery!) When buying bags of apples, potatoes, etc. be sure and weigh them. Packages are allowed to vary by as much as half a pound. You might as well get the most for your money.

Remember you can freeze sliced bananas for shakes, grapefruit in sections with juice, and melon balls in orange juice if you find a good buy on these items. Store the tomatoes stem down and not in the refrigerator. Be sure and be adventurous and try a few of the different vegetables in season. (Have you tried steamed parsnips sprinkled with a little nutmeg and melted butter yet? Ooh!)

Buy plenty of relish items (celery — pick the bunch that is the lightest shade of green, radishes, green onions, carrots, etc.) Clean them as soon as you get home, and they'll be ready for snacking. Don't shove that bunch of celery in the fridge on the lowest shelf only to find a flibbily bunch next week that you'll have to throw out. When buying the small, cleaned carrots, I put them into a different zip bag along with a few folded paper towels. They keep better this way. As you are cleaning the celery, put the leaves on a paper grocery sack and set aside to dry. When they are crisp and dried, put them in a jar to use as seasoning. I also do this with the tops of green onions (chopped) instead of discarding them.

When buying onions, you know as one starts to spoil, they all go — like the Osmond's old song about one bad apple spoils the whole darn bunch! I save my old panty hose. Then I separate each leg, drop in an onion, tie a knot, drop in another onion and tie a knot until the "leg" is full. I hang these in the basement. It's so handy to snip off an onion, the air can circulate around them, and they keep so much longer. (Doing a TV show in Houston once, displaying my ideas, I had a stagehand pick up my "stocking" of onions and say "Hum! I was out with a girl that had legs like that last night!" Poor girl!)

Citrus fruits have many uses. I avoid thick, bumpy rinds and look for heavy fruits. Orange and grapefruit shells make great "cups" in which to serve sherbets. Any rinds can be shredded and dried to use as seasonings. I dry and save citrus peels to toss in the fireplace. What a delightful aroma! I also save a bag of "peels " in the fridge to toss into a hot bath after a hard day of work or shopping. It smells like you are vacationing in Florida, and the oils are good for your skin. If you have accumulated some lemon halves after juicing, try placing your elbows in them for about ½ hour while watching your favorite TV show or reading a book. You'll be surprised how soft and light your skin will be!

Think ahead as you purchase produce to eliminate as much waste as possible.

As we round the corner there is a whole aisle of drinks. Be sure and read the labels here. You may not be getting the juice you think you are. There are drinks, -ades and punches. These items can be a real budget drainer, and like we say at our house, "nothing beats good water." I can't believe how many people spend their limited food budgets buying soda, etc!

Next to the dairy case. Watch prices and brands of milk. These can vary greatly, too. And always check the expiration date on all dairy products. Sometimes if you plan to use the item immediately you can find a real bargain — especially on whipping cream (and I hope you are using the real stuff and not that topping in a tub.) I'm amazed how many young people don't realize you can "whip your own." There really is no comparison. Always look for the cartons of whipping cream that say "heavy cream." Period. Avoid the ones with gelatins and gums or other additives. By the way, if I have a little whipped cream left over, I drop dollops on a lined cookie sheet and freeze them. Then I store them in a plastic bag. They are WONDERFUL on a cup of hot chocolate.

Much can be said about cheeses. Just remember again to read the labels. The protein content goes down with cheese — cheese food — cheese food spread — and "imitation, pasteurized, processed, cheese food spread." At that point, I would choose peanut butter! There are many types of cheeses available to us now. Don't get in a rut. Try some different varieties. I like to choose several — cheddar, Muenster, jack and Colby — and cube them and keep a bag in the freezer. They make great snacks for the grandkids or to take in the car with some crackers and fruit. You can freeze most cheeses. Just never in blocks bigger than ½-1 pound. Then let it thaw on the counter and then place it in the fridge to use. Some types crumble more after freezing but are great for cooking. I buy my grated Parmesan cheese at an Italian market for less per pound than the canned variety at the supermarket. No fillers — and grated fresh. We smiled when our grandson, Jake, was over for spaghetti and after sprinkling his helping with our Parmesan cheese, said, "Gee, this stuff melts!" There's nothing like the real thing!

I feel eggs take a "bum rap." They are economical, versatile and good for you (just like everything else, in moderation.) There are so many sizes and prices available now that the easiest thing to remember is 7c. If you can go the next size up for less than 7c you are getting the most egg for your money. Eggs should always be refrigerated and keep well. Just watch the expiration date. If you're in doubt about any eggs that you have, place them in a bowl of water. They should sink. If they float, get rid of them. As soon as I purchase eggs, while I'm putting my groceries away, I hard-boil a few. They are so handy for salads, sandwiches, or snacks. AND save that water! Let it cool and water your houseplants. They love it! I even save the egg cartons. The foam ones are washed well in soapy water and used as extra ice cube trays or freezing small amounts of sauces, gravies, etc. The cardboard cartons we fill with charcoal briquettes and keep to take on a picnic up the canyon. Just set the carton on a grill, light the carton, and as it burns, all the briquettes catch on fire (no fire-starters!)

With eggs, remember the color of the shell or the intensity of the yellow of the yolk really doesn't make any difference. It depends on the breed of chicken and the type of diet it ate. Include eggs in lots of ways in your meals — French toast, puddings, chef salads, omelets, and sandwiches.

When it comes to spreads, at our house we prefer butter. Used sparingly, I feel it is better for you (being a natural product) than margarine; and it sure tastes better! However, I do use some margarine and Crisco in my baking. Be careful using and switching margarines in baking because the water content and oil content can really make a difference. I used Blue Bonnet margarine in several of my recipes, and suddenly they didn't turn out the same. I then noticed they changed their formula. I now use Nucoa with success, but that could change, too. I have always had good consistent results with Crisco products. Avoid all of the "whipped" products. You can whip them full of air and water at home, if that's what you prefer.

Butter and margarine freeze well, and of course, Crisco requires no refrigeration. When storing cottage cheese, sour cream, etc. in the refrigerator, place the cartons upside down. They keep much better.

If you are in a rush to bake and discover the margarine is frozen, simply shred it into the mixing bowl. It will cream up nicely with your other ingredients.

Let's move on around to the meat department now. It is usually spread clear across the back of the store to tempt you as you turn down each aisle. Meat is one of our most expensive items on the grocery list, but there are so many fun and exciting ways to prepare meals. Don't let it intimidate you. First, remember to think in terms of meals! Watch the price per pound, not the price of packages, and plan to use every bit.

Beef — When buying ground beef, I always buy the lowest in fat content (it is listed on the packages). Otherwise you are throwing away half of your purchase in grease and fat. Roasts or round steaks can be a great buy per pound. Buy the largest you can afford. I often purchase them to cut up for stroganoff, stew, chili, spaghetti, stir fry, etc. — and any trimmings left make great soups.

Always watch for the code date on meats, and any ground meat should be sold the day it is ground.

When cooking meats, never pierce with a fork. You will lose flavorful juices. Never salt meat as it is cooking as it also draws out juices. The exception would be when making soups and stews when you want the juices in the broth.

If I am making a dish that requires the meat to be floured, such as Swiss steak, I pound the flour into both sides with the edge of a saucer and then let the meat stand for 10-15 minutes.

Don't waste money on expensive tenderizers. Use marinades such as lemon juice, fruit juices, vinegar or tomato juice.

As you prepare any ground meat for cooking — hamburgers, meat loaf, meatballs, etc. — be sure and handle the meat gently. Never pack ground meats solidly into shape!

If you are grilling steaks, always remember to make small slashes around the outside to keep the fat from curling as it cooks.

Pork — This is a super buy and is also very versatile. My favorite is the whole pork tenderloin. I watch for a sale, and then cut it crossways in meal-size pieces. These I use as a pork roast with potatoes, cooked with sauerkraut, cubed and stewed to serve over noodles, cut up for stir fry, or sliced thinly for a delicious sandwich. Pork is now a very lean meat and very tender if not overcooked! We've all had pork chops that were like shoe leather, right?

I don't use much bacon because it is mostly used as flavor — not much food value. Ham is always my choice. I prefer the bone-in variety. Remember these hams are usually cut in half — butt and shank. If the package says "butt half" or "shank half," you are getting the choice center section, also, that is often cut into steaks. If the package says "butt portion" or "shank portion," the nice center slices have been removed. The best purchase is a butt half for the most meat. Simply roast it in a 325* oven uncovered, fat side up. A piece of foil over the cut side will keep it from getting too brown. I usually do about 30-40 minutes a pound and then slice. You'll never taste more delicious ham. After cooking, freeze bags of the slices to be used in scalloped potatoes, ham and noodles, omelets, salads, for breakfast with a waffle, or a lunch sandwich. Then you have that fantastic bone for a pot of tasty soup with beans, carrots, and potatoes. This ham is a real budget stretcher.

Poultry — I love turkey, both as a budget saver and as a wonderful convenience food. Besides, it's good for you! Try my absolute favorite way with this great bird! It's always the best buy to get the biggest turkey you can, no matter how small your family. Ask the butcher to saw it in half lengthwise and then crosswise (on an angle so you get all the breast together.) I package these quarters individually in plastic bags and freeze them. The breast sections I can roast with barbecue sauce, a can of cream of chicken soup, or just placed over some stuffing and baked. It's a delicious white meat roast. Now with those "hind" quarters — just place one in the biggest kettle you have (your canner works well), cover it with about six quarts of water, an onion, carrot, celery stalk, and salt and pepper. Bring to a boil, and then cover and let simmer six hours or more until meat is very tender. Then strain the broth and pick the meat from the bones as soon as it's cool enough to handle. This gives me six quarts of nice broth and six packages of meat. (You can package the broth and meat together if you plan to use it that way.) I then freeze the broth and meat, and it really makes a neat convenience meal. Put a quart of broth and meat in a pan, add some noodles, rice or dumplings, a few carrots and peas, some salt and pepper if needed and a dash of sage. Boy, that's the best you'll ever taste. Or you can thicken the broth, add some leftover vegetables and the meat, and put on a crust for a great meat pie.

Luncheon meats are very rarely seen in my grocery cart. When there are so many delicious real meats to serve for lunch, why resort to ones with fillers and chemicals. We prefer sliced left-over roast, meat loaf, canned fish, turkey, ham, chicken pieces, egg salad, peanut butter and even baked bean sandwiches. All better for you and saves money, too!

Wow, it's time to step around to the cereal aisle. Overwhelming, isn't it? I heard someone say once that never before have we bought so little food in such big boxes! True, true. If your family insists on these boxes, at least read the labels and get the most nutrition possible. Some of the sugared varieties give you the equivalent of 12 spoons of sugar per bowl. Even purchased granola can be a culprit. It's so simple to make your own.

Now is a perfect time to start varying your breakfast menu. There are so many whole grains in addition to the usual cream of wheat and oatmeal. But even oatmeal can become interesting — just add currants or raisins, nuts, and cinnamon and nutmeg as it cooks. Then spoon it into the hollow of a baked apple (that you baked in the oven the night before, as supper was cooking). Top with a little half and half and some brown sugar. Yum! Our Jessica loves cooked rice. This, too, can be dressed up with a few raisins or other dried fruits. Why not a creamy rice pudding, a hot tasty bread pudding, easy whole grain muffins, a quick veggie omelet, multi-grain French toast, even breakfast tacos or pizza. You'll soon discover you can whiz down this "cereal" aisle in a hurry.

It seems like the other rows of food in the store are classified as convenience! Many are just fancy (and misleading) names. Boxes of crumbs? My goodness, I have plenty of crumbs of my own! Have you ever analyzed a meat pie? Two little squares of carrot and 3 peas! A complete serving of vegetables? I think not! Beans and franks? Who can't slice a wiener into a can of beans and save 50¢? And so many pictures on boxes that don't come close to resembling the inside contents!

We pay so much for the so-called convenience. We really sacrifice nutrition. Nearly everything is loaded with synthetic flavors, colors, and preservatives, and often the average homemaker can put together these same items in less time than it takes to assemble the so-called convenient package. In addition, it will taste much better and be more nutritious for you.

Learn to be a label reader when you do your shopping. Here are some things you should look for and be aware of —

1. The brand name. This should serve as a guide to the goodness of the product. Don't always assume that the store brand is cheapest. Check and compare. On the other hand, if the store brand is a good buy, buy one can and give it a try. You may like it as well as the name brand and also save a few pennies.

2. Check weight and volume. Many times packages and cans are exactly the same size but contain different weights. Almost all grocery stores now have the "price per unit" listed on the shelf below the item. This is a fast way to tell which package is the best buy. For instance, it will tell the price per ounce below the regular box of Tide and also under the large family pack. You can then see which is the best price.

3. Address of distributor. It is always good to have the address in case you are unhappy with the item. Don't hesitate to let them know!

4. Variety and style of food. Don't buy canned fancy whole tomatoes if you're only going to use them in chili or a stew. To save a few calories, avoid fruit packed in heavy syrup. Canned fruit tastes more like fresh fruit if the syrup is light.

5. Ingredients listed in descending order. The ingredient listed first is what there is the most of in the can or package. So, a can of beef and gravy would have more meat than a can of gravy and beef. Of course, my advice here regarding anything they combine in packages or cans, is we can do the same thing for less money and much better quality at home. The list of ingredients should be checked on all things, though, for items like sugar, water, salt, etc., so you know what you are paying for.

6. Watch pull dates. These tell you how fresh the product is. Remember that the item is not going to spoil exactly on that day. They usually allow for a few days on the family kitchen shelf or refrigerator.

Just remember — read labels and know what you're buying!

Usually we find the simpler the better. You can't beat a piece of good cheese, a loaf of healthy bread and a fresh picked tomato! Who can't bake a potato, broil a piece of fish and toss a salad? (And in less time than it takes to open boxes, cans and packages to put together!)

Speaking of healthy bread, shop around for those great tasting whole grain breads. No more of this "Styrofoam" stuff. There are so many breads on the market today, and this item alone can give your daily menus a lift. Try rye, pumpernickel, English muffins, biscuits, Italian crusty rolls, croissants, garlic bread sticks or good whole wheat. Cinnamon raisin makes great toast or a cream cheese and grated carrot sandwich. It's amazing what a difference bread varieties can make in sandwiches.

Nearly everything that is fixed for you in the frozen food section, you can freeze yourself. Those leftovers after dinner make a nice frozen "TV" dinner for another meal. Soups and stews freeze very well in meal-size containers. Why not have a family pizza party? Assemble several pizzas and freeze for a quick supper. Heavens, they even try to sell us frozen pancakes, French toast, and waffles. If they can freeze them, so can we. And who doesn't have a few leftover pancakes after breakfast?

Commercially produced salad dressings are so expensive! These are also easy to mix up in a glass jar, and you'll have a quart for pennies, opposed to 8 oz. (one cup) for dollars!

Have you tried your hand at the flavored vinegars and oils? They're quick and easy, but so flavorful. We also really enjoy balsamic vinegar. It has a sweet/sour, but full, robust flavor. It's dark brown in color and really adds pizzazz to a dish. A little added to a typical oil and vinegar dressing really sparks up the taste. Especially with spinach, strawberries and greens. Roy likes it straight, splashed on greens with salt, pepper and freshly grated parmesan. A little balsamic drizzled over a beef roast is delicious. Try it sprinkled on an omelet or pasta dishes, as well. Always add it toward the end of cooking or some of the flavor dissipates. Even a few drops sprinkled over fresh strawberries will give a pleasantly surprising taste treat.

Herbs and spices can also liven up your meals. Learn about them, experiment with them and have fun!

As we approach the bakery aisle, hold on to your taste buds. "Anything they can do, you can do better!" A few little tips on cookie baking. If you like a crisp cookie, use butter. If you prefer a softer cookie, increase the flour just a little. Never over-bake cookies. When you peek in the oven and think they are just about done, they ARE! Get them right out. The shortening bubbles will continue to "cook" the cookie for a minute or two. Never cool cookies on a rack. The shortening or butter bubbles will absorb right back into the cookie and will cause a softer cookie to become hard or a crisp cookie to be "flibbily." They will also become rancid or stale sooner. I cool mine on brown paper sacks from the grocery store. They are free and are wonderfully absorbent for the excess grease. You'll be surprised at the ring each cookie leaves, and as I tell Roy, it's a dead give-away when someone swipes a cookie as they are cooling!

If you have a need for lots of cupcakes and not enough cupcake pans, simply put some mason jar rings on your cookie sheet and place a cupcake paper in each ring. You can bake a big bunch at a time.

In any baking, remember that shiny pans are not the best choice. A dull or darkened pan gives a lot better finished product. This is especially true with bread pans.

Avoid the expensive baking items if a substitute will do.

Substitutes

1 c. cake flour = 1 c. minus 2 T. all-purpose flour (1 T. cornstarch can be added for an extra fluffy cake)

1 square baking chocolate = 3 T. cocoa and 1 T. margarine or butter

1 c. sour milk or buttermilk = 1 c. milk and 1 T. lemon juice or vinegar (let stand a few minutes)

2 mashed garlic cloves in a 1 lb. box of salt = lots of garlic salt

1 vanilla bean in a canister of sugar eliminates the need to add vanilla to a recipe when baking or cooking. (With the price of vanilla, this really saves.)

1 clove garlic = 1/8 tsp. garlic powder

1 c. granulated sugar = 1 c. packed brown sugar or 2 c. powdered sugar

1 c. sour cream = 1 c. plain yogurt

1 whole egg = 2 egg yolks

1 regular marshmallow = 10 miniature marshmallows

1 c. sugar = ½ to ¾ c. honey (adjust liquid in recipe by ¼ cup)

1 T. cornstarch = 2 T. all-purpose flour (for thickening)

Broth, tomato juice, fruit juice or a little vinegar in water can be substituted for alcohol in recipes.

Mint extract can be used instead of crème de menthe.

7-Up or ginger ale can replace beer.

Never throw away leftover fruit juices or the fruit syrup drained from a can of fruit. Thicken it with a little cornstarch to use as a glaze or sauce, add it to jello in place of some of the water, mix it with a little mayonnaise for a great fruit salad dressing, or use it to flavor a glass of milk and surprise the kids!

Why not just pass up the bakery department and give your family that fresh baked goodness?

We spend a lot of "grocery" money on cleaning products. Many of these can be eliminated, also. We don't need a separate cleaning item for each job. Double up your usage on some of the things you normally purchase, and remember plain baking soda is cheap and works wonders on many things. I even prefer my own window cleaner –

    4 T. household ammonia
    4 T. rubbing alcohol
    1 pint water

You can even add a few drops of food coloring if you like (it doesn't have to be blue!)

One of the most exciting things for me is the challenge I feel to feed my family wisely, save money and have fun. Take a look at your normal shopping patterns and see where you might make a big difference in your family's health and your pocketbook. Think of all the fun things you can do with your new-found money. Don't just buy "bargains." Nothing is a bargain if your family won't eat it, or it isn't good for them.

Much of our food budget can slip through our fingers by simply being disorganized. Do you run to the store for something when you have some hiding in the back of the fridge? Do you throw out those fresh vegetables because you didn't get them cleaned and now they are spoiled? Did someone forget to wrap up the bread or cover the cake and now it's hard? I come from the old school that taught "use it up, wear it out, make it do or do without!" It's not such a bad lesson to teach our children. We are so fortunate to live in a land of plenty, let's appreciate it and use it well.

"Eating out," a substitute for cooking at home, can also be a big drain on your budget. We try to not eat out on the same night that we go to a movie or program. That way we have two special evenings. If we are going out with friends, we enjoy an appetizer or dessert at home together. Roy and I nearly always split an entrée in a restaurant, and with an extra salad, we have plenty. With a little planning you really can double your pleasure for half the cost.

This September let's set some new goals as we settle in getting our "nests" in order. I remember a story of a mother measuring a hem for her little boy's new school pants. With determination and conviction he said, "Leave a BIG hem 'cause I'm gonna grow a lot this year!" Wouldn't it be great if we each approached our lives with such an attitude. Put a big hem in your plans this fall, and grow with determination and a positive attitude. You can do it!

September Food for Fun
Recipes Guaranteed to Please Your Budget

My freezer is never without some containers of Minestrone. It is such a tasty and versatile soup. You can add about anything you like. On the day I bake Italian bread or bread sticks, this soup is a must.

Minestrone

Into a large, heated kettle place 2 slices bacon, a cup or so of leftover ham scraps, and some beef trimmings and bones that you've cut off a roast or round steak before cooking. (I always trim my meats and keep the trimmings in a bag in the freezer). Use any scraps you have. Cook these together well until nicely browned.

Add: 2 qts. hot water. Cover and simmer for about 2 hours.

Strain the broth and pick off any meaty beef or ham pieces and add back to the stock.

Then add:
- 2 sliced carrots
- 1 small chopped onion
- 2 c. canned or fresh tomatoes
- 1 c. lima beans (or green beans)
- 1 stalk chopped celery
- 2 peeled and diced potatoes
- 1 chopped zucchini
- 1 c. cut-up cabbage
- 1 c. uncooked broken spaghetti or macaroni
- 1 T. parsley
- 2 bay leaves
- ½ tsp. basil
- ½ tsp. oregano
- salt, pepper, and garlic to taste

Let simmer about 45 minutes until all vegetables are tender.

Stir in: ¼ c. Parmesan cheese

Heat through and serve. Makes 2 ½ quarts.

¤ ¤ ¤ ¤ ¤

For a quick, economical lunch try this great soup with some French bread and a tossed salad. It is so-o good!

"Perky" Tomato Soup

In food processor, combine:
- 3 T. fresh basil
- 1 clove garlic
- 1 T. romano or parmesan cheese
- a dash of coarse black pepper

Process until smooth.

Combine in a saucepan with:
- 1 can tomato soup
- 1 can milk

Heat, stirring often.

¤ ¤ ¤ ¤ ¤

Grab a bag of corn chips and make a big tossed salad — we're going Mexican tonight. You will love this easy soup! I usually just cook a couple of chicken breasts in a couple of quarts of water (seasoned with carrot, onion, and celery, salt and pepper) for about 1 hour to get my broth and meat. Then the soup goes together in minutes.

Sopa Fiesta

Combine:
- 2 quarts turkey or chicken broth
- 1 ½ c. cut-up cooked turkey or chicken meat
- 1 small can green chili peppers
- 2 c. corn
- 1 chopped zucchini
- 1 ½ c. canned or fresh tomatoes
- 1 T. minced fresh onion
- dash of cumin
- salt and pepper to taste

Bring to a boil, cover and simmer for 30-45 minutes.

¤ ¤ ¤ ¤ ¤

My sister-in-law, Dolores, came up with this dressing. Now it's a family favorite.

The Scheel Family Fabulous Blue Cheese Dressing

Beat together with mixer:
- 1 qt. mayonnaise
- ½ c. Miracle Whip
- 1 ¼ c. buttermilk
- 1 tsp. garlic salt
- 1 tsp. onion salt
- ¼ tsp. sugar
- ¼ tsp. salt
- 1 T. lemon juice

Then crumble and add 4-6 oz. blue cheese.

¤ ¤ ¤ ¤ ¤

One item I could not be without is my jar of taco seasoning. It is just so simple to mix up and saves me many dollars. When I add it to browned ground beef, I use 2 T. and add 1 cup of hot water and then simmer for 10 minutes. Great for tacos, enchiladas, tostados, burritos, etc.

Mexican Taco Seasoning Mix

Mix together:
- ¼ c. dried minced onion flakes
- 4 tsp. cornstarch
- 2 T. salt
- 4 T. chili powder
- 3 tsp. cumin
- 1 ½ tsp. oregano
- 3 tsp. dried minced garlic
- 3 tsp. crushed hot red pepper flakes
- 2 tsp. beef bouillon

Store in tightly covered container.

2 T. mix equals 1 commercial package.

¤ ¤ ¤ ¤ ¤

Ask my daughters what dessert they want and you can bet it will be this one. They have been known to "hide" the last piece for later! It's so chocolatey and good, you really aren't aware of the dates.

Date Delight

Bring to a boil: 1 c. chopped dates
                   ¾ c. water
                   ¼ tsp. salt

Simmer for 3 minutes. Add: 2 c. miniature marshmallows.

Stir until marshmallows are dissolved. Cool.

Then add: ½ c. chopped pecans.

Crush 14 Oreos. Spread ½ of crumbs in 8x8 inch pan. Spread date mixture over cookie crumbs.

Whip ½ pint whipping cream and spread over date mixture. Sprinkle with the rest of the crumbs. Then sprinkle with chopped pecans.

Chill overnight. Enjoy!

¤ ¤ ¤ ¤ ¤

My freezer is always stocked with a supply of these yummy treats.

Surprise Cupcakes

Combine: 8 oz. softened cream cheese
1 egg
1/3 c. sugar
½ tsp. salt

Beat together until smooth. Stir in 1 c. chocolate chips. Set aside.

Mix together: 3 c. flour
2 c. sugar
½ c. cocoa
1 tsp. salt
2 tsp. soda

Add and mix until smooth: 2/3 c. oil
2 c. water
2 tsp. vanilla
2 T. vinegar

Fill cupcake pans not quite 2/3 full, top with a heaping teaspoon of filling.

Bake at 350* for about 25 minutes.

Makes 2 ½ to 3 dozen.

¤ ¤ ¤ ¤ ¤

It's hard to beat this cobbler; the topping is so light and tender (never heavy and doughy.) You'll make it over and over with every kind of fruit and berry available.

Bev's Fruit Cobbler

In saucepan, combine:
- ½ c. sugar
- 3 T. cornstarch
- ½ tsp. cinnamon
- ½ tsp. nutmeg
- 1 qt. fruit and liquid (apricots or peaches, etc.)

Cook until nicely thickened. Pour into a 1 ½ qt. casserole.

Combine:
- 1 c. flour
- 2 T. sugar
- 2 tsp. baking powder
- dash of salt

Mix well together, then cut in: 1/3 c. Crisco.

Cut until fine, then gently stir in with a fork:
- 4 T. milk
- 1 beaten egg

Drop by spoonful over fruit mixture. Bake at 375* for about 30 minutes.

September Grocery Bag

I'm always excited to see fall come because I love the foods that are available then — apples, cabbage, winter squash, pumpkins, grapes and pears. We can start making all those delicious soups, chowders and stews, and they are all easy on the budget. The nice part about this time of year is that there are still a few tomatoes, corn and peppers around to include in our meal planning.

With Labor Day approaching, children returning to school and all of us resuming a regular routine again, I'd like to encourage you to begin planning three basic healthful meals a day with everyone enjoying them together. Mealtime should be the most special time of day!

Include broccoli, brussel sprouts, cauliflower, carrots and winter squash in your vegetable list. They are very reasonable now and just loaded with vitamins and minerals.

There will be more pork specials this month and, of course, chicken will still be a good buy. Watch for beef prices to start climbing upward.

Cereal prices will be climbing. Now is the time to enjoy delicious cooked cereals. The whole grains are better for you, much, much cheaper, and so delicious and satisfying.

You should also be able to find fresh, good quality **pears** at reasonable prices this month. Their season is just beginning. Look for firm pears and let them ripen on your kitchen counter. Pears are never picked ripe, so they are rarely ready to eat when purchased. Avoid pears that are wilted or shriveled and that have soft spots on the blossom end. Pears are mild and blend great with other flavors. We like them with cheeses, minted, or in fruit salads with bananas and berries.

One of our favorite vegetables that comes with fall is **yams**. Yams are a popular variety of sweet potato. They are moist and sweet with a bright orange color. Because they are so sweet, you don't need sugar, honey, or molasses. We prefer them baked whole in the oven and then served with lots of butter and salt and pepper. Yams are so versatile and go well with pork chops, turkey, and especially ham. They are also good combined with oranges, apples or pineapple. They're even good in desserts. For some variety try substituting them for white potatoes in soups and stews.

Another of our favorite ways to prepare them are deep fried yam slices. Just peel and slice, then soak in ice water for a while, pat dry and deep fry in hot oil. You can't believe how good they are. Almost taste like cookies. You'll be able to enjoy yams at low prices for quite a while now, so experiment and find out how your family likes them best.

Watch for **canned goods** on sale this month. Be sure to watch your grocery ads and stock up on the things you use. Since you'll eventually be buying them anyway, you might as well save on the price when you can.

Why not surprise your family with some **pomegranates** this month? They are also a good buy. This is a fruit most people avoid because it is unfamiliar. Grenadine syrup is made from pomegranates, and the little red seeds are delicious in a big fruit salad. When you choose a pomegranate, remember the heavier and larger it is, the juicier it will be.

Pomegranates can be eaten several ways. The kids love to roll them with pressure on the countertop (like you would a lemon) to break the seeds down, then cut a little hole in the side and suck out the juice. They can also be cut, the seeds picked out (this is the part you eat) and kept in a plastic container to use in salads or desserts. Just beware, pomegranate juice is a permanent dye, so don't get it on any clothes!

This is certainly the month to stock up on all varieties of **grapes**. They are at their peak of flavor and freshness. When they have been allowed to ripen on the vine, they keep all their nutrition and sweetness. Look for well-colored, plump grapes still attached to the stem, and refrigerate them as soon as you get them home. This way they'll keep a good week. Just wash them before you eat them.

For a real taste treat, put a panful of freshly washed grapes in the freezer for a couple of hours. Your family will eat them like candy, and you'll feel good knowing they are loaded with vitamin A and potassium. Happy Eating!

September Why Didn't I Think of That?

Don't overlook popcorn as a nutritious snack for after school.

¤ ¤ ¤ ¤ ¤

Frozen orange juice should not be thawed and mixed ahead of time and allowed to stand. As soon as it's thawed, it begins to lose nutrients, so make it fresh each morning. By the way, if you mix it in the blender, it returns some of the air to the juice and it really tastes fresher.

¤ ¤ ¤ ¤ ¤

A couple of little tips will make lunch-box time easier for little ones. I split my cupcakes in the middle and frost sandwich style; it makes them easier to eat. Also, draw arrows on the top of the thermos so they know which way to turn the lid. This can be a trying experience; I've watched many frustrated children trying to open their thermoses.

¤ ¤ ¤ ¤ ¤

A few drops of vanilla in your pancake, waffle or french toast batter really adds a nice touch.

¤ ¤ ¤ ¤ ¤

I like to add a few basil leaves to each quart as I can tomatoes.

¤ ¤ ¤ ¤ ¤

Dried squash, pumpkin or melon seeds are great to feed the birds.

¤ ¤ ¤ ¤ ¤

For those of you with Venetian blinds, save your old gloves for dusting. I can remember how fast my Grandma Benson was able to clean her blinds this way. It's kinda fun, too.

¤ ¤ ¤ ¤ ¤

Glue and labels will come right off of glass things with a little nail polish remover.

¤ ¤ ¤ ¤ ¤

If you're doing any painting this fall, line your paint roller pan with a plastic bag. Then when you're finished, the clean-up only takes seconds.

¤ ¤ ¤ ¤ ¤

Roy also always punches a few nail holes in the rim of the paint can so any overflow runs back in the can. With the lid snapped on tight the holes are sealed. (He does all the painting at our house. Roy says I'm the only person he knows who has more paint on the handle of the brush than the bristles.)

¤ ¤ ¤ ¤ ¤

If you have different-sized mattresses, have certain colors or designs for certain-sized sheets. Saves unfolding each one. Or keep sheets for each room in that room.

¤ ¤ ¤ ¤ ¤

We use glass jars in the cupboards for all our dried things — cornstarch, noodles, popcorn, rice, raisins, cornmeal, etc. As soon as I open a container, it goes into a jar. If there are special cooking instructions — like with rice, oatmeal, etc. — I just tape them to the lid with masking tape or write the proportions on the tape. It's a good way to keep your shelves neat — and to discourage bugs!

¤ ¤ ¤ ¤ ¤

I stick the filter from my stove vent into my dishwasher. It sure beats nicked up fingers.

¤ ¤ ¤ ¤ ¤

"How beautiful are the leaves in their last days."

October

October

Golly, isn't this a pretty time of year? Makes me want to stand back and count my blessings. The colors outside are breathtaking, and all the produce frozen, canned, and stocked on the shelves makes such a pretty picture. It's great just to be alive! And such a fun time of year! The cool evenings with the beautiful autumn leaves, the smell of bon fires in the air, and those crisp apples and huge orange pumpkins just waiting to be picked! I don't think anything is more invigorating than refreshing, fantastic, fall days. To have my larder stocked for winter, my house cleaned for the season ahead and sewing projects planned, I'm ready to roll up my sleeves and prepare for the "love-filled" holiday time.

Food for Thought

"An Acorn or a Nut"

Emerson said, "The creation of a thousand forests is in one acorn." I think of this so often and ask myself what kind of forest I am creating. My mother taught me an appreciation for trees and the lessons they can teach us. So many people admire trees in all their beauty, with leaves, flowers and adornment. Yes, they are beautiful then, but the true appreciation comes in the winter when all the covering has fallen and you can see the true shape and soul of that creation. It is so enlightening to drive down the road on a clear, crisp winter day and observe the personalities of the trees. There's the sad undecided tree that has bent this way and that, with the forces of the world, not knowing what way to go and ending up with no true form of his own. Then there's the weak one bent over with the wind at every opportunity and eventually found himself unable to stand straight again. There's the abused, neglected one that shows scars, blemished and broken branches but struggles to hold its trunk up high and reach for help. Of course there's the one that is trying to be like the tree next to him and has twisted and wound himself around until no one can tell what his potential really is.   There are the strong, straight trees that have stood tall sending out small roots at first, step by step until one day they had a strong mass with which to hold tight. All of these trees have a character and a personality of their own with a purpose. It may be a little nest of bunnies protected under that gnarled and crooked tree, or a tender seedling getting its start under the shade of the abused and broken tree, but all are of worth!

I remember one Christmas a few years ago, we decided to go as a family to cut our Christmas tree. When we arrived at the farm on a beautiful snow covered hill near Chardon, Ohio, the sun vas shining so brightly we jumped out of the car and felt like we were in a glistening fairy land forest. Naturally the kids scattered in every direction to find the most beautiful tree on the farm. Before long Kristen came running back shouting, "I've found it! I've found it!" We all ran to see what wonderful creation she had found. Well, we couldn't believe our eyes. Kristen was standing next to the most scrawny, bent, and sagging tree I have ever seen. When the family started to object, tears filled Kristen's eyes and she said, "But Mom, it's been trying so hard, it probably didn't get as much water and sunshine clear over here and no one will ever want it. Look, it even has a left over nest in its branches. We can take it home and love it. Isn't that what Christmas is all about?" Needless to say, we bought the little tree (nest included) and it became the focus of one of the nicest Christmases we ever had.

Too often we become confused in this life and think that what's on the outside is what counts. The happiness we give to others comes from what's inside. It's so easy to get caught up in a rut and spend our lives keeping up with the Jones'. Have you heard about the naturalist that was studying the processionary caterpillars? This particular variety of caterpillar eats pinecones. They follow each other with their eyes half closed and their heads butted up against the caterpillar in front of them. One day the man very carefully lifted a row of caterpillars onto the rim of a flowerpot. Inside the flowerpot he put a large supply of pinecones to sustain them. But as is their habit or custom, they went round and round the flower pot rim with their heads down and eyes half closed. Not realizing they were within an inch of food, they dropped in exhaustion and starvation. How like the caterpillar we can become, caught up in a rut, mistaking activity for accomplishment.

By observing trees, I have learned that there is an order to all things in life, a time and a season, and ups and downs. It is so exciting in the Spring to know we can count on the willows to pop out, followed by the red bud and wild plum. Soon there's that familiar tinge of green everywhere you look. It seems like one day the trees are bare and the next day the buds are appearing but, we all know there is a PLAN.

As we journeyed across the country a couple of years ago, we started in the lush pine forests in Washington State. The towering trees were really a marvel to us as they stood strong against the snows on Mt. Rainier. Soon we were in the fertile flowering fruit orchards near Wenatchee. Within a day we crossed a barren strip in Wyoming where a lone tree was struggling for existence. Isn't it amazing how like life, a journey like that can be? Do you have days when the going is tough but you feel strong against the storms? Other time when just everything seems to be going right and life is blossoming for you, and then times when you feel all alone? Isn't it a comfort to know there is an order to things — a time and a season — and as Roy always says, "The scriptures say 'It came to pass'!" (not to stay.)

I have always been fascinated by legends. On Easter Sunday morning I used to take the little grandchildren on a tour through our yard and gardens. They loved to hear the story of the red bud tree and how it was the red bud tree from which

Judas hung himself and that's why the leaves are tinted pink. The dogwood tree is said to be the tree they used to make the cross for Jesus, and he said "From this day forth the dogwood tree would never grow tall enough to be used for this purpose." Its flower also forms a cross with brown nail prints and a red drop of blood on the petal. Sharing nature with the little ones provided me with a great teaching tool. Not long ago as Nathan ran by our hawthorn tree, I saw him stop and tell little Cameron how the thorns were used to make a crown for Jesus' head. As they pricked their fingers on the sharp points I'm sure understanding and sympathy filled their hearts.

I feel very blessed to have "tree" friends as well as "people" friends all over the country. Though they may be far away, the memories and lessons will always be with me.

- The two cedar trees that banked my Grandma's mail box — aah! The smell of cedar still brings back memories of brushing against those branches.

- The two huge willow trees in Grandpa's front yard that he constantly complained about because they were a nuisance. I never could understand why, because they provided me a cool private place to play on a hot summer day.

- The large stand of linden trees on our Nebraska farm. They were family to me, and I spent many hours playing beneath them.

- That beautiful old holly tree standing in front of our first little apartment in Olympia, Washington. It provided holly for all my relatives in Nebraska that Christmas. How proud we were to share such an extravagance!

- The fragile little apple tree we planted and nurtured in the yard of our very first home. We didn't live there long enough to harvest fruit, but it's still standing and I'm sure has brought happiness to many.

- Our beautiful snowball tree in Kansas City, Missouri for the bouquets it provided for our table.

- That huge, stately pine in our backyard under which we buried our fun loving little dachshund "Hans."

Trees, like people, are all so different and have so many things to offer. Don't weed them out or ignore them until you really understand what they are about. They may become your best friends.

Three lovely things life gives to me
Whatever else fate sends
My heart is filled with gratitude
For trees and books and friends.

– Robert Mc Cann

As you whiz down the highway in your automobile, or take a walk in the park, enjoy those trees! Do you see one that reminds you of someone, or brings to mind a lesson in life you could learn? One day while reflecting on these things, I felt inspired to write this little poem.

That little, bitty acorn has a lesson for us all.
It looks just like a simple nut that took a long, long fall.
But while it quivered on the branches and the winds were blowing strong,
it said, "I have a destiny to help the world along.
Right now I'm brown and shiny and add beauty to the tree,
but soon I'll fall to earth and a miracle I'll be.
The Lord will help me grow up tall, send rain to water me.
He will support me when I'm weak, and soon a mighty oak I'll be."
From that one small, but mighty, acorn a thousand forests will erupt,
if he but catches of the vision that he's an acorn not a nut!

What kind of forest are you creating?

October Food for Fun
Satisfying, Comfort Food for Crisp, Fall Days

On a busy day, I vote for this pork stew recipe — inexpensive, easy, hearty, and a healthy dish to satisfy everyone. I love it!

Pork Stew

Cut a 1 lb. pork tenderloin into cubes. Shake cubes in flour, then brown in 3 T. hot oil.

Add: 2 cut-up carrots
1 sliced onion
1 ½ c. canned tomatoes
1 c. water
1 ½ tsp. salt
½ tsp. caraway seeds

Bring to a boil, cover and cook slowly for 45 minutes.

Add: 4 c. coarsely shredded cabbage

Cover and cook for 1 more hour. Serve over noodles.

¤ ¤ ¤ ¤ ¤

For a fun change with sauerkraut, give this polish version a try. It's one of Roy's favorites from a dear friend of ours.

Ted Gorka's Polish Sauerkraut

Dice ¼ lb. bacon finely.

In a large, heavy pan, sauté until crisp. Add: 3 medium finely chopped onions

Cook until golden. Add:
- 1 qt. rinsed sauerkraut
- ½ c. dark brown sugar
- 2 ½ T. caraway seed
- 1 tsp. dill weed
- 1 ½ tsp. freshly ground black pepper
- 1 c. beef bouillon

Cover and cook over low to medium heat for a total of one hour. Stir every 10 minutes for the first half hour. Keep it covered, and if the liquid cooks away, add a little water.

For the last 15 minutes, add ½ lb. chopped mushrooms

A dish of this with some Kielbasa sausage and black bread makes a delicious supper.

¤ ¤ ¤ ¤ ¤

An Autumn party wouldn't seem right at our house if we didn't serve our favorite Mexican dish. It's so fun because everyone adds their own colorful toppings. It is a one dish meal, easy to prepare and absolutely "the best."

Beans Ole

Soak 1 lb. pinto beans in 7 8 c. water overnight.

In the morning, add: 2-3 lb. pork loin roast (uncooked)
       ½ c. chopped onion
       2 cloves minced garlic
       1 T. salt
       2 T. chili powder
       T. cumin
       1 tsp. oregano
       1 can (4 oz.) chopped green chilies

Combine all in a large Dutch oven, cover and simmer for 5 hours (or longer).

Take out roast and pick all meat from the bones. Add meat back to the pot, discarding the bones and fat.

Cook another ½ hour or so, uncovered, to desired thickness.

Serve in bowls with shredded lettuce, diced tomatoes, chopped onions, chopped avocados, shredded cheese, and corn chips.

¤ ¤ ¤ ¤ ¤

These cool October days just seem perfect for our hot German Scones. They are so easy to make. The dough keeps in the refrigerator for a good week, and it is so fun to fry a few for a treat when you'd like. Be sure and eat them hot. They aren't good kept, so fry them fresh. Sure beats any doughnuts, hands down. We like to sprinkle them with sugar or drizzle with honey or jam. Yum!

German Scones

Dissolve 2 pkg. yeast in ½ c. warm water. Add 1 T. sugar.

Pour 1 c. boiling water over: ½ c. sugar
½ c. margarine
2 tsp. salt

Let cool until warm, then add: 3 beaten eggs
yeast mixture
2 c. flour

Beat with mixer until smooth. Add 2 ½ c. more flour and stir in with wooden spoon. Let rise for 1 hour, stir down, then cover and refrigerate.

When desired, roll out very thin and cut in 2 inch squares. Fry in hot oil.

¤ ¤ ¤ ¤ ¤

Now, let's get down to the goodies! What could be better than a slice of this nut bread, fresh from the oven, topped with a little butter or cream cheese. However, it does slice better the next day! Darn!

Aunt Minnie's Applesauce Nut Loaf

Combine: 2 c. flour
               ¾ c. sugar
               3 tsp. baking powder
               1 tsp. salt
               ½ tsp. soda
               ½ tsp. cinnamon

Stir in 1 c. chopped walnuts.

Heat together: I c. applesauce
                      2 T. Crisco.

Add to dry ingredients and stir lightly.

Add 1 beaten egg.

Mix together and pour into a greased 8 inch by 4 inch bread pan. Bake at 350* for hour.

Let cool before slicing.

¤ ¤ ¤ ¤ ¤

We love Caramel and Cinnamon popcorns at our house. I promise you it won't last long!

Microwave Caramel Corn

In a glass bowl, place: 1 stick margarine
　　　　　　　　　　　　I c. brown sugar
　　　　　　　　　　　　¼ c. white corn syrup
　　　　　　　　　　　　½ tsp. salt

Microwave on high for 4 minutes, stirring twice.

Remove from oven and stir in: ½ tsp. soda
　　　　　　　　　　　　　　　1 tsp. vanilla

Put "popped" popcorn (I pop about 1 cup of kernels for this recipe) into a paper bag and pour syrup over.

Fold over the top of the sack. Microwave for 1 ½ minutes on high, stir well. Again fold over sack and microwave for 1 ½ minutes on high. Stir again, close sack and microwave again for 30 seconds on high.

Cool on cookie sheets.

¤ ¤ ¤ ¤ ¤

Microwave Cinnamon Corn

In a glass bowl, place: ½ c. margarine
　　　　　　　　　　　　½ c. sugar
　　　　　　　　　　　　¼ c. corn syrup
　　　　　　　　　　　　¾ c. red hots

Microwave on high for 6 minutes, stirring twice.

Remove from oven and stir in: ¼ tsp. soda
　　　　　　　　　　　　　　　1 tsp. vanilla

Put "popped" popcorn (I pop about I cup of kernels) into a paper bag and pour syrup over.

Fold over the top of the sack. Microwave for 1 ½ minutes on high, stir well. Again fold over sack and microwave for 1 ½ minutes on high. Stir again, close sack and microwave again for 30 seconds on high.

Cool on cookie sheets.

¤ ¤ ¤ ¤ ¤

Fritters are a tasty treat with a meal or by themselves. We especially like them with hot chocolate in the evening.

Apple Fritters

Combine: 1 c. flour
3 T. sugar
1 ½ tsp. baking powder
½ tsp. cinnamon
¼ tsp. nutmeg
½ tsp. salt

Stir in: 1 beaten egg
¼ c. milk
2 ½ T. melted butter

Stir only until mixed. Fold in 1/3 c. diced fresh, tart apples.

Drop by teaspoonfuls into hot oil and deep fry for about 2 minutes until nicely browned and crisp. Drain, sprinkle with powdered sugar, and serve hot!

¤ ¤ ¤ ¤ ¤

I couldn't share my favorite apple recipes without this Apple Butter recipe from my dear friend, Mary. It's an old family recipe, and gosh is it good on a fresh baked roll or hot crispy toast! The method is a little different, but it really works!

Mary's Apple Butter

In a large kettle with a lid, combine: 2 gallons of apples
   (cored and chopped but not peeled)
5 ¼ c. sugar
2 T. cinnamon
1 T. nutmeg
1 T. allspice

Cover and let stand at room temperature overnight.

In the morning DON'T REMOVE LID but bring to a boil and simmer for 2 ½ hours.

Put through a colander. Pour into sterilized jars and process in boiling water bath for 15 minutes.

¤ ¤ ¤ ¤ ¤

While apples are so plentiful now, be sure and try my Apple Macaroon. Serve it warm with a scoop of ice cream. It can't be beat!

Apple Macaroon

Fill pie pan with 4 medium apples sliced.

Sprinkle with: ½ c. sugar
½ tsp. cinnamon
½ c. chopped nuts

Beat: 2 eggs

Add: ½ c. sugar
1 c. flour
1 stick melted margarine

Mix together and pour dough over apples.

Bake at 300* for 1 to 1 ¼ hours.

October Grocery Bag

This is definitely "**apple** month," and there is much to be said about this tremendously versatile fruit. The pilgrims brought apple seeds and cuttings to the Massachusetts Bay Colony, and with the help of modern technology there are now more than 7,000 named apple varieties on record! Ten or twelve varieties have become the most popular. Among these are: the Red Delicious (the world's most popular eating apple which is available nationwide), the Jonathan and Stayman (tart varieties primarily for eating), the Golden Delicious (a sweet apple that doesn't turn brown when cut), and the McIntosh, Cortland, and Winesap (very flavorful and juicy apples used primarily for eating). The tart varieties work best for cooking and baking, and the most popular are the Rome Beauty (whose flavor is brought out by baking) and the Newtown Pippin and Rhode Island Greening (both crisp, tart, green apples). Not all apple varieties are common in all locations, so become familiar with the varieties available to you.

Plan on about 3 medium apples to I pound. Don't be tempted by those huge beauties; the smaller ones are more tasty. Watch for bruised and soft ones in prepackaged bags. Keep apples refrigerated.

Apples are a good source of vitamins A and C and are rich in minerals. Eaten raw, they aid the digestive juices, helping to combat intestinal disorders. Apples are also called "nature's toothbrush" because of their crisp, crunchy texture which is so stimulating to the teeth and gums. You know what they say, "An apple a day keeps the doctor away."

There are so many ways to use and preserve apples. Used fresh, they can be sliced in pies and cobblers, diced in salads, or grated in cakes, muffins, and breads. Try this quick and easy taste treat: slice 2-3 apples in ½ inch thick slices. Melt ¼ cup butter in a skillet and add ¼ cup brown sugar, 1 tsp. cinnamon, and a dash of salt. Add apple slices and sauté over low heat until tender. This is just delicious served with eggs and bacon! Buy those beautiful apples by the bushel and use them baked as a breakfast or dessert treat; cut up in a salad with celery, walnuts, grapes or bananas, and some mayonnaise; fried in slices; cooked up into sauce with a dash of cinnamon and nutmeg (remember, don't add any sugar until they're fully cooked and they will require less). Use them diced up in muffins, pancakes, waffles or fritters and in bread pudding. Of course, an apple pie or cobbler is a treat everyone loves.

In the produce section take advantage of broccoli and Brussels sprouts as well as squash, pumpkin and yams. Apples, cranberries and pears are the best buys in fruit.

Broccoli is loaded with Vitamin C and is very low in sodium. Look for a large number of small stems, bright green color and compact heads. We love broccoli served raw with a vegetable dip. Steaming is the best way to cook broccoli, or use just a small amount of water and don't overcook it. I throw a clove of garlic in the pot as I steam broccoli and, golly, it really makes the mild flavor of broccoli come alive.

Winter squash(Acorn, Butternut, and Hubbard) is usually quite plentiful and reasonably priced in most areas. These should be heavy for their size and show no bruising or decay spots. I prefer to cut them in large pieces, bake in a 375* oven until tender, and just serve with butter and salt and pepper. Since the acorn squash tends to have a little drier type meat, I invert the halves on a cookie sheet or pie pan with a little water in the bottom of the pan. These are also good baked with a stuffing in the cavity. A little browned sausage added to the stuffing mixture is good. It adds moisture and flavor to the squash. All squash is rich in vitamin A.

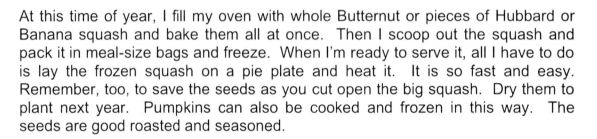

At this time of year, I fill my oven with whole Butternut or pieces of Hubbard or Banana squash and bake them all at once. Then I scoop out the squash and pack it in meal-size bags and freeze. When I'm ready to serve it, all I have to do is lay the frozen squash on a pie plate and heat it. It is so fast and easy. Remember, too, to save the seeds as you cut open the big squash. Dry them to plant next year. Pumpkins can also be cooked and frozen in this way. The seeds are good roasted and seasoned.

Look for **carrots** with the tops on if you can find them — they will be fresher. Remove the tops as soon as you get home so they don't continue to sap the nutrition and sweetness from the carrots. Store the carrots in a plastic bag. Avoid carrots that are too large — they won't be as nutritious. When preparing cooked carrots or raw carrot sticks, please don't peel them; just scrub them well. Most of the nutrition in vegetables is either in the skin or right under it. If you must peel, do it thinly! For a taste treat, try shredding some carrots and mixing with peanut butter and maybe a few raisins. Then spread on fresh whole wheat bread. This is really good!

When choosing **cauliflower** look for firm white heads; avoid brown spots or molding on the head. Clean the head as soon as you get it home and cut or break it into cauliflowerettes. Keep in a plastic bag in the refrigerator, and you're always ready with a fresh snack with a dip if you like or with a ready to cook vegetable. Don't overcook; use just a little water. Then serve with a cheese sauce or plain with a dab of butter.

Now about **onions** — avoid any onions that are sprouting or wet. They should be firm and dry. Yellow onions are used primarily in cooking, white onions are more delicate in flavor, and the red onions are sweeter and really good for slicing on hamburgers. We like sliced red onions or onions and cucumbers combined in a glass jar and covered with vinegar and lots of salt and coarse ground pepper. Let stand in the refrigerator overnight. They're delicious. Don't store onions with potatoes. The potatoes give off moisture and will hasten spoilage. Also don't throw those tops away from the green onions. Chop them, dry on a paper towel, and store for seasoning.

One of the most popular vegetables is the **potato**, so let's talk about them for a minute. When buying potatoes, watch for decay spots, sprouting, or large green areas. Some red potatoes and yams are dyed. The white, or Idaho potato is a dry, mealy type; the red, round potato is moister and holds its shape after cooking. I suppose it's personal preference, but I prefer the white for baking and the red for potato salad, scalloped potatoes, mashed, and so on. Don't overlook the small, red potatoes. They are delicious cooked in their skins and served with butter and parsley or creamed with peas. All potatoes are rich in vitamin C and are a good source of fiber in the diet. When possible, cook with the skins on — there is a powerhouse of nutrition in and just below the potato peel. All potatoes should be kept in a dark, cool, dry place. Light causes them to turn green, and refrigeration causes the starch to turn to sugar.

Remember how we talked about not peeling our fruits and vegetables? Since we are concerned with both saving and nutrition, try this: whenever you have just one thing to go in the oven, such as a cake, never waste all that surrounding oven space and heat. Scrub and wrap in foil all the potatoes that will fit into the leftover space and bake them, too. I always try to keep a supply of these baked potatoes in my vegetable crisper. They make terrific hash browns (don't even remove the skins). They are also much more flavorful in potato salad or any dish where you would usually use peeled and boiled potatoes. Try potato pancakes served with warm applesauce and sausage — yum yum! Delicious! If you should ever peel potatoes, remember to peel them thinly and then don't throw away the cooking water. It's a great addition to breads and yeast doughs. However, do refrigerate it if you aren't ready to use it right away.

Buy or bake plenty of whole grain breads this month to add variety to lunchtime. Egg prices are holding their own and eggs are always a good buy in the protein family. Watch for cheese specials this month. Use cheese in a main dish meal at least once a week to really cut back on your meat bill.

There are so many varieties of pastas, dried beans, peas and lentils. Why not try serving a different type each day? Your meals will be more exciting, and you'll save money, too.

Use your sales resistance and avoid all those fancy frozen things that will be featured this month. Stick to the basics and enjoy simple, honest to goodness food!

HAPPY SHOPPING!!

October Why Didn't I Think of That?

On Halloween why not set up a card table on the porch and serve some warm cider and scones or doughnuts to the parents when they bring their little ones around trick-or-treating. It's a great way to get acquainted with the neighbors, and it also gives them a pleasant little "pause". We always set up our big electric fry pan and cook my German scones.

¤ ¤ ¤ ¤ ¤

Another fun idea for Halloween is to have your children go "pick-and-treating" instead of "trick-or-treating." Fix a big cardboard box or tray with strawberry boxes or baskets full of bittersweet, apples, popcorn balls, homemade cookies, etc. Then make a list of the children who are unable to go trick-or-treating (Johnny with the broken leg, Mary just getting over the flu, or maybe even the elderly couple on the corner). They will be so delighted to see you with your "pick-and-treat" box, and it's such a satisfying experience for your family. Halloween's not just for kids, anyway!

¤ ¤ ¤ ¤ ¤

A fun activity for youngsters on a rainy day is potato block printing. Just cut a potato in half and carve a design (circle, letter, etc.) on the cut side. Put some food coloring on a moistened sponge, and then simply press the potato against the color on the sponge and stamp the design onto paper. Maybe you could even make a jack-o-lantern. This is a fun way to make greeting cards, stationary, wrapping paper or just pictures to hang on the family bulletin board.

¤ ¤ ¤ ¤ ¤

For an October birthday party, "Pin the Grin on the Pumpkin" is a fun game to play.

¤ ¤ ¤ ¤ ¤

Make a Halloween mobile. Use a branch from a tree and suspend witches, ghosts, pumpkins, owls and a quarter moon. Witches could be cutouts hung by their paper cone hats. Put a tissue over a small wad of newspaper for the ghosts.

¤ ¤ ¤ ¤ ¤

If you're having a party, send the invitations in ghost writing. Write the message on white paper using a toothpick and milk or lemon juice. Let dry thoroughly.

Instruct your prospective guests to read the invitation by holding it close to a warm light bulb or running an iron over it. The heat will make the letters darken.

¤ ¤ ¤ ¤ ¤

You can make a cute tablecloth and decorations by using a white sheet. Make pumpkin appliques using an orange felt circle, green felt stem, orange yarn for the lines on the pumpkin, and a black felt face.

¤ ¤ ¤ ¤ ¤

Refreshment ideas are plentiful, too. One favorite is gingerbread jack o' lantern cookies with goblin Jello. Make orange Jello and pour it into serving bowls. While it is still warm, stir in a spoonful of yogurt. Part of the yogurt will swirl through, making ghost trails and a small amount will remain as the ghost. Or try a jack o' lantern fruit cup and cut out cookies. Cut the top section off an orange and scoop out the middle. Make a fruit salad (be sure to use the orange pieces you scooped out) and refill the orange. Put the top back on and secure with a green toothpick "stem." Draw a face on the front with a black marker and you're ready to go. For cake and ice cream, make a round pumpkin batter cake and frost with orange frosting. Make the jack o' lantern face with toasted coconut, candy corn and licorice. Serve with small balls of chocolate, vanilla and orange ice cream.

¤ ¤ ¤ ¤ ¤

Besides the traditional bobbing for apples and other games, play "drop the clothespin into the bottle" with candy corn. Or blindfold a "witch" and have all the "goblins" take turns making spooky noises. If the witch guesses the goblin's name, the goblin becomes the witch. Or have a race transferring pumpkin seeds from one cup to another with a straw (you have to suck on the straw to pick up and move the seeds). Or make a spider web outside or in the basement. Give everyone a ball of fairly sturdy string (preferably different colors). Have each person tie the end around a tree and wind it around bushes, under swing sets, over clotheslines, around fences, etc. You can make really pretty webs. If you want, after the web is made, have a race to see who can wind up his string first. (This can get hectic but it saves clean up later!) Whatever you do this Halloween, relax and make it fun. You can always blame the mess on the little goblins and spirits no one has control over!

¤ ¤ ¤ ¤ ¤

To remove splinters easily, soak the area in cooking oil for a few minutes. Numbing the area with ice also helps. Tell a child to yell while you are removing the splinter, and he won't even know when you do it.

¤ ¤ ¤ ¤ ¤

Marinating meat overnight adds variety to your menus and can cut the cooking time almost in half.

¤ ¤ ¤ ¤ ¤

Remember if a package is called "economy size" or " budget pack" it has to sell for at least 5% less than the usual size. Words like "jumbo," "giant" and "super" are just descriptive words to make you think you are getting a good deal. Be careful and check.

¤ ¤ ¤ ¤ ¤

Remember to take bread from the pan as soon as you take it out of the oven and cool it on a rack, out of drafts.

¤ ¤ ¤ ¤ ¤

You get a complete protein when you combine a potato and a milk product.

¤ ¤ ¤ ¤ ¤

Know your grocery store's schedule. Find out what day(s) they get their fresh produce shipments and be aware of when they run the most specials.

¤ ¤ ¤ ¤ ¤

On fall outings be sure and collect pine cones, seedpods and other interesting natural items. Pine cones dipped in a little melted wax makes great fire starters in the fireplace. A basket of these make a pretty gift.

¤ ¤ ¤ ¤ ¤

We also like to make nature wreaths to use over the holidays or take to friends as a gift. Cut a piece of one quarter inch ply wood to the desired shape and size. I usually cut a circle about sixteen inches in diameter with the center cut out. Then coat the board with about one fourth inch thick covering of linoleum paste. This stays soft for quite awhile. Then start putting on your dried materials. Do the outer and inner edges first. I like to use milo, wheat, or tiny pine cones for the edges. Then fill the major portion of the wreath with larger cones and pods, filling in the little nooks and crannies with the tinier objects. Be sure to press each object into the paste well. They are so fun to make and easy, too. After they are completely set and dry, I spray them with a coat of varnish or a sealer of some kind. The many natural shades of brown shine through and are really beautiful. Sometimes we make smaller wreaths out of the centers we removed from the larger wreaths. I use these to stand a big candle in as a centerpiece! (Don't waste a thing, remember?)

¤ ¤ ¤ ¤ ¤

If you are using a natural theme, another pretty wreath can be done the same way, using plywood and linoleum paste. Just outline the board and do a design in rope. Then fill in with different kinds of nuts. Finish by spraying with clear varnish.

¤ ¤ ¤ ¤ ¤

Isn't it funny how one idea or suggestion can trigger another or how, out of necessity, we come up with money and energy-saving hints? We always kept a box of old socks, and when the kids played in the snow, they wore these as mittens. There was always a dry change every now and then, and if one was "holey," they could double up and wear two on that hand. No more cold, wet hands!

¤ ¤ ¤ ¤ ¤

Always cool your pumpkin or custard-type pies on a cooling rack. Never set them directly on a cool, solid surface or your crust will get soggy.

¤ ¤ ¤ ¤ ¤

For a fun after-school or TV snack, mix equal parts of cream cheese and hot pepper jelly and spread on apple slices or crackers.

¤ ¤ ¤ ¤ ¤

Try a split English muffin spread with apple butter and a slice of sharp cheddar cheese popped under the broiler until bubbly — mmm! Good!

¤ ¤ ¤ ¤ ¤

Have you tried dipping dried pear slices in chocolate? Yum!!

¤ ¤ ¤ ¤ ¤

Why not serve a piping hot bowl of chili over mashed potatoes with a sprinkling of grated cheese on top!

¤ ¤ ¤ ¤ ¤

When making apple pie I always drizzle a little real maple syrup into the filling and cut back a little on the sugar! Boy, is that good!

¤ ¤ ¤ ¤ ¤

I guess its the German in me, but have you ever tried my favorite snack — Braunschweiger spread on an apple slice? Terrific !!!!

¤ ¤ ¤ ¤ ¤

Rather than making carameled apples, we like to slice crispy apples into bowls, drizzle with caramel sauce and sprinkle with chopped pecans. A great finger food while watching TV!

November

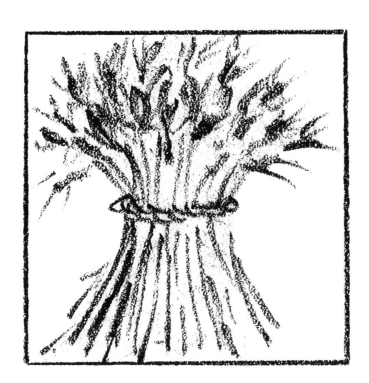

November

As we surround our tables on Thanksgiving Day, I'm sure we will all give our formal thanks for health, happiness and the abundant life we enjoy. But throughout the month, let's stop and reflect on the many simple blessings that are ours every minute of each day.

I'm thankful for the sunshine, each fresh new day that greets me, families, smiles, grandchildren's laughter, the birds, their song, flowers, trees in all forms, crunchy autumn leaves, the moon, the crisp night air, rainbows, fluffy clouds, the smell of woodsy smoke, the freedom to vote, candlelight, a good night's sleep, the honking of the geese,- - - my goodness I could go on all day, but most of all — a loving husband. I'll spend this month really concentrating on how blessed I am. Why don't you do the same? Then let's remind ourselves that when Thanksgiving comes our blessings won't end, and we can continue counting for months to come. What a wonderful winter will lie ahead of us!

Food for Thought

With the holidays just around the corner, many of us are focusing on gifts. I'd like to share with you some thoughts on one of the best gifts that we give ourselves, and that's a friend. We all know that to have a friend we must be one. What would life be without special people in our lives?

About nine years ago Roy and I retired and moved to South Jordan, Utah, to a condo community. We soon realized we were in a little part of "Heaven." Every day is an adventure, learning and sharing with these wonderful people. Each has a unique story to tell, if only we have ears to listen.

It didn't take long to discover the zest for life that LaVon has. Early one morning she was on top of her RV scrubbing and polishing, getting ready for a trip. Her husband says she thinks she's 16 years old, and I believe she does. (She's really in her 70's.) What an attitude!

A person can't help but be motivated as we see June bustling down the street every day at full speed, walking her five miles. The nice part is, she always wears a smile and has a kind word for everyone.

There goes Hal on his bicycle, making the rounds to replace a light bulb on someone's porch or fix a loose hinge on a gate. Where would we be without him?

Vern, next door, recently lost his wife to Alzheimer's, and the love and devotion he showed to her was truly an example to all of us. Such a loving, giving man!

Many of our interests and goals have been developed through these wonderful friends. Sweet Wilma and the wonderful poetry she shares with everyone gives us inspiration. Ruby is always there with encouragement and enthusiasm and helps me feel I can accomplish about anything. We all have times of self-doubt and insecurity. Where would we be without a friend? Don't we all need the stamina and positive outlook of Murhl? She is in her 80's with only 25% of her heart working, and she just bought a new car and is making plans for the holiday dance.

When our young Leona had a brain tumor and extensive surgery, the outpouring of love as well as physical help was unbelievable — a listening ear, a warm hug, a hot meal, a pretty card, a bunch of flowers, but most of all, time, attention, and genuine caring.

Jay, our oldest resident, loves to sing in the church choir and raises his voice in beautiful song each week. It wasn't until several weeks had passed that we learned he was nearly blind and brought a tape recorder to each practice so he could learn the bass part!

Whether it's the quick wit and humor Helen shares with me or the soft spoken kindness LaDonna radiates, I feel loved and blessed with these great people in my area.

Have you looked, listened and learned from your neighbors lately? The interest and love you share with others will reflect back to you a hundredfold.

I read a quote the other day from Anais Nin, "Each friend represents a world in us, a world possibly not born until they arrive and it is only by this meeting that a new world is born." I know the greater part of what I am has been shaped over the years by the friends I have known. Have you paused to think of past friendships lately? Have you told them how much they mean to you? Have you thanked them for lessons learned or apologized for things left unsaid?

We live in such a mobile world today that often we find ourselves many miles away from those we love and were once close to. I have been fortunate to "collect" friendships all over the country through my books, television and radio shows. Gosh, how I treasure the notes and letters I have received. From a simple, "Super recipe — made it for dinner! Thanks!" to a many page letter from a young mother who was discouraged and feeling very inadequate. After watching the show, she felt like she had a friend and a new lease on life. I've heard from her many times now and often on a day when I needed a boost!

A good friend of mine in Cincinnati never missed an opportunity to drop someone a note, and I have tried to emulate her habit. This busy and often cold, uncaring world of ours needs a little sunshine and cheer. Do you hesitate to write a line or two to someone because you think if may sound corny or be misunderstood? Do you say you're too busy? Then you are both missing out. True, the phone is handy, but don't you love to read over and over those words of love, cheer or encouragement?

A while back when my daughter, Kristen, had a new baby I headed to Utah to help out for a few days. When I returned home, I received an envelope in the mail. Much to my surprise it was a poem written by my son-in-law, Mark. An unexpected expression of love. I treasure this poem, framed it, and read it often.

The Unironed Shirts

a birthday poem by mark seethaler
August 18, 1986

The unironed shirts lay in a pile
When my mother-in-law said with a smile
Although it's my birthday, I think I'll pitch in
And help out dear son-in-law, since he is kin

And help out she did, till the pile became small
And played down the praise, "heck, it weren't much at all"
But the shirts that she hung in the closet with care
Sure helped out son-in-law, provided him wear

And her daughter too, she got quite a lift
For with a new baby she needed a shift
From full-time mother, lover and wiff
There just wasn't much she could do in a jiff

But there's more to this story about this jewel of the Midwest
For she did more than shirts, yes she did all the rest
She washed and she cleaned and she played with such zest
That our three oldest children knew she was the best.

And cooking delighted all three when they shared
A bowl and two beaters when cake was prepared
They played her at "Sorry" and played bat and ball
But it's the bears that she brought them they loved best of all

She says she must leave, what a terrible thing
To go back to her home, shows, husband and things
We'll miss her for sure, us and the bears
For we love her a lot and she knows that we care

Do you have a friend, neighbor or family member who could use a note of caring, love or thanks? Simple words mean the most so don't put it off thinking you should be eloquent or clever with words. Just be generous with your praise and feeling. Don't we all love to read nice things about ourselves? Nearly every day I can find something nice to thank or praise someone for. The secret is to do it! I keep a little basket, lined with a pretty doily, filled with note cards, thank you cards and stationery along with some colored pens, address book, and stamps. It makes it much easier than hunting for something to write on or a pen. I can carry my basket out on the patio in the sunshine or in by the cozy fire and my favorite chair to jot a note or two. I even put it in the car when we travel ready to send a thought to someone!

Just a thought, as you are sending those Christmas cards this year, please take the time to add a handwritten note. It will mean so much to many who have made your world a little richer.

I hope you are all keeping those touching notes that you have received over the years. I have a big box of letters I love to read over when I'm feeling down. Some date back to childhood notes from my best friend Suzanne, teenage boy friends, and many choice people along my path in life. I also have a loose-leaf notebook for each of the 23 grand children, using plastic poly-vu page covers. Every note, picture they've drawn me, or letter goes into their book. Some day, I hope they will treasure them. Even now, as teenagers they love to look through them and chuckle at their writings as a 6-year old.

Recently when Roy received a much-needed new wallet for his birthday, I watched as he transferred cards, etc. into the new from the old. A worn, tattered little folded paper fell to the floor, and he blushed as he quickly picked it up. Then with a tear in his eye he shared with me a little poem I had written to him many years ago. It had a special place in every wallet since then. I'm sure it was not a very expertly written poem, and it wasn't long, but it touched his heart. A famous (and wise) British statesman, Edmunde Burke, once said, "Nobody makes a greater mistake than he who did nothing because he could only do a little!"

Now may I offer one little bit of advice — it it's not too late, say thank you today. To Mom for the caring, trust, and love she gave you. To Dad for the hours of playing, working, and being there. To the friend for listening to your troubles, understanding, helping you with projects, and loving you through it all. To the husband, wife, neighbor, or child. Don't wait until tomorrow or later when all there is, is "If only!" Say a big "thank you very much" TODAY!

There are many ways we can bring happiness into the lives of others. Small things like a smile or gentle touch can mean so much.

A little more kindness, a little less creed,
A little more giving, a little less greed.
A little more smile, a little less frown,
A little less kicking a man when he's down.
A little more we and a little less I,
A little more laugh, a little less cry.
A little more flowers on the pathway of life,
And there will be a little less heartache at the end of the strife.

My sister, Maxine, always gathers seeds in the fall from all her plants to carry over until next spring. She recently gave me a little envelope full of these seeds, decorated with a little "cut out" and a label saying "Courtesy Seeds." On the back of the envelope was written —

Sowing — sow with care and kindness. Sow daily with service.
Germination — begin to grow with daily applications of love, understanding and charity.
Cultivation — weed daily all inappropriate thought. Water with determination and commitment.
Maturation — these will be beautiful and rare plants. All the flowers of tomorrow are the seeds of today.

Wouldn't this be a beautiful sentiment and fun idea to use at each plate for your Thanksgiving dinner!

It is such a joy to do nice things for others, especially those in need. But just one word to those on the "receiving end" of good deeds. Don't deprive your friends and loved ones of the joy of sharing. It's been said it's more difficult to receive than to give, but it is also one of the nicest things you can do for someone. Have you ever seen the dejected look in a child's eyes as he tries to share a cookie or favorite toy with someone who brushes him aside and says, "No, that's all right. I don't want it." Nothing breaks my heart more than seeing someone longing to share an exciting bit of news or an enthusiastic idea that falls on deaf ears. Even the sharing and helping that comes from a complete stranger holding the door at the supermarket, offering a seat on a crowded bus, or picking up a package that was dropped, should be met with a smile and a thank you.

Don't deprive others of the joy of sharing. I had a grandmother who had a very hard time receiving anything graciously. She was a happy, fun-loving person, and she loved to give, but just had difficulty accepting. How many times my heart broke because I wanted to do something nice, and she wouldn't accept it. Grandma is gone now, and I wish so much I could have done things for her. She deserved it so! Please, accept pleasantly the little things others do — the bunch of dandelions in a child's hand, a shared cookie, vegetables from their garden, or a helping hand when you're struggling. They will feel good and so will you. It takes so little to make two people happy.

There are so many ways to convey our feelings to friends — the written word, the spoken word, and the simple but powerful influence of touch. This lesson was brought home to me when I was a young mother in Kansas City. Marge was a dynamo of a woman, capable of any task, and a friend to everyone. One day I was feeling especially grateful to her for some things she'd done for me, so on the spur of the moment, I fixed a plate of cookies I had just made, stopped and picked up a few fresh flowers and went by her house. When she came to the door and saw me standing there with my cookies and flowers, tears welled up in her eyes. She invited me in and told me what a special gift that was. Everyone thought Marge could do everything and consequently didn't need anything! I'll never forget her telling me to always remember that even the busiest people need love, and never, ever pre-judge. A valuable lesson learned. The hug I got that day will never be forgotten.

In this busy, pressure-filled world of ours, is there anything more reassuring or comforting than the touch of a loved one's hand? Too often we forget the powerful influence touching can have in our lives.

When that little one slides a tiny hand into yours, it's like a chick cuddling under its mother's wing, warm and soft, saying, "I'm here. Love me and guide me." Suddenly you feel ten feet tall and are on your way to becoming the perfect person he sees you as.

When you and your mate walk down the street and he gently takes your hand in his, a whole lifetime of loving and living passes between you. A complete conversation is carried on with simply a squeeze of the hand.

How much that hand on the shoulder can mean to someone who is about to start a new adventure in life. It seems to say "I care and I know you can do it!"

When a loved one lies in a hospital bed, afraid and trembling, you take his hand and it says, "I love you and everything will be all right."

Holding hands and touching is our very link with life. May we always feel the love of those around us and extend our love by saying, "Here, take my hand."

November Food for Fun
Simple Foods, with Thankfulness in Our Hearts

I think our family looks forward to the stuffing more than the turkey! Its s-o-o-o good!

Delicious Bread Stuffing

Melt: 2 sticks margarine

Add: ¾ c. chopped onion
1 ½ c. chopped celery

Cook until transparent.

Add: 12 c. bread cubes
1 T. salt
1 tsp. pepper
1 T. sage
2 well-beaten eggs
enough broth or hot water to moisten

Mix well. Makes enough for a 12 lb. turkey or serve with other meats. This can be baked in a pan separately for about an hour or placed inside the turkey. Never "stuff" until ready to bake.

¤ ¤ ¤ ¤ ¤

We all look forward to this satisfying, heart-warming chowder after the "big day"!

Thanksgiving Chowder

Fry 8 slices of bacon until crisp. Drain and reserve.

Sauté until tender: ¼ c. bacon grease
                      2 c. chopped onions

Then add: 4 c. chopped potatoes
            ½ c. chopped celery
            2 c. turkey broth
            ½ tsp. salt

Simmer (covered) until potatoes and celery are tender.

Add: 4 c. turkey (cooked and cut up)
       1 can whole kernel corn
       1 can cream-style corn
       1 pint half-and-half
       dash of coarsely ground pepper

Heat thoroughly.

When serving, crumble the bacon on top and sprinkle with a little parsley.

Makes 6-8 servings.

¤   ¤   ¤   ¤   ¤

Whether for a party or a TV snack, we love this shrimp dip with crackers. It is so economical and delicious!

Shrimp Cocktail Dip

Blend together (in a blender):   1 pkg. (8 oz.) softened cream cheese
                                 6 oz. cocktail sauce

Stir in: ½ c. finely chopped celery
         1 c. tiny salad shrimp (or as many as you like)

¤   ¤   ¤   ¤   ¤

A wonderful idea for serving at your next bazaar are these delicious potato toppers. It's a great money maker, and everyone loves baked potatoes. (Your family will love them, too.)

Baked Potato Treats

Italian Potatoes

Prepare sauce of:
- 1 can (6 oz.) tomato paste
- 1 can (8 oz.) tomato sauce
- ¾ c. water
- 1 small chopped onion
- 2 tsp. parsley flakes
- 1 tsp. each basil, oregano, garlic salt
- 1 T. sugar
- 1 c. chopped pepperoni

Simmer sauce about 45 minutes to blend flavors. Top a large baked potato with sauce, chopped green pepper, sliced mushrooms, lots of mozzarella cheese. You can substitute sausage for the pepperoni, and other favorite pizza toppings can be added. Serves 6.

Mexican Potatoes

Brown together:
- 1 lb. ground beef
- 1 small chopped onion

In blender, blend 1 lb. can whole tomatoes with a small can of diced green chilies.

Combine with ground beef in saucepan and add:
- 1 T. sugar
- 1 tsp. cumin
- 1 tsp. chili powder

Heat until sauce is warmed. Pour over baked potato and top with grated cheddar cheese, chopped black olives, crushed corn chips, sour cream or yogurt and guacamole. Serves 6.

Back to Nature Taters

Make a cream topping by combining:
- 1 c. cottage cheese
- ¼ c. water
- 1 T. lemon juice
- dash of salt
- dash of paprika

Whir in blender until smooth and pour over baked potato. Top with chopped green onion and lots of sliced mushrooms.

¤ ¤ ¤ ¤ ¤

Treat those guests over the holidays to a special breakfast. Served with orange juice, a cup of piping hot chocolate and a homemade cinnamon roll, they'll never forget their visit at your house.

Bev's Farmer's Omelet

Fry ½ lb. bacon until crisp in a large skillet. Drain the bacon and set aside.

In the bacon grease (you can pour off some if you like), fry 1 chopped onion.

Then add:
- 2 c. chopped or shredded cooked potatoes
- 1 c. cubed bread (French bread is good)
- ½ c. shredded cheese
- 6 beaten eggs
- salt and pepper to taste

Cook until eggs are set. Add crumbled crisp bacon. Stir in and serve.

¤ ¤ ¤ ¤ ¤

No pumpkin pie is simpler or better than this!

Nye's Pumpkin Pie

Beat together:
- 1 large can (29 oz.) pumpkin
- 1 tsp. salt
- 3 ½ c. milk
- 5 eggs
- 1 1/3 c. white sugar
- 2 ½ tsp. cinnamon
- 1 tsp. ginger
- ½ tsp. cloves

Pour equally into three 9-inch unbaked pie shells. Bake at 425* for 30-40 minutes or until knife comes out clean.

¤ ¤ ¤ ¤ ¤

After the big Thanksgiving dinner has settled and you're ready for an evening treat, try this delicious, refreshing drink.

Holiday Cranberry Cream

In the blender combine:
- 1 c. cranberry juice
- 1 carton (8 oz.) yogurt
- 1 large scoop vanilla ice cream (about ½ c.)

Blend all together and serve with a sprinkling of nutmeg of top.

November Grocery Bag

With lots of holiday baking just around the corner, let's take a closer look at **nuts** this month. A nut is a dry fruit or seed with a hard, separable shell and an edible interior kernel. This applies not only to the common nuts, but to chestnuts, coconuts, and edible seeds like sunflower, pumpkin, and sesame seeds as well. Most nuts have a lot to offer as they are from 10 to 25 percent protein and are a rich source of Vitamin A, iron, thiamine, and phosphorous. The fat portion of nuts is highly unsaturated, in contrast to the saturated fats added to our diet by most other protein foods such as meat, cheese, and eggs. Except for chestnuts, which are only available during the winter months, all other nuts are available in some form year-round.

Nuts are available both shelled and unshelled; however, cashews are never sold in the shell. The shell is a natural container which maintains freshness and preserves nutritional value. The shell also acts as a barrier against chemical processing. A treatment of lye and gas is used on almost all nuts to soften and loosen the shell. In addition, all shells are bleached and some are colored and waxed, but none of this processing can penetrate the shell. Pistachios are an exception, so try to avoid those that are dyed red. Nuts sold in the shell will be the freshest, highest in nutritional value, and free of chemical additives. They are also the least expensive as the work of shelling is passed on to you. I like to keep a bowl of nuts and a nutcracker in the family room readily available for snacking.

Shelled nuts are sold either raw or roasted. Those that are raw will be in pieces, slivers, or whole. Almonds are covered with an outer skin that is edible and acts as a protective coat, but they are usually blanched in a hot-water bath to remove this skin. Once the skins and shells are removed, the nut is left unprotected and is subject to deterioration by light and air. Those sold in see-through bags give us the chance to check the quality, but vacuum-packed cans will protect the nuts for a longer period of time.

"Roasting" is a process of frying the nuts in oil that is continually being heated and reheated, and then they are heavily salted. "Dry roasted" nuts don't have the oil but do have added salt, starch, spices, and in some cases, sugar and preservatives. To roast your own nuts, spread them on a cookie sheet and bake at 350* until lightly browned (5-10 minutes). For more even browning, add a teaspoon of oil per cup of shelled nuts and stir well before spreading on pan.

If properly stored, nuts will last 6-8 months without losing their quality or going rancid. They must be protected from heat, air, and moisture. Keep them in covered jars or containers, out of direct sunlight, and at room temperature. During the summertime, they should be kept in the refrigerator or freezer. Always be sure your containers are air and liquid tight.

There are many ways to use nuts, and because they contain such a large amount of protein, you can add to the quality of protein in your meals by combining them with dried beans, dairy products, and grains. To start with, add a handful of chopped nuts to all your baked goods and sprinkle them on top of cooked cereals and puddings. Also try adding them to your stuffing for meats and poultry, especially your Thanksgiving turkey. Use sunflower seeds to add a little "crunch" to all of your salads, and stir them into your rice and vegetable dishes. The possibilities are endless, and nuts are so good for you!

We'll start seeing lots of **cranberries** in the stores this month, and Thanksgiving dinner wouldn't be complete without them. I always associate these bright red berries with the festivities of the holidays that are just around the corner, and there are many ways to use them.

Try making your own cranberry sauce this year by combining 4 cups of fresh cranberries, 1 ½ cups water, and 2 cups of sugar in a saucepan. Bring to a boil rapidly for about 5 minutes (or longer, depending on how thick you like you sauce). Serve as it is or chill it, and it will become jelly-like. It's so simple and a lot more flavorful than commercially prepared cranberry sauce. To vary the flavor, try adding a few whole cloves and a cinnamon stick or some grated lemon peel while the berries are cooking.

Cranberries are also delicious chopped and added to nut breads, cookies, muffins and salads. For a delicious raw cranberry relish, mix some chopped orange sections with chopped cranberries and sweeten to taste with a little honey or sugar. I'm so glad to see cranberries coming on in abundance (and reasonable in price) because they are so good for everyone. They're full of vitamins and a great tonic for the kidneys. They freeze well and can be ground or chopped right from the freezer.

Speaking of your freezers, remember you can freeze many of the items you'll be needing for the holidays, so take advantage of any sales you see now to stock up on **freezeable items** you'll be using later on. Just be sure anything you freeze is tightly sealed in its package. All the following freeze well: all nuts, raisins and all dried fruits, potato chips and all other type chips and cracker snacks, bread products, casseroles (leave out any potatoes or pasta as they tend to get mushy, and add when serving), all candies, cereals, pies (I like to freeze mine before baking — they taste fresher), all cakes and cupcakes, cookies, nut breads, soups, cheeses, and whipped cream.

At our house, November signals the beginning of one of our favorite times of year, and I can hardly wait to start baking all those goodies that are so irresistible as we come in out of the cold after an afternoon of raking leaves or watching a football game.

There are still lots of **pumpkins** around. Use them also for a lot of good nutrition for your family. Just cut them into chunks, scoop out the seeds and bake the pieces on a cookie sheet at 375* until tender. Serve hot with butter and salt and pepper. It makes a delicious vegetable. The pieces can also be covered with water, boiled until tender, then mashed or "smooshed" in the blender to use in pies, breads or cakes.

Please don't throw away the seeds when you use your pumpkins. Did you know that they are 29% protein, compared to only 20% in a porterhouse steak? It's so easy to roast them. Rinse them well in a colander, then simmer them in salted water (2 T. salt to 1 qt. water) about 20 minutes and pat dry; or simply salt them, then spread on a cookie sheet and bake for about 20 minutes. Be careful not to burn them. I give them a stir every now and then. They are delicious as well as being full of vitamins and protein.

Watch for some good canned goods specials this month; also specials on pork and turkey. The new crops of beans and rice should be on the market now and are a terrific bargain in price and nutrition.

Be careful using coupons. Too many homemakers are tempted to buy nutritionless, empty-calorie foods just because they have a coupon for a few cents off. It's still cheaper to buy good, wholesome food, and your family will feel better, too. Put on a pot of soup, and sit down and plan your grocery list with good health and happy eating in mind. We'll beat those high prices yet!

November Why Didn't I Think of That?

To "liven" up those canned green beans, I give them a shake of seasoning salt, a few onion flakes and a drop or two of liquid smoke!

¤ ¤ ¤ ¤ ¤

In your winter car kit, along with the ice scraper, spare gloves etc., keep an old-fashioned blackboard eraser. It's great to wipe the moisture off the windows.

¤ ¤ ¤ ¤ ¤

Stop saying, "What ever happened to…" and go find out!

¤ ¤ ¤ ¤ ¤

My friend, Wilma, once sent me an idea to get your home and yourself in good shape. "Stretch when you shine, hop when you mop, and wiggle when you wax. Soon you'll be neat as a pin and just as thin!"

¤ ¤ ¤ ¤ ¤

"Treat your family like company and your company like family!"

¤ ¤ ¤ ¤ ¤

A few mothballs between your window and storm window should chase away the bugs and spider webs.

¤ ¤ ¤ ¤ ¤

"God has two dwellings — one in Heaven and the other in a thankful heart." Izaak Walton

¤ ¤ ¤ ¤ ¤

Be a friend. Instead of "Call me if you need me," or "Let me know if I can do anything," be there and do it.

¤ ¤ ¤ ¤ ¤

"It's not the schilling I give you that counts, but the warmth that it carries with it from my hand."

¤ ¤ ¤ ¤ ¤

"It profits little to bury the hatchet and leave the handle sticking out."   Dwight L. Moody

¤   ¤   ¤   ¤   ¤

Even a strong man cannot lift himself.

December

December

This is the month to live in the spirit of the season! I often hear people comment that they dread the holidays or just wish they would hurry and pass so life could return to "normal." What a shame!

Now is the time to return to the true spirit and meaning of this beautiful time of year. Not costly gifts, but genuine feelings of sharing, loving and giving. Think back to when you were a child — the most cherished holiday memories are never tied up with expense but with the warmth and caring of loved ones. Our favorite memories are the simple things — the smells of cookies and gingerbread, the scent of ashes and wood, the crunching of snow beneath our feet, the comfy old quilts brought from the cedar chest, and the laughter of our loved ones around us.

The most important thing you can give your family and friends is "happy memories." Material things come and go, but happy times linger in our hearts and minds forever. We are all so blessed! Let's make this a season of sharing, and if you have nothing to share but your smile, give it to everyone you see!

Food for Thought

We all have times of the year that we cherish. December is that time for our family. As the years roll by, experiences become traditions and then even more important. As we share them with others, we've laughed, shed tears, and shared many hours of conversation reflecting on what this month means to our family and friends. May you feel the warmth of the holiday season as we share them with you.

Our son, Stephen, will always treasure our gingerbread house tradition. Every year after Thanksgiving we gathered as a family and made these fun houses. Everyone used their own creativity — there were pretzels for fences, marshmallows for snow men, rock candy for fireplaces, licorice swing sets, cotton for smoke on the chimneys, jelly bean and mint sidewalks, cookie wafers to make a sled, animal crackers for pets, and of course, our standard icicles hanging from the roof. Before Christmas we chose several of our houses and took them to special friends as we went caroling (it's fun to put their house number on the front door of the gingerbread house with icing). On New Year's Day, between watching ball games (another tradition) Stephen took our gingerbread house outside and placed it in a tree. How much fun we had watching the birds enjoy our Christmas gift to them! They pecked away at the gingerbread and occasionally even peeked in the little door or window! Nothing ever went to waste. If you plan to include the birds in your family experience, you can use bird seed, pieces of dried fruit and bread and cracker crumbs as your decorate your house. The fragrant aroma of the gingerbread baking, the fun and laughter you share as you "create," the beauty and scent it adds to you home for the holidays, and finally the sharing with nature makes this one of the most memorable traditions you can enjoy with your family. (If you have tiny children in your family, they can use graham crackers to build their houses.)

Stephen enjoys this project so much he has been known to do Valentine houses, spring flower cottages and even haunted houses for Halloween (for these he makes uneven pieces of gingerbread for his house parts, even burning part of them. Then there are cob webs, scare crows, bails of hay from shredded wheat, and even bats made from opening a pitted prune and putting an almond in the middle for a body!) Isn't it amazing what one little idea done with your family can grow into?

Roy and I still treasure a plastic star decorated with nail polish and sequins. It was our first Christmas ornament, given to us by sweet little, 80-year old, Mrs. Lane who was our landlady. We were newly married, in the Army, and stationed at Fort Lewis Washington with hardly a dime to our name. Our "star" has a place of honor in our home every Christmas.

Each year as we start our Christmas baking, the list comes out and there is not one item we want to delete. As I press Grandma Scheel's butter cookies with the tines of a fork, I can see that big crock she kept hidden under the staircase filled with these yummy treats. Cinnamon rolls and caramel pecan rolls raising on the counter take me back to Mom's farm kitchen in Nebraska. My "grown" grandson, Christian, still loves them the best. He was my buddy baking rolls and would watch through the oven window in awe as they "poofed" up. Some day I know he'll be sharing this with his children!

Grandson Nathan wouldn't pass up a visit to our house just for our chocolate raisin clusters. As he grew older, they were always included in a gift box mailed to him. Now, he can make them!

Mark always prefers the Christmas fudge and toffee, Kristen insists on the Date Delight (see July recipes), and Heidi loves to decorate sugar cookies (see February recipes). It wouldn't be Christmas without Roy's mint sandwich cookies, and my favorites are the chocolate-covered nuts, so — our list continues! Each recipe brings memories of someone's love into our kitchens!

One of our friends gives everyone is their family new nightgowns and PJ's to be modeled on Christmas Eve. I'll never forget the Christmas many years ago when our son Mark, age 4, insisted he wanted a night shirt and cap for Christmas! He was an avid story lover, and I guess he picked up the idea from a story. I stayed up nights sewing a red checked nightshirt with matching cap, and he wore them with pride until they were threadbare.

We are all part of this wonderful, big world, and I love the idea of including traditions from other lands and cultures. We've learned about the Menorah, spun Driedles, sung Feliz Navidad in Spanish and O' Tannenbaum in German, and enjoyed our advent wreath, lighting a white candle each Sunday before Christmas and a red one on Christmas Day. Invite friends and neighbors over and have them share their traditions and culture with you. You'll learn so much and may start a new idea growing at your house. Our grandson, Jake, is in Holland as I am writing, and I'm sure we'll be including "wooden shoes" in our Christmas celebration next year as he returns home.

When our daughter, Kristen, married Mark she joined with him in one of his traditions of ringing sleigh bells on Christmas morning to wake the family. We now enjoy that fun time with them each year.

One of the ideas we started when our children got married was to give them each a special place setting for their first Christmas. This doesn't have to be expensive China; we've even used a bright, cheery red unbreakable setting. This one special setting is used for Johnny for a good report card, Dad when he has a special happening at work, or even for Mom when she's had a hard day. They have all enjoyed this tradition and use that place setting often. Roy and I have one, too, and it's such a nice, sweet surprise when he sets the table and gives me the special plate with a kiss to cheer me up!

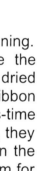

As you know, I believe in using lots of turkey and chicken in my meal planning. So I heartily recommend a wishbone basket to everyone — we save the wishbones each time a chicken or turkey is prepared. When they have dried well, we rub them with a little sandpaper, paint them white, and tie a red ribbon on the top of each one. I keep them in a basket under our tree at Christmas-time along with a ballpoint pen. As each guest comes to visit over the holidays, they write their name on a wishbone, make a wish for themselves, and tie it on the tree. We take the wishbones off when we take down the tree and keep them for next year, adding new ones each year. It is so fun as we hang the wishbones from Christmases past to reflect on each guest and the fun time we had.

This year with 23 grandchildren, we drew names and set a one dollar limit. Now I realize today that might not seem like much, but we were absolutely amazed at the cleverness and ingenuity that went into those gifts. After a chili supper, a night of caroling (we felt like the Tabernacle Choir!), and opening those fun gifts, it was one of our best Christmases ever.

Of course, our most important tradition, and one we have done for 50 years now, is on Christmas Eve to sit by the fireplace and candlelight and have Roy read the Christmas story found in Luke from the old family Bible.

I really love spending this month preparing for the holidays. Getting ready for Christmas is really the best part. This is a lesson we can learn from the little ones. They will soon forget the toys and gifts they receive, but they long remember the paper chains they worked so hard cutting and pasting, the pencil holder they labored over in Cub Scout meeting, the pin cushion made for mommy, or the plaster hand print they painted in pretty bright colors. These gifts are the magic of Christmas, truly coming from the heart (and a few hammered thumbs, pricked fingers and stained hands.)

Stringing popcorn and cranberries is something everyone can do. Use the largest needle you have and heavy "carpet" thread. Buy yellow popcorn to pop because the kernels are larger and not quite as tender as the white variety. Then after Christmas be sure to set your tree out in the backyard with the strings still on for the birds to enjoy.

Christmas wouldn't be complete without a pomander ball. I have a bowl of them in the living room. They smell so good. You'd better make them right away, because they need a few weeks to age. Start with a medium-sized orange (not thin-skinned). Begin sticking the stems of whole cloves in the orange until it is completely covered. (If you have trouble piercing the orange, you can poke the holes with a knitting needle first.) Then roll the balls in cinnamon, or equal parts of orrisroot and cinnamon, until well coated. Let set in a warm, dry place. When it's dry, shake off the excess powder and decorate with a bow if desired. I like to use them plain in a pretty bowl. Lemons and apples can be done this way, too.

Something that is a little more work, but something you'll love and use often, is a Christmas table top. It is simply a large circle cut of masonite or plywood to fit over the top of your card table. Clean the board well and then cover with and glue on pretty Christmas cards in a patchwork pattern or a design that you prefer. When the top is completely covered and the glue is dry, coat it with several coats of shellac, varnish or poly coat. (You can get a varnish that is hot and cold resistant if you will be serving food on it.) These table tops are so pretty and useful. You'll receive many compliments. Be sure to hang it up for storage so that it doesn't warp.

The candle that I think is the prettiest is the old-fashioned ice candle. To make these you start with a half-gallon waxed milk carton. Wash it out well, dry it, set a 10" table candle in the center and completely surround it to the top of the carton with coarsely cracked ice cubes. Then quickly pour 1 ½ pounds of melted paraffin wax over the ice. Let it cool for about an hour, then cut away the carton. These can be decorated with a sprig of holly or tiny flower on the side, or a pretty ribbon or bow. Let your imagination guide you. They are so pretty as they burn.

Do you make Christmas candy wreaths at your house? Kids love making these (and eating them, too). Just get a 10" foam wreath, a couple of boxes of flat wooden toothpicks, and a good supply of gumdrops or candy kisses and let them begin. Break the toothpicks in half. Push a piece of candy on the end of the pick and then push the rest of the pick into the wreath. The paper-wrapped hard candies work well, too. You'll be surprised at the pretty designs they come up with. Add a big bow and your wreath is ready to hang by the door for those hungry little visitors.

I would like to suggest a very special gift for someone you love. Why not write your life story? It will be very satisfying and therapeutic for you and a prized legacy for whoever receives it. Tell about your childhood — favorite games, toys, clothing, memories of activities on holidays, stories of family members, lessons you've learned in life, and an expression of feelings and love for your loved ones!

Kits are a neat gift to give (and receive!) and can be made to fit any personality. Try a letter-writing kit including stationery or tablet, envelopes, stamps, a new address book, and a new pen for a student or grandmother. Try a dress-up kit including old dresses, hats, scarves, jewelry, and shoes for a little girl. Or a banana split kit including a variety of toppings, nuts, bananas, ice cream, long-handled spoons, and banana split boats for the ice cream lover. A spice kit is a favorite of any cook, young or old, male or female. Include a variety of whole spices, a grater, and a mortar & pestle. Just consider the interest of the person it's for, and I'm sure you'll be able to concoct dozens of kits — it's easy!

Living plants are always appreciated. The thoughtful friendship expressed through them lasts long after the hustle and bustle of the holiday season is over. A favorite among many is the bright red "flowered" poinsettia. The flowering poinsettia plant was brought into the United States over 100 years ago from Mexico. It's been incorporated into holiday decorating ever since.

I've recently learned to appreciate orchids. They really are easy to grow and take care of and now are quite inexpensive. Just buy them from a reputable flower shop and follow their instructions. With the right varieties, you can have blooming orchids nearly all year long.

The Christmas cactus, along with narcissus and hyacinth bulbs which are planted indoors, bloom during the holiday season. They all add an air of festivity to any décor. Long ago laurel and rosemary, now used mostly in cooking, were commonly used as Christmas plants. Evergreens — holly, mistletoe, and ivy — have been symbols of life since before Christ. Most people in the U.S. do not think of ivy as a Christmas plant. This is a popular tradition in England. An old English custom, brought out in the traditional English carol, "The Holly and the Ivy," portrays holly as masculine and ivy as feminine.

Making a terrarium for gift-giving would be an enjoyable activity for any family. Using any of the Christmas plants would be an unusual and appreciated gift. If holly is used, remember that holly sprigs do not have roots, so they will only last a few weeks, but they can easily be replaced with other plants.

Ever since the night of Christ's birth, animals as well as birds have played an important part in the celebration of Christmas. In many countries in Europe, animals receive gifts (usually in the form of extra food) at Christmas. Let's not forget them here. In the Scandinavian countries, there is a tradition of giving the winter birds a "bird pole." The farmers save tall sheaves of grain after the fall harvest, tie them together and set them out for the birds to enjoy. An attractive way to decorate our yards and feed the birds at the same time is to follow this Scandinavian tradition. We need to remember to maintain the tree throughout the winter, though, because the birds can easily become dependent on it. If you don't have access to a yard with trees, take a few minutes and make a "bird pole" by filling a large flower pot with soil, stones, or sand and arranging a bunch of sturdy branches in the container. Evergreen branches are good to use.

When feeding our feathered friends, there are a few important rules to remember. The two most important items in a bird's winter diet are fat and seeds. They generally love bread, but bread will not produce body heat, and birds will freeze to death if their diet is not balanced. Birds also love peanut butter, but make certain it is mixed with over twice as much seed as peanut butter. Also make sure that fruit is in balance with the rest of their diet. Too much of this can also cause health problems. Most birds prefer cooked fat (i.e. bacon fat that has re-hardened). A string of cranberries looks pretty and adds color, but it will be eaten much better if pieces of apple are alternated with the cranberries. The key is to remember that birds need a balanced diet just like we do, and replace things as they are eaten. Also remember that birds have different eating habits, so place the variety on sturdy branches as well as the outer limbs. You'll have a happy yard and happy hearts knowing you shared the Christmas spirit.

So many of our single friends, young and old, appreciate being remembered but seem to be swamped with goodies for a day or two at Christmastime and then forgotten. We came up with a couple of ideas that we have lots of fun with. We often buy a pretty calendar for the new year and take it to our friend with a small plate of cookies. Then on the 25th of each month of the new calendar is written a treat to expect — maybe a piece of cherry pie in February or some fried chicken in July. This way the pleasure is spread out for them with something to look forward to, and it's no trouble to include that item in my dinner preparation (just remember to keep a list for yourself!)

Oftentimes we select a single person or lonely couple and play Christmas pixies for the twelve days of Christmas (secretly). On the 14th of December after a knock on the door, they might find a package and a note that says, "On the first day of Christmas what does Mrs.____see? A potted plant as pretty as can be." The next day, "two lovely candles...." Continue with 4 ornaments, 5 flowers, 6 little soaps, 7 cookies, 8 candy canes, and on to Christmas with a stocking filled with 12 little gifts — gum, stamps, jelly, etc. I promise you it will be a Christmas they will long remember. Roy and I still have precious memories of little Mrs.

Murphy, next door, trying so hard to catch those "pixies!" It takes so little money to give so much love to someone. Choose your gifts wisely!

After the shopping is done and the gifts are made, it's time for some creative gift-wrapping. One of our prettiest Christmases I wrapped everything in brown paper bags, cut up, then tied each package with strips of bright calico and gingham fabrics cut with a pinking shears. It looked so cheerful and fit right in with our pioneer theme. Some other ideas to use for wrapping are: use the Sunday comics and a bright red bow for a child, a brown paper bag (cut up) with a brown velvet ribbon and small pine cones, a road map with a tiny road sign on a toothpick on top for a man's gift, the financial page tied with a gold ribbon and a gold seal, and old sheet music for a music lover. Toy paper dollars glued together with a few pennies pasted to the ribbon in a great way to wrap a penny bank. Fabric tied with rick-rack or yarn with spools of thread attached wraps a nice sewing gift. Aluminum foil is a good way to wrap an odd shape. If the gift is just too big to wrap, we always wrap up a little package with a note inside saying, "Look inside the closet," or "on the front lawn" or whatever. Or maybe send them on a treasure hunt. Sometimes the note just says, "Close your eyes and think sweet thought, my dear. When you open your eyes, a nice gift will appear." Then we bring in the gift and set it in front of them. Have fun personalizing your gifts!

We all love to see Santa arriving with his bag of goodies, but my favorite visitor is the mailman with greetings from our scattered friends and family. None of us get too thrilled over the "signature only" cards or the endless pages of wonderful accomplishments, but isn't it fun to see a picture of the new baby or art work by a grandchild, a little poem cleverly written, a family favorite recipe or highlights of an interesting trip?

Everyone looks forward to the Christmas letters written by our son-in-law, Mark. He picks a theme each year and the letter is done in that perspective. One was written from their dog, Clayton's, view and started with, "Dear Human-kind." Another was from the Seethaler Team (a word from the coach). There was the "Annual Report" with "receivables," "liabilities," and "transactions." When they moved into a new home, their letter featured a picture of their house with each one's picture in a window; the letter was their reactions to the move. One of my favorites was "The Wanderers" with a brief report of their gallivanting! Mark's letter is always just one page, easy to read, and includes a picture, drawing, or visual of some type. I have received phone calls from people upset because they missed his letter!

If you have a few pictures you'd like to share with friends, why not make a collage or grouping on a page. These can be copied well, reduced if necessary, or made even more fun with little captions. Oftentimes sharing a memory with a dear friend means more than a year-long report. Reminisce about that special time together. Stay in touch with loved ones in a meaningful way this year!

Just a word about Bazaars. I'm sure at this time of year you may be involved in this activity. At your first meeting, the date, time, place and theme should be decided. Also, set your budget. Assign chairmen and make decisions on items to sell. 1) Is it worth spending money on? 2) How much could it sell for and what profit would be made. 3) Will it look professional? (You don't want any poorly made items, and this could require diplomacy!) Plan your bazaar with the local weather in mind, also convenience in location, traffic and parking. Decide what your community's needs are, the age of your shoppers, and some of the things that make your area unique.

Christmas décor booths, of course, are always popular, but other ideas are — baby and children's booths. Parents and grandparents love finding quilts, bibs, clothing, towels, wall décor, mobiles and toys. White elephant tables are always successful. There is always something for everyone, and who doesn't love a bargain. Remember, "One man's trash is another man's treasure." Set your prices low here. Since everything is usually donated, you should get a good "return" on this booth. Plant and flower booths are lots of fun. Many "starts" can come from one plant, and pots can be decorated and trimmed in many ways. The needlework booth is usually the most popular. These items can be time-consuming, but many women enjoy sewing, knitting, embroidery etc. Those who don't can be involved in collecting and donating yarn, fabric pieces, patterns, etc. and by packaging the finished items. Include a wide range of merchandise from simple pot holders to quilts and hand-knit sweaters. Feature the talents of your group.

Most importantly, have fun together. I remember many strong bonds of friendship built while working on bazaars in the past — friends I will always cherish.

I know this will be a busy, busy month for all of us, no matter if we're young or old, single or with families. Let's all resolve to just do our best and then have no regrets. We have had a wonderful year, filled with sunshine. President Howard W. Hunter gave us some wonderful thoughts to end this year and begin anew on a bright new year. "Mend a quarrel. Seek out a forgotten friend. Dismiss suspicion and replace it with trust. Write a letter. Give a soft answer. Encourage youth. Manifest your loyalty in word and deed. Keep a promise. Forgo a grudge. Forgive an enemy. Apologize. Try to understand. Examine your demands on others. Think first of someone else. Be kind. Be gentle. Laugh a little more. Express your gratitude. Welcome a stranger. Gladden the heart of a child. Take pleasure in the beauty and wonder of the earth. Speak your love and then speak it again." Wonderful words to live by!

Thanks so much for spending this time with me. Let's "Keep our faces toward the sunshine and let the shadows fall behind us."

December Food for Fun
Happy, Holiday Eating!

This is so fun to do with the kids.

Our "Veggie" Christmas Tree

Cover a large piece of cardboard with aluminum foil.

With the tip of a spoon lightly draw the outline of a Christmas tree, nearly covering the board. Fill in the "tree" with a vegetable dip, spreading carefully with a knife.

Then start covering the "spread" with small pieces of fresh vegetables — broccoli, cherry tomatoes, tiny carrot strips, red and green pepper pieces, etc., to create a "tree."

As each person picks up a little veggie, it already has some dip on it! Fun, and pretty to serve!

¤ ¤ ¤ ¤ ¤

I first tasted this treat in the Amish country in Pennsylvania. After that first bite, I was sold. It's a nice addition to a holiday appetizer table.

Pickled Ham Salat

Cut 2 lbs. boneless pre-cooked ham into one-inch cubes (remove any fat).

Combine with:
- 1 T. pickling spice
- 2 ½ c. water
- 2 c. white vinegar
- 2 diced onions
- ¼ tsp. coarsely ground black pepper

Place in a covered container (not metal) and refrigerate for 24 hours. This is a good keeper.

¤ ¤ ¤ ¤ ¤

Isn't it fun to have tasty treats made ahead to serve holiday guests? This is a real delight and so pretty to slice on your dessert tray.

Festive Holiday Bread

Cream together: ½ c. Butter Flavor Crisco
¾ c. brown sugar

Beat in: 2 eggs
3 sliced, ripe bananas

Then add: 2 c. flour
1 tsp. soda
1 tsp. baking powder

Stir in: ¾ c. chopped nuts
½ c. chocolate chips
1/3 c. finely chopped dates
1/3 c. chopped maraschino cherries

Pour into two nut-bread pans (7 1/2 x 3 1/4 inch).

Bake at 350* for 30-40 minutes. Cool, wrap, and let sit overnight before slicing.

¤ ¤ ¤ ¤ ¤

Try this new and different drink to go with your delicious cookies and nut breads. YUM!

Hot Cranberry Float

In a saucepan, bring to a boil:
- 1 c. water
- 6 T. brown sugar
- dash of salt
- dash of nutmeg
- ¼ tsp. cinnamon
- ¼ tsp. allspice
- ½ tsp. cloves

Simmer together for 5 minutes.

In a blender, combine:
- 1 can (16 oz.) jellied cranberry sauce
- 2 c. unsweetened pineapple juice

Then add cranberry blend to sugar mixture.

Add: 3 c. water

Bring all ingredients to a boil and serve hot with a dab of butter on top (be sure to use real butter.)

¤ ¤ ¤ ¤ ¤

Our holidays would never be complete without "toasting" with a cup of Syllabub. It is absolutely delicious. (I'm told this was a favorite treat of Thomas Jefferson, and that's good enough for Roy!)

Syllabub

In a large container, stir together:
- 2 ¾ c. apple cider
- 1/3 c. sugar
- ½ c. milk
- ¾ tsp. vanilla
- a dash of salt

Then whip 1 pint heavy whipping cream.

Gently whisk the cream into the liquid mixture and store in the refrigerator.

Each time you serve it, "whisk" it well again and top each cup with a grating of fresh nutmeg!

¤ ¤ ¤ ¤ ¤

If you have any "dunkers" in your family, this will be a favorite. It is an old German recipe — spicy and good!

Aunt Minnie's Pepper Nuts

Combine: 1 c. dark Karo syrup
             1 c. sugar moistened with 3 oz. hot water
             ½ c. Crisco
             ½ tsp. baking powder
             1/8 tsp. each of salt, pepper and soda
             ¼ tsp. each of cinnamon, cloves, allspice, ginger, nutmeg, cardamon, vanilla, lemon extract and anise seed
             2 tsp. coriander seen or 1 tsp. ground coriander
             4 ½ c. flour
             ¼ c. milk

Mix all together, and let stand, covered, in the refrigerator overnight.

Roll out like a one-inch thick stick on a floured board and cut diagonally in 1 ½ inch pieces.

Bake at 350* for 10 minutes.

Let set out until hard as desired, and then store in tightly covered jars or cans. They keep for a long time.

¤ ¤ ¤ ¤ ¤

I like to add these to a tray of candies. They are colorful and tasty.

Dipped Pretzels

Dip each pretzel (the twists, not the sticks) in melted chocolate or white chocolate. Shake off excess and let harden on waxed paper. Then drizzle red, green, white or chocolate (melted pieces) across each pretzel with the tines of a fork.

¤ ¤ ¤ ¤ ¤

We couldn't share our favorite family recipes without these. But be sure to make plenty — they disappear in a hurry!

Ritzy Chocolate Wafers

Melt chunk chocolate over very low heat in a heavy pan.

Add a few drops of flavoring to taste. (For mint, use peppermint oil from the drug store. It has a much more pleasant and intense flavor than extract and takes only a couple of drops. We also like orange extract or cherry-almond.)

Then dip Ritz crackers into chocolate, one at a time. Using tweezers (that's right) turn cracker, shake off excess chocolate, and place cracker on a plastic wrap-lined cookie sheet.

Let cool so chocolate hardens.

¤ ¤ ¤ ¤ ¤

These are always a hit!

Dipped Apricots

Simply melt chocolate over low heat. Then take each dried apricot half and gently dip half in the chocolate. Shake off excess and lay on waxed paper to harden.

¤ ¤ ¤ ¤ ¤

Everyone can do this, and it's so yummy.

White Chocolate Bark

Melt white chocolate over low heat. Stir in any combination of almonds, dried cranberries, pecans, macadamias, etc. Spread mixture on a cookie sheet lined with waxed paper and let harden. Break into pieces and serve.

¤ ¤ ¤ ¤ ¤

These are a little messy to make, but ooh! So good to eat! It really helps to have two people working together.

Christmas "Twigs"

Use the "rod" pretzels that are about 8 inches long.

Dip pretzel into melted caramel, leaving about 2 inches plain on the end to hold on to. Lay on waxed paper to harden.

Then dip into melted chocolate, shake off excess and roll in chopped nuts (always leaving the end plain). Again, lay on waxed paper to harden.

You'll get the hang of it after one or two and will be so glad you did!!

¤ ¤ ¤ ¤ ¤

A delicious favorite filling for cakes, cookies or small cream puffs drizzled with chocolate.

Orange Filling

Beat together until thick: 3 c. whipping cream
3 cans (6 oz. each) orange juice concentrate
½ c. sugar

Can be made in thirds.

¤ ¤ ¤ ¤ ¤

If you like chocolate like I do, this cheesecake is "to die for." I believe Cameron could eat the whole thing!

Chocolate Cheesecake

For chocolate crumb crust, combine: 1 ½ c. vanilla wafer crumbs (very fine)
½ c. powdered sugar
1/3 c. cocoa
1/3 c. melted margarine

Smoosh into a 9" springform pan.

Beat until fluffy: 3 pkgs. (8 oz. each) softened cream cheese

Gradually beat in: 1 can (14 oz.) sweetened condensed milk

Beat until smooth. Add: 2 c. melted chocolate chips
4 eggs
2 tsp. vanilla

Mix well. Pour into pan on top of crust.

Bake at 300* for 1 hour and 5 minutes or until center is set.

Cool. Chill.

Serve with raspberries and a dollop of whipped cream.

December Grocery Bag

We will all be doing more grocery shopping than usual this month with the holidays, entertaining, and the busy pace we will be keeping. Remember to avoid all those high cost, so-called convenience things for quick meals. Plan ahead and keep a big kettle of stew, soup, chili or chowder in the refrigerator. If you are buying lots of fresh fruits, vegetables, and nuts, team up with a neighbor or two and go to your nearest wholesale supplier. You'll be amazed what you will save on a box of oranges, apples, etc.

This month take advantage of the great buys on **citrus fruits** — oranges, grapefruit, tangerines, and lemons. It's been said that vitamin C plays an important part in preventing colds, so that gives us even more reason to add more citrus fruit to our diets this winter. One medium orange contains at least the minimum daily requirement for vitamin C and has only 75 calories.

Not only are **oranges** delicious just to peel and eat, there are also lots of ways to use the sections, juice and peel in recipes. Did you know that squeezing fresh orange juice into your fruit salad will bring out the sweetness of the fruit and eliminate the need to add sugar? Think of the calories you can save by taking advantage of their natural sweetness.

If you prefer a sweet dressing for your fruit salads, try blending ½ c. mayonnaise with ¼ c. light corn syrup. Then add 2 T. fresh orange juice and 1 T. finely grated orange peel. Finally fold in ½ c. whipped cream and ¼ tsp. nutmeg; pour over fruit and mix well. This makes about 1 ¼ cups of dressing.

Our favorite way to eat **grapefruit** is simply halved and sectioned. But using our imaginations, there are lots of delicious grapefruit "toppers" right in the cupboard. Try brown sugar, molasses, powdered sugar, or honey on top; or mix a tablespoon of maple syrup with a dash of cinnamon and nutmeg and stick under the broiler for a few seconds. Let your family experiment, and you'll come up with many more.

When grapefruit is at its lowest price, we buy it by the case to freeze. It's a great family activity as it involves a lot of work for just one person — the more hands, the faster and more fun it is! We divide the jobs — one halves the fruit, one cuts the sections, one scoops sections out and puts them in jars, and another squeezes in the juice from the empty halves. You don't have to add anything else — just be sure to leave room in the jar for expansion while freezing.

Look for grapefruit that seem heavy for their size. Thin-skinned fruit is juicier, and the coarser the skin, the thicker it tends to be. Except for large soft spots, skin defects usually aren't an indication of what lies inside. A wrinkled and rough skin, however, tends to indicate tough, dry fruit. Store your grapefruit in a cold room or refrigerator, and they'll usually keep two to four weeks.

Tangerines are a pretty addition to your fruit bowl, and children love them because they are so easy to peel. Look for brightly-colored fruit with loose-fitting skin (they won't feel firm). Avoid those that are very pale or have skin punctures. For a delicious holiday pancake syrup, melt ½ c. butter or margarine in a saucepan and add 2 T. grated tangerine peel. Stir in 1 c. of maple syrup. Peel 3-4 tangerines, section and seed them, and add to syrup. Cover and let simmer 5 minutes. Then serve warm over your favorite pancakes or waffles. This is so easy to make, it doesn't need to be reserved just for "company" – treat your family to a special breakfast while they are home on vacation. Don't forget to remind Santa to drop a few tangerines in each of the kid's stockings as a wholesome "goodie!"

Always try to keep a few **lemons** on hand as they can add lots of "zip" to your meals! Lemons keep well in the refrigerator for at least two weeks. Look for rich yellow color and smooth skin. Those that are heavy for their size usually have the most juice. Avoid those that have hard or shriveled skin and soft spots, punctures, or mold. Before you use a lemon, place it in warm water for five or ten minutes. Then roll it around on the counter with the palm of your hand. This way you'll be sure to get all of the juice — sometimes twice as much as you'd get from a hard lemon.

For your baking needs buy in bulk, also, and avoid all those pre-mixed packages. They really don't save much time, and you are so limited. There are oodles of delicious recipes that are simple to make, good for you and much cheaper.

The vegetables to plan on are broccoli, cabbage, yams, cauliflower and parsnips. Potatoes will be a good buy, also. Of course, there will be specials on turkeys, hams and pork in the meat department, but plan to extend your meat dollars with the plentiful grains and beans. By combining a small amount of meat, cheese, or grain with dried legumes (beans, etc.) you gain the complete protein with all the amino acids.

Shop wisely and enjoy those healthy meals this month.

December Why Didn't I Think of That?

When I'm baking, I always use my extra oven rack as a cooling rack on my kitchen counter. If you're desperate for extra cooling space, a muffin pan turned upside down works great, too.

¤ ¤ ¤ ¤ ¤

Leftover frosting spread between graham crackers makes a yummy, quick treat. Chocolate frosting with a "hint" of mint extract is terrific. Heidi liked these so much, she thought I should make frosting just for these treats!

¤ ¤ ¤ ¤ ¤

If you are making cookies or a cake recipe that calls for raisins, set the raisins in your preheating oven to warm through before adding to the batter. This will keep them from sinking to the bottom.

¤ ¤ ¤ ¤ ¤

When baking in glass, always lower the temperature 25 degrees.

¤ ¤ ¤ ¤ ¤

When making a recipe, I always read it clear through first and then assemble my ingredients before I start. This saves time and energy. It is nice if you can arrange your cupboards with all the baking needs in one area, the "lunch-making" necessities together, and so on. Mom always said, "Use your head and save your feet!"

¤ ¤ ¤ ¤ ¤

A friend of mine color-codes her recipe cards — red for desserts, green for main dishes, blue for salads, and so on. She also sticks a color-coded star sticker by each recipe to indicate personal favorites. Yellow means Don's favorite, and silver is for Mary. I like that!

¤ ¤ ¤ ¤ ¤

To save dirtying bowls when I make cookies, I cream my shortening and sugar together in a large bowl, push it to one side and beat the eggs on the other side in the same bowl, and then mix it all together and add the rest of my ingredients. I guess I'm lazy, but it sure works!

¤ ¤ ¤ ¤ ¤

When measuring my ingredients, I always put the eggs in the measuring cup first and then measure my shortening, molasses, or whatever, and they'll slip right out of the cup. It also works to rinse the measuring cup in real hot water before measuring the shortening. Again, it will slip right out.

¤ ¤ ¤ ¤ ¤

I like to fold my napkins and put them in the glasses. It looks so pretty on the table.

¤ ¤ ¤ ¤ ¤

Save those broken peppermint sticks and crush them up to add to brownies, chocolate cookies, or to top a chocolate frosted cake.

¤ ¤ ¤ ¤ ¤

Leftover eggnog sure makes super French toast. I add a little extra cinnamon and nutmeg.

¤ ¤ ¤ ¤ ¤

Save paper towel rolls and toilet tissue rolls, and spray with adhesive glue and cover with pretty paper. Fill with candies, etc. and wrap and tie using colored cellophane and ribbon or gold cord. Keep a basket of these by the door. Guests love to take one home with them!

¤ ¤ ¤ ¤ ¤

Use a cinnamon stick as a dowel to hang those mini-Christmas quilts — cute!

¤ ¤ ¤ ¤ ¤

Old mason jars filled one third with sand make fun votive candle holders to set around the house for the holidays.

¤ ¤ ¤ ¤ ¤

The way a gift is given is more important than the gift itself.

¤ ¤ ¤ ¤ ¤

Why not bake a birthday cake for the Baby Jesus, and each family member can do a good deed as a present to Him.

¤ ¤ ¤ ¤ ¤

Set out all your Christmas storybooks in a basket to be picked up and read each day. Children never outgrow their love of being read to.

¤ ¤ ¤ ¤ ¤

How about a "progressive" family dinner this holiday?

¤ ¤ ¤ ¤ ¤

To cut up a large amount of candied fruit, I use my kitchen scissors and keep a glass of hot water handy to keep dipping the blades in. It's so quick and easy.

¤ ¤ ¤ ¤ ¤

To make the holiday (or anytime) stay more memorable for your house guests —

- Brighten up the room with a green plant or fresh flowers.

- Candles give the room a warm and inviting glow.

- Have a basket of magazines and reading material and maybe a bowl of fruits and nuts for a late night snack.

- Make the bathroom festive, also, and don't forget plenty of towels.

- Have an extra Christmas stocking for each guest. They will be so pleased you included them in this tradition.

- Finally, save some of the baking and decorating chores until your guests arrive. They love to be included!

Thanks again, friends, for stopping by for a visit. It has been fun for me, and I hope we'll all resolve to be a little happier, healthier, and more creative. Let's let our enthusiasm and encouragement come shining through whether we're a parent, mate, grandparent, aunt, uncle, sister, or brother, and make life a little better for those around us! We can do it!

Smile Always,

Bev Nye

Bev Nye

Recipe Index

Soups

Bavarian German Chowder........ 40
Cabbage Patch Soup............... 41
Country Style Corn Chowder.... 178
Delicious Hot and Sour Soup...... 99
Ham and Bean Soup................ 68
Minestrone......................... 202
Perky Tomato Soup............... 203
Potato Soup......................... 42
Roy's Chicken Soup with......... 100
    Velvet Dumplings............... 101
Sopa Fiesta........................ 203
Southern Peanut Soup............. 42
Thanksgiving Chowder........... 244
Velvety Chicken Asparagus Soup... 67

Salads and Vegetables

Aunt Viola's Cucumbers.......... 121
Baked Potato Treats........ 245-246
Country Rice........................ 69
Kristen's Yummy Potatoes........ 48
Mandarin Orange Salad.......... 102
Mexican Vegetable Bake......... 157
Opal's Baked Beans.............. 156
Oriental Salad..................... 118
Our Veggie Christmas Tree...... 263
Pickled Ham Salat................ 263
Spinach Salads.............. 101-102
Springtime Tomato Aspic Salad.... 121
"The Best" Potato Salad.......... 156
Zucchini Pasta Salad............. 179

Main Dishes

Barbequed Brisket of Beef....... 158
    Barbeque Sauce............... 159
Beans Ole.......................... 221
Bev's Farmer's Omelet........... 246
Bev's Pasta Primavera........... 119
Bev's Taco Salad.................. 155
Cajun Hot Halibut................. 180
Chicken Magnifico................ 103
Chinese Chili....................... 43
Dutchman's Pizza.................. 44
Frenchie Dips....................... 17
Hot and Cold Chicken Salad..... 120
Italian Sloppy Joes................ 180
Mexican Bake...................... 16
Mexican Pizza...................... 45
Mom's Salmon Loaf............... 103
Monday Salad..................... 137
Noodles Mexicano................. 46
Pinata Burgers..................... 157
Pork and Sauerkraut.............. 138
Pork Stew.......................... 219
Roy's Country Supper............. 47
Roy's Hot Buffalo Wings.......... 137
Ted Gorka's Polish Sauerkraut. 220
Tex-Mex Burgers.................. 158
Three Cheese Pasta & Zucchini... 181
Virginia's Ham Loaf with......... 122
    Mustard Sauce.................. 122
Yummy Beef Stew................ 138
Zucchini Monterey................ 123

Breads

Aunt Minnie's Applesauce Loaf. 223
Bev's Fluffy Corn Bread............49
Breakfast Sunshine Muffins......140
Easy No-Knead Bread............19
Festive Holiday Bread.............264
French Toast and Varieties... 20-21
German Scones....................222
Grandma's Lemon Pecan Bread. 70
Melt In Your Mouth Rolls...........18
Sourdough Muffins...................51
Sourdough Pancakes...............50
Sourdough Starter...................50
Southern High Rise Biscuits.......49
Sweet Rolls and Variations....19-20

Desserts

Apple Fritters.......................225
Apple Macaroon....................226
Aunt Minnie's Pepper Nuts......266
Bev's Fruit Cobbler................207
Bread Pudding......................71
Chocolate Cheese Cake.........269
Cream Puffs........................71
Date Delight........................205
Donna's Everyday Cookies......104
Grandma Scheel's Butter Cookies...52
Heidi's Sugar Cookies.............52
Jennifer's Springtime Parfait.....123
Jessica's Glorified Rice Dessert..22
Nye's Pumpkin Pie.................247
Roy's Lemon Meringue Pie with
   Easy Pie Crust and............139
   Perfect Meringue...............140
Sourdough Chocolate Cake.......51
Surprise Cupcakes.................206

Candies

Christmas Twigs................... 268
Dipped Apricots.....................267
Dipped Pretzels.....................266
Ohio Buckeyes......................182
Ritzy Chocolate Wafers...........267
White Chocolate Bark.............267

Miscellaneous

Blender Drink........................25
Chili con Queso....................159
Delicious Bread Stuffing..........243
Delicious Granola.................. 141
Holiday Cranberry Cream........247
Hot Cranberry Float............... 265
Mary's Apple Butter.................225
Mexican Taco Seasoning Mix...204
Microwave Caramel Corn.........224
Microwave Cinnamon Corn......224
Mom's Lemonade................. 160
Mom's Lemon Sauce.............. 72
Orange Filling...................... 268
Raisin Sauce........................ 69
Salsa................................48
Scheel's Bleu Cheese Dressing....204
Shrimp Cocktail Dip................244
Syllabub............................ 265